# Awareness Bound and Unbound

# Awareness Bound and Unbound

*Buddhist Essays*

DAVID R. LOY

Published by
State University of New York Press, Albany

For information, contact State University of New York Press, Albany, NY
www.sunypress.edu

Production by Diane Ganeles
Marketing by Michael Campochiaro

**Library of Congress Cataloging-in-Publication Data**

Loy, David, 1947–
    Awareness bound and unbound : Buddhist essays / David Loy.
        p. cm.
    Includes bibliographical references and index.
    ISBN 978-1-4384-2679-2 (hardcover : alk. paper)
    ISBN 978-1-4384-2680-8 (pbk. : alk. paper)
    1. Buddhism—Doctrines.   I. Title.

BQ4165.L68 2009
294.3'42—dc22                                                    2008050507

10 9 8 7 6 5 4 3 2 1

# Contents

# Acknowledgments

Earlier versions of these essays have been published previously. Permission from the following journals and publishers to reprint this material is gratefully acknowledged.

"Awareness Bound & Unbound: On the Nature of Attention," *Philosophy East and West* 58, no. 1 (April 2008): 223–243.

"Language Against Its Own Mystifications: Deconstruction in Nagarjuna and Dogen," *Philosophy East and West* 49, no. 3 (July 1999): 245–260.

"Dead Words, Living Words, Healing Words: The Disseminations of Dogen and Eckhart," *Healing Deconstruction: Postmodern Thought in Buddhism and Christianity*, ed. David Loy (Atlanta: Scholars Press, 1996).

"Zhuangzi and Nagarjuna on the Truth of No Truth," in *Essays on Skepticism, Relativism, and Ethics in the "Zhuangzi,"* ed. Paul Kjellberg and Philip J. Ivanhoe (Albany: State University of New York Press, 1996).

"CyberBabel," *Ethics and Information Technology* 10, no. 2 (2008): 251–258.

"A Zen Cloud? Comparing Zen Koan Practice with *The Cloud of Unknowing,*" *Buddhist-Christian Studies* 9 (1990): 43–60.

"The Dharma of Emanuel Swedenborg: A Buddhist Perspective," *Arcana* 2, no. 1 (Autumn 1995): 5–31. Reprinted as the afterword to D. T. Suzuki, *Swedenborg: Buddha of the North* (West Chester, PA: Swedenborg Foundation, 1996).

"The Karma of Women" in *The Religious Roots of Violence Against Women*, ed. Judith Plaskow and Marvin Ellison (Cleveland: Pilgrim Press, 2007).

"The West Against the Rest? A Buddhist Perspective on Huntington," *Confronting Technology, Globalization, and War: Challenging the Gods of the Twenty-first Century*, ed. David Hawkin and Michael Hadley (Albany: State University of New York Press, 2004).

"Terror in the God-Shaped Hole: A Buddhist Perspective on Modernity's Identity Crisis," *Journal of Transpersonal Psychology* 36, no. 2 (2004): 179–201.

In addition to those acknowledged in the notes, I am grateful to SUNY Press editors Nancy Ellegate, Allison Lee, Diane Ganeles, and especially Wyatt Benner for all their assistance.

# Introduction

## Myth Broken and Unbroken

If we can no longer believe in transcendence—an eternity with God in heaven, or a nirvana that subsists apart from samsara—then we are faced with a choice. We can simply dismiss such beliefs as superstition, perhaps a necessary stage in the development of humanity but a crutch to be outgrown as modern science discovers more about the world (and modern psychology reveals more about ourselves).

Alternatively, we can understand religious language as metaphor that fails when taken literally. Paul Tillich distinguished "unbroken myth" from what he called "broken myth," stories no longer believed to be historically true yet still resonant with meaning. The argument of this book is that broken myths and metaphors can point to a different type of salvation or deliverance: not liberation from this world but *into* it. We can fantasize about going somewhere else where everything will be okay, or we can "wake up" to realize that this world is different from what we thought it was. What do we need to do to become truly comfortable with—at one with—our lives here and now?

This more hermeneutical approach encourages sensitivity to implications of religious claims, implications that are becoming more important as the legacy of modernity becomes more questionable. If burgeoning social and ecological crises are tied to increasingly dubious ways of understanding what the world is and who we are, where should we look for a better understanding? Our manifest inability to take care of our collective home (and mother) suggests the need for a more nondual worldview: a new version of secularity that is just as much a new vision of sacrality.

The chapters that follow develop this alternative approach in various ways. They offer primarily Buddhist perspectives, because Buddhist teachings lend themselves to this sort of hermeneutic. That is not to say that such perspectives are uniquely Buddhist, only that Buddhist categories provide especially receptive and productive ways to address these issues. (See the chapters on

Swedenborg and *The Cloud of Unknowing* for some remarkably similar non-Buddhist categories.) Like other religious claims, Buddhist doctrines need to be interrogated and deconstructed; what is distinctive about Buddhism is how often the tradition has performed that deconstruction on itself, the better to reconstruct itself. In addition to fruitful comparisons with other traditions (especially Taoism and various versions of Christianity), several of these chapters engage in what might be called "internal dialogue" to clarify an issue by bringing together what different Buddhist teachers and teachings have had to say about it. It is academically fashionable, and often important, to focus on differences and tensions within a tradition, to highlight the difficulties that dog most generalizations. "Buddhism" is certainly susceptible to that sort of critique, yet my main concern in what follows is to emphasize the continuities that can contribute to a more or less consistent worldview, one that challenges what we have been taking for granted.

Chapter 1 takes seriously the many Buddhist admonitions about "not settling down in things" and the importance of "wandering freely without a place to rest." Its simple thesis is that delusion (ignorance, samsara) is awareness trapped, and liberation (enlightenment, nirvana) is awareness unstuck because freed from grasping. This means that the key issue is attachment. Our basic difficulty is not letting go of (things in) this world, in order to experience something else; attachments are problematic because they are the forms on which formless awareness has become fixated. "Awareness" here does not mean Mind or Consciousness—concepts with transcendental pretensions—but nothing more grandiose than (the true nature of) our attention. According to the Japanese Zen master Hakuin, the difference between Buddhas and the rest of us is like that between water and ice: without water there is no ice, and without Buddha there are no sentient beings. Are we "frozen" Buddhas?

Our basic attachment—the main place that awareness gets stuck—is the ego-self, which is not a self (a subject) but a psychological/social/linguistic construct (a mental object). Understanding "my" awareness as the vehicle of "my" ego-self, as something that *belongs to me*, is a delusion. We are normally preoccupied with relating bodies and possessions, hopes and fears, and so forth, to something that does not exist except as an unstable, always insecure, always incomplete construction better understood as a process than as a thing. In fact, that ongoing act of relationship is how the sense of self is constructed and maintained. Ironically, then, while all experience is related to this ego-self, it has no reality except as that to which all experience is supposedly related. This lack of own-being is a persistent source of considerable anxiety—in Buddhist terms, the root of our *dukkha*, "suffering."

The ego-self does not act; being fictional, it cannot do anything, any more than a character in a novel (a being composed only of words on a page) can actually do something. The literary metaphor is a good one, because we can lose ourselves in the plot and identify with the protagonist (usually in opposition to other characters), overlooking the fact that all the people and situations in a novel are creations of the same imagination. The same thing happens when I identify with (the supposed interests of) my own ego-self . . . but then who is this "I"? *What* imagination identifies with the ego-self? Some of the chapters offer a demythologized account of how one finds the answer to that question.

Emphasizing the distinction between delusion (awareness bound) and awakening (unbound) is consistent with basic Buddhist teachings and provides insight into some of the more difficult ones, including the relationship between samsara and nirvana, and the Mahayana claim that "form is no other than emptiness, emptiness not other than form." It is also important to see the implications of this perspective for the social issues that concern us today. The constriction or liberation of awareness is not only a personal matter. What do societies do to encourage or discourage its emancipation? Is attention to be controlled and exploited, or cultivated and awakened? Is awareness to be valued as a means to some other goal, or should its liberation be cherished as the most valuable end-in-itself?

This approach also has implications for how we understand language. Those who meditate are familiar with warnings about clinging to concepts, which can interfere with one's practice and hinder enlightenment. To awaken is to experience that which transcends language, whatever that means. This has provoked some unresolved and perhaps irresolvable controversies about whether there is a formless "pure consciousness" distinguishable from thought and language. If, however, the basic issue is whether awareness is stuck or unstuck, there is another possibility: not liberation from language but *into* language. Do we use language or does language use us? What happens when we realize that (as philosophers such as Heidegger emphasize) we *are* language?

Chapter 2 addresses these questions. It compares two important Mahayana thinkers—Nagarjuna and Dogen—who are linked (if we accept the traditional account) by a common transmission lineage yet also separated by vast geographical, historical, and linguistic differences. Those differences are reflected in their divergent textual styles: Nagarjuna, the philosopher's philosopher, notorious for his laconic, knife-edged logic, versus Dogen, the allusive and transgressive poet, willing to reinterpret or misinterpret Buddhist texts in order to devise new semantic possibilities. It is remarkable, then, that their dissimilar methods end up emphasizing similar Buddhist insights. That is because they deconstruct the same types of delusive dualisms, most of them versions of our commonsense distinction between substance and attribute, subject and predicate. They provide alternative demonstrations of how language can work against its own mystifications.

Nevertheless, although both undermine dualistic ways of understanding ourselves "in" the world, they reach different conclusions about the possibility of language conveying a "true" understanding of the world. For Nagarjuna, language at its best (that is, deconstructive philosophy) ultimately self-negates, to reveal a beatitude or serenity (*shiva*) in which there is no Buddha to teach and nothing to be taught. For Dogen, however, concepts and metaphors are not just instrumental means to communicate truth; they themselves manifest the truth—or rather, since that is still too dualistic, they are themselves the truth that we need to realize. If we have a problem with language, why blame the victim? When I do not try to extract some truth *from* a metaphor, it can be a way "my" awareness consummates itself. Although symbols can be redeemed only by mind, awareness does not function in a vacuum but is activated by—or better, *as*—symbols. In short, the path leads not to the elimination of concepts but to their liberation.

Chapter 3 offers examples from different traditions (including Derridean deconstruction) that demonstrate how language can operate in a more liberated and liberating fashion. Hui-neng, Dogen, and Eckhart—arguably the greatest Chinese Chan master, the greatest Japanese Zen master, and the greatest medieval Christian mystical writer, respectively—are so elevated in the spiritual pantheon that we tend to overlook how freely and opportunistically they employ words. (There I go again, dualizing between *them* and *their language*!) In addition to the blithe way that Hui-neng contradicts traditional Buddhist teachings when it suits his purposes (that is, when it might prompt an awakening), there are striking parallels to Dogen's semantic transgressions in Eckhart's Latin neologisms, which he uses to subvert the usual bifurcations of language—for example, when "thy will be done" in the Lord's Prayer becomes "will, be thine." For Eckhart, the dualism that most needs to be deconstructed is between myself "inside" and God "outside," and there are linguistic ways to undermine their duality.

The Mahayana doctrine of interpenetration (e.g., Indra's net) implies that each dharma is both cause and effect of all other dharmas, and that applies to language as well. This means that linguistic expressions are at the same time both relative—they always refer to other terms and things—and ends in themselves. To dwell only on the instrumental and referential aspect of language overlooks what Dogen calls the *ippo-gujin*, "total exertion of a single dharma," of words and symbols. They are *ippo-gujin* because they remain, like everything else, groundless—that is, lacking any self-nature or self-presence of their own. Isn't our philosophical quest for Truth a sublimated response to the same groundlessness? We try to fixate ourselves somewhere, if only (for intellectuals like me who write these words and you who read them) on some produced linguistic effect. Such searches for unconditioned grounds and origins are doomed to fail, for our philosophizing too sails in an unfathomable ocean without any secure harbors to anchor within. Yet when language is not used to compensate for our own groundlessness—when we do not grasp at it in order to extract something else from it—then language can become a way awareness consummates itself.

Chapter 4 compares Nagarjuna with the Chinese sage Zhuangzi, whose eponymous reflections comprise the most profound and provocative text of ancient China. Again, the geographical, historical, and linguistic differences are vast, yet their targets and conclusions are remarkably similar. The *Zhuangzi* offers a bewildering succession of anecdotes and arguments whose shifting tone makes it difficult to determine which voice represents the author. This postmodernist playfulness, which prefers posing questions to drawing firm conclusions, functions quite differently from Nagarjuna's univocal dissection of this and that logical alternative. Instead of refuting all candidates for a master discourse, Zhuangzi subverts our need for such a master discourse, for that perfectly reason-able position Zhuangzi loves to mock.

What if there is no such Truth? Or is this insight itself the Truth? Is that a contradiction (and therefore self-refuting) or a paradox (which encourages a "leap" to a different level of understanding)? Zhuangzi has been labeled a relativist and/or a skeptic, Nagarjuna a skeptic and/or a nihilist, yet such designations put the cart before the horse. We cannot appreciate their skepticism without considering what motivates our commonsense belief in objective knowledge. We cannot determine whether Zhuangzi is a relativist without considering what the rest of us expect from the truth. Instead of asking what kind of a skeptic or relativist Zhuangzi is—that is, which of our conceptual boxes he should be squeezed into—this chapter reflects on the relationship between knowledge and other important themes for him: especially no-self, mind-fasting, and dreaming. By no coincidence, these topics happen to be very important for Buddhism as well. The most interesting issue, however, is not whether the "skepticism" of Zhuangzi and Nagarjuna is consistent with other claims such as no-self. That question needs to be turned around: What context do common themes such as no-self, meditation, dreaming and waking up, and so on, provide for their understanding of our understanding of knowledge?

Chapter 5 brings us back from ancient India and China to twenty-first-century technologies. To be only *here*, and for here to be always *now*: Would that be the fulfillment of our dreams, or a nightmare? New cyberenvironments have begun to compress space and time so radically that they may be altering awareness itself. Is that transformation something to be embraced or deplored?

Unsurprisingly, there are sharp differences of opinion. In *Real Time: Preparing for the Age of the Never Satisfied Customer*, Regis McKenna acclaims our digital conquest of space and time, with its new possibilities for e-business. Paul Virilio's *Open Sky* is less sanguine: instantaneous communication and almost-as-fast transportation are producing an "ultimate state of sedentariness" in a society without future or past, since "there is no more here and there, only the mental confusion of near and far, present and future, real and unreal—a mix of history, stories, and the hallucinatory utopia of communication technologies" (Virilio 1997, 35). Why should we make the effort to go anywhere or do anything if everywhere is already here, if everytime is now?

Virilio's critique adds a new dimension to the distinction between awareness bound and awareness unbound. To be attentive to everything telepresent would spread one's awareness so thinly that it becomes indistinguishable from ignore-ance. Infinite possibility implies paralytic indecision. How do I decide what to do when nothing is more present than anything else?

From this paradox Thomas Eriksen derives a general law of the information revolution: "When an ever-increasing amount of information has to be squeezed into the relatively constant amount of time each of us has at our disposal, the span of attention necessarily decreases." Data-glut tends to make each instant "ephemeral, superficial and intense. . . . Everything must be interchangeable with everything else *now.* The entry ticket has to be cheap, the initial investment modest. Swift changes and unlimited flexibility are main assets" (Eriksen 2001, 119). Margaret Gibbs points to one of the consequences: "We've become a society where we expect things instantly, and don't spend the time it takes to have real intimacy with another person" (in Crary, 2006).

From a Buddhist perspective, accelerating cybertime aggravates rather than reduces the delusive dualism between things (including ourselves) and the time they are "in." Perhaps technological preoccupation with ever-increasing speed is not the solution but the problem. The difficulty here is liberating awareness not from fixations but from inability to focus—which, as meditators know, can be just as great a challenge. To counteract Eriksen's law, Buddhism provides contemplative practices that increase our attention span by slowing us down. This enables us to "forget ourselves" so that we can realize the true nature of awareness and become one with whatever we do.

Chapters 6 and 7 compare Buddhism with two versions of Christianity that are very different from each other. Both comparisons demonstrate how the path to liberation has been conceptualized and practiced in other ways that turn out to be remarkably congruent with basic Buddhist teachings. *The Cloud of Unknowing,* an anonymous fourteenth-century English mystical text, is a manual of contemplative practice that eshews doctrinal claims. The voluminous writings of the eighteenth-century Swedish scientist, philosopher, and mystic Emanuel Swedenborg offer just the opposite: a grand metaphysical system whose structure unexpectedly resonates with Buddhist perspectives on such issues as the delusion of self and the nature of karma.

Buddhist awakening involves the realization that there is no ontological self and never was. Nevertheless, there are provocative similarities in the ways that some other spiritualities emphasize the need to "die to the self." Christianity, for example, urges a change of heart (*metanoia*) so drastic that it requires a kenosis (Phil. 2:6), a total emptying of the self so that "not I but Christ lives in me" (Gal. 2:20). Evidently Christ's own death and resurrection are not enough: we ourselves must be crucified and reborn in order to realize that "the Kingdom of God is at hand" here and now.

Chapter 6 compares two specific contemplative practices. Zen koans are paradoxical problems that in principle cannot be solved rationally. One of the best known is "Joshu's Mu": "A monk in all seriousness asked Joshu: 'Has a dog Buddha-nature, or not?' Joshu retorted: 'Mu!' " The koan point—the problem to be solved—is: What is "Mu"? Practitioners are usually instructed to treat "Mu" as a kind of mantra to let go of other mental activity. In order to become enlightened, I must lose myself completely in "Mu." Since the sense of self is a psychological construct sustained by habitual ways of thinking, cutting off all such activity with "Mu" can undermine it.

This process was described by the thirteenth-century Japanese Zen master Dogen: "To study Buddhism is to study yourself. To study yourself is to forget yourself. To forget yourself is to perceive your intimacy [nonduality] with all things. To realize this is to cast off the mind and body of self and others." When this practice is ripe, a teacher can sometimes help by cutting the last thread: an unexpected action or sound may startle the student into letting go. "All of a sudden he finds his mind and body wiped out of existence, together with the koan. This is what is known as 'letting go your hold' " (Hakuin). The shock of an unexpected sensation can cause it to penetrate to the very core of one's being—in other words, it is experienced nondually as the sense of self momentarily evaporates.

The practice described in *The Cloud of Unknowing* has a different goal: to attain "with a loving stirring and a blind beholding unto the naked being of God himself only." The text takes its title from the meditation method recommended. Those who want to experience God should wrap themselves in "a darkness or a cloud" that "treads down" all thinking: "[T]ake thee but a little word of one syllable, for so it is better than two.... And such a word is this word GOD and this word LOVE. Choose whichever thou wilt, or another: whatever word thou likest best of one syllable. And fasten this word to thine heart, so that it may never go thence for anything that befalleth" (McCann 1952, 16).

A detailed comparison between the two practices discovers many other parallels, which prompt the inevitable question: If I can "forget myself" either by becoming one with "Mu" or by fastening the word "love" to my heart and never letting it go, what does that imply about the results of these not very different techniques? The Zen experience of *kensho*, "seeing into one's own nature," reveals the *shunyata*, "emptiness," of the self and other phenomena, while a practitioner of *The Cloud* beholds the naked being of God himself. Whether or not they can be equated, the source of our attachments has been mortally wounded: realizing that the ego-self is an insubstantial construct frees awareness from the delusion that most binds it.

Chapter 7 summarizes a very different vision of human and postmortem existence, one that contrasts sharply with our postmodernist suspicion of grand narratives. No narrative could be grander than Swedenborg's, yet his perspective (like Buddhism's) is postmodern insofar as it denies an ontological self. The love of self, which closes our inmost parts to the "divine influx," is the main problem to be overcome. With the help of his rationality man has corrupted the output of the spiritual world within himself "through a disorderly life. So he must be born into complete ignorance and be led back from there into the pattern of heaven by divine means" (Swedenborg 1988, section 108).

The claim of a rebirth into ignorance suggests a Buddhist-like critique of conceptualization. Insights, being outward truths, do not by themselves save us; we are saved by the way those insights change us. Innocence is the essence (*esse*) of everything good, which invites comparison with *tathata*, the "just this!"-ness that describes the unselfconscious way an enlightened person lives. To be spiritual is nothing more than being open to, and thereby one with, the whole. We are in heaven right now if our "internals" are open, according to Swedenborg, even as nirvana is to be attained here and now, according to the Buddha.

Like that of Shakyamuni Buddha and, for that matter, of Christ himself, Swedenborg's account of evil and its retribution emphasizes intention, for that is how evil becomes tied to its own punishment.

> Every evil carries its punishment with it, the two making one; therefore whoever is in evil is also in the punishment of evil. And yet no one in the other world [afterlife] suffers punishment on account of the evils that he had done in this world, but only on account of the evils that he then does; although it amounts to the same . . . since every one after death returns into his own life and thus into like evils; and the person continues the same as he had been in the life of the body. . . . But good spirits, although they had done evils in the world, are never punished, because their evils do not return. The Lord does not do evil to anyone. Evil has

its own punishment, thus hell, and goodness its own reward, thus heaven. (Swedenborg 1990, sec. 9033).

This remarkable passage is, in effect, a sophisticated account of karma that avoids both the problem with a mechanical understanding of moral cause and effect (common in popular Buddhism) and also the difficulty with a juridical understanding of hell as punishment for disobeying divine authority (common in popular Christianity). The crucial insight is that people are "punished" not for what they have done but for what they have become, and what we intentionally do is what makes us what we are. My actions and my intentions build my character—my "spiritual body"—just as food is digested to become my physical body.

As in Buddhism, Swedenborg's version of karma undercuts our usual distinction between the one who intends and the intention itself. One's habitual tendencies to act in certain ways—one's *samskaras*, according to Buddhism—are what construct and maintain the sense of self. A person with unwholesome *samskaras*—a "bad character"—cannot be saved, because he or she *is* those *samskaras*, which cannot dwell in Swedenborg's heaven because they would not be comfortable there. "Evil" people suffer in the afterworld for the same reason that good people are blessed there: they end up living with others just like themselves.

Whether or not there is such an afterlife, the issue becomes how our attention—in this case, as *in*tention—is bound or unbound, here and now. The previous chapter focuses on contemplative practices that can release awareness from its usual patterns. Swedenborg's understanding of evil and its punishment helps to clarify the problem: how habitual tendencies keep our attention circling in familiar, comfortable ruts.

Karma remains a serious problem for contemporary Buddhism. Taken literally, it not only rationalizes racism, caste, birth handicaps, and genocides, but also justifies the authority of political elites, who must deserve their wealth and power, and the subordination of those who have neither. It provides the perfect theodicy: if there is an infallible cause-and-effect relationship between one's actions and one's fate, there is no need to work toward social justice, because justice is already built into the moral fabric of the universe.

What does that imply about "the karma of women," the subject of chapter 8? Although responsibility for the inferior status of women in Asian cultures cannot be placed solely upon Buddhism, there is nevertheless a Buddhist explanation: those born as women are reaping the fruits of their inferior karma—which includes, in many cases, prostitution.

Thailand has probably the largest sex trade in the world, a business that some temples profit from. Women and prostitutes are encouraged to offer *dana,* "gifts" such as money and other valuables, in order to ensure a better rebirth next time. This classic example of "blame the victim" overlooks the Buddha's emphasis on *cetana* "motivation." By "ethicizing" karma he made it into the key to spiritual development: one's life situation can be transformed by transforming the motivations of one's actions right now. Karma is not something the self *has*; it is what the sense of self *is*, and that sense of self changes according to one's conscious choices. "I" (re)construct myself by what "I" intentionally do, because "my" sense of self is a precipitate of habitual ways of thinking, feeling, and acting.

Once again, the issue comes down to what we choose to do with our attention—yet that way of making the point is upside down, if attention-habits are what construct *us.* Understood in this fashion, the karma doctrine does not imply passive acceptance of any type of violence against women, but encourages us to confront the unwholesome motivations of those who maintain patriarchal systems of domination.

The last two chapters broaden the discussion of awareness, bound and unbound, to consider more collective and institutionalized versions. Do group ego-selves share a group awareness, subject to the same problems and possibilities? Chapter 9 addresses Samuel Huntington's infamous thesis that the world's new battle lines are the fault lines between world civilizations. Is this a prescient observation, validated by the September 11 terrorist attacks and what has happened since then, or better understood as a dangerous example of group delusion, because it rationalizes policies that may make it into a self-fulfilling prophecy?

Religion turns out to be the crucial factor for Huntington. His test case, of course, is Islam, which provides strong support for his argument, since the Islamic world is having so much trouble getting along with any other world.

Or so it seems from a Western perspective. That perspective, however, is hardly objective or neutral. For most of their histories, the Christian West and the Islamic world have been each other's chief rivals. Unlike Jesus and Shakyamuni, however, Muhammad was not only a spiritual teacher but a political and military leader. Because neither Jesus nor Shakyamuni provided that sort of leadership, it has been easier to adapt their teachings to secular nationalism, capitalism, and consumerism. The need to "have faith" that corporate globalization will eventually work to benefit everyone implies what is increasingly difficult to overlook: that the West's economic system now serves a religious function as well, providing a worldview and set of values whose religious role we miss only because they do not refer to anything transcendent.

That is not the only problem with Huntington's "clash of civilizations" thesis. In the only place where he identifies Western values, he trots out the usual shibboleths: "individualism, liberalism, constitutionalism, human rights, equality, liberty, the rule of law, democracy, free markets, the separation of church and state" (Huntington 1996, 26). But what is the relationship between these Western *values* and Western *interests*? Huntington never addresses this uncomfortable question, perhaps because it is difficult to reconcile these ideals with the ways that the United States continues to treat other nations when its own short-term interests are at stake. Would the West get along better with other civilizations if we were less greedy for their resources and markets?

Should religious terrorism be dismissed as just another example of violent fanaticism, or is it a reaction to some failure of modernity? Chapter 10 argues that religious fundamentalism is not a return to premodern religiosity but a response to the "God-shaped hole" at the core of secular modernity.

The key issue in this case is identity, especially the dis-ease that lack of secure identity arouses. Traditional religions ground us in an all-encompassing vision of the sacred that explains the cosmos and our role within it. Modernity and postmodernity question such transcendental narratives and leave us anxious about the apparent meaninglessness of the universe and the ungroundedness of our lives within it. We no longer have a way to cope with death, or with the sense of lack that haunts the sense of self.

The violent religious movements that Mark Juergensmeyer has studied differ in many ways, but they agree in rejecting modern secularity. Although their responses only make things worse, I think there is nonetheless something perceptive about that rejection: it realizes that secularity is an ideology that pretends to be the everyday world we live in. This secular view of secularity, its own self-understanding, is not necessarily something to be accepted at face value.

From a Buddhist perspective, the basic problem with modernity (and postmodernity) is that our sense of *lack* festers regardless of any distinction we may make between sacred and secular worldviews. The disappearance or devaluation of transcendence means we end up trying to resolve that *lack* by compulsively grasping at something or other in the (secular) world—in ways that are doomed to fail

We are brought back to the distinction between awareness bound and unbound. According to Mahayana, our identity is always *shunya*, "empty," yet realizing that is not problematic, because our emptiness/formlessness is liberated to take on the form or forms appropriate to the situation. If form is empty, emptiness is also form. This implies that the "spiritual home" awareness seeks can be found only in some transformation of its homelessness.

When such problems with secularism are acknowledged, we realize that what remains important about religion today—what survives its corrosive encounter with modernity—is its role in encouraging such personal transformation. Buddhism helps us to see that dogmas and practices can be useful in accomplishing that. We should have no illusions that such an understanding of religion will soon or easily become the most prominent, but it may become necessary if religions are to fulfill the role that is most needed today.

This final chapter is an appropriate way to conclude, because it highlights some of the social implications of the Buddhist perspectives offered in earlier chapters. Whether awareness is bound or unbound is not only a matter for individual concern. Swedenborg's claims about the afterworld (including the claim that he visited it himself!) and the *Tibetan Book of the Dead* notwithstanding, these chapters offer a demythologized version of the Buddhist understanding of our situation and the path we need to follow. Transcendence and myth—for example, the law of karma—are not rejected but "broken open" and interrogated in Tillich's sense. Comparisons with other religious traditions, and within the various Buddhist traditions, play a vital role in helping to distinguish what has become extraneous from what remains insightful—indeed, essential—today.

We end up with a spiritual path that focuses on the liberation of awareness: to say it again, release not from this world but into it. If the main issue is the ways our attention/intention gets trapped, the main place it gets stuck is the ego-self. Inasmuch as the sense of self is that to which everything else is related, it is the fundamental delusion and the basic source of our *dukkha*, since the constructed ego-self can never gain the secure identity it cannot help craving.

Do those claims have any special salience today? One could make a strong argument that the ecological and social breakdowns that have begun are consequences of our collective inability to digest this basic realization about the problem of the ego-self, individual and institutional. Before we dismiss religious perspectives as outmoded and irrelevant to modern challenges, we should reflect on the fact that in their different ways the world's religions have been emphasizing this insight for millennia.

# ONE

# Awareness Bound & Unbound

## On the Nature of Attention

No wisdom can we get hold of, no highest perfection,
No Bodhisattva, no thought of enlightenment either.
When told of this, if not bewildered and in no way anxious,
A Bodhisattva courses in the Tathagata's wisdom.
In form, in feeling, will, perception and awareness
Nowhere in them they find a place to rest on.
Without a home they wander, dharmas never hold them,
Nor do they grasp at them. . . .
The Leader himself [the Buddha] was not stationed in the realm which is
    free from conditions,
Nor in the things which are under conditions, but freely he wandered
    without a home:
Just so, without a support or a basis a Bodhisattva is standing.

                    —*Ashtasahasrika Sutra*, 1:5–7, 10

Subhuti: "How is *prajnaparamita* [the highest wisdom] characterized?"

Buddha: "It is characterized by non-attachment. To the extent that beings
take hold of things and settle down in them, to that extent there is defilement.
But no one is thereby defiled. And to the extent that one does not take hold
of things and does not settle down in them, to that extent can one conceive
of the absence of I-making and mine-making. In that sense can one form
the concept of the purification of beings, i.e., to the extent that they do not
take hold of things and do not settle down in them, to that extent there is
purification. But no one is therein purified. When a Bodhisattva courses
thus, he courses in *prajnaparamita*."

                    —*Ashtasahasrika Sutra* 22:399–400

Do we miss the nature of liberated mind, not because it is too obscure or
profound to understand, but because it is too obvious? Perhaps, like Edgar

Allen Poe's purloined letter, we keep overlooking it: rummaging around hither and thither, we cannot find what we are searching for because it is in plain sight. Or, to employ a better metaphor, we look for the spectacles that rest unnoticed on our nose. Unable to see her reflection in the well, Enyadatta wanders about looking for her head. Mind seeks for mind.

Such, at least, has been a central claim of the Mahayana tradition. How central? How much insight might be gained by taking seriously and literally the many Buddhist admonitions about "not settling down in things" and the importance of wandering freely "without a place to rest." Although a few qualifications will need to be made later, my basic thesis is simple:

> Delusion (ignorance, samsara): attention/awareness is fixated (attached to forms)

> Liberation (enlightenment, nirvana): attention/awareness is liberated from grasping

Although the true nature of awareness is formless, it becomes "trapped" when we identify with particular things, which include mental objects (e.g., ideologies, one's self-image) as well as physical ones. Such identifications happen due to ignorance of the basic "nondwelling" nature of our awareness. The familiar words "attention" and "awareness" are used to emphasize that the distinction being drawn refers not to some abstract metaphysical entity ("Mind" or "Consciousness") but simply to how our everyday awareness functions.[1] To appropriate Hakuin's metaphor in *Zazen Wasan*, the difference between Buddhas and other beings is that between water and ice: without water there is no ice, without Buddha no sentient beings—which suggests that deluded beings might simply be "frozen" Buddhas. I hope to show that this straightforward distinction is not only consistent with basic Buddhist teachings but also gives us insight into some of the more difficult ones. Moreover, this perspective may illuminate some aspects of our contemporary life-world, especially the particular challenges of modern technology and economics.

Before developing the above claim about awareness, bound and unbound, it is necessary to emphasize how widespread and important it is within the Mahayana tradition, for it is found in many other canonical and commentarial texts besides the *Perfection of Wisdom in Eight Thousand Lines*. Thus, the most-quoted line from a better-known Prajnaparamita text, the *Diamond Sutra*, encapsulates the central doctrine of the *Ashtasahasrika Sutra* in one phrase: "Let your mind come forth without fixing it anywhere." According to the *Platform Sutra* of the sixth Ch'an patriarch Hui-neng, this verse precipitated his great awakening, and certainly his teachings make and remake the same point: "When our mind works freely without any hindrance, and is at liberty to 'come' or to 'go,' we attain liberation." Such a mind "is everywhere present, yet it 'sticks' nowhere." Hui-neng emphasized that he had no system of Dharma to transmit: "What I do to my disciples is to liberate them from their own bondage with such devices as the case may need" (Yampolsky 133).[2] Po-chang Hui-hai, another Chan master who lived about a century later, elaborated on the nature of liberated mind:

> Should your mind wander away, do not follow it, whereupon your wandering mind will stop wandering of its own accord. Should your mind desire to linger somewhere, do not follow it and do not dwell there, whereupon your mind's questing for a dwelling place will cease of its own accord. Thereby, you will come to possess a non-dwelling mind—a mind that remains in the state of non-dwelling. If you are fully aware in yourself of a non-dwelling mind, you will discover that there is just the fact of dwelling, with nothing to dwell upon or not to dwell upon. This full awareness in yourself of a mind dwelling upon nothing is known as having a clear perception of your own mind, or, in other words, as having a clear perception of your own nature. A mind which dwells upon nothing is the Buddha-mind, the mind of one already delivered, Bodhi-Mind, Un-created Mind . . . (Hui-hai, in Blofeld 1969, 56)

Lest we think that such a capitalized Mind is something other than our usual one, Huang-po Hsi-yun deflates any illusions we may have about its transcendence:

Q:          From all you have just said, Mind is the Buddha; but it is not clear as to what sort of mind is meant by this "Mind which is the Buddha."

Huang Po:  How many minds have you got?

Q:          But is the Buddha the ordinary mind or the Enlightened Mind?

Huang Po:  Where on earth do you keep your "ordinary mind" and your "enlightened mind"?

                                        (Blofeld 1958, 57–58)[3]

A familiar corollary to such claims, therefore, is the Chan/Zen insistence that enlightenment is nothing special, it is just realizing the true nature of our ordinary activities:

Zhaozhou:    "What is the way?"

Nan-ch'uan: "Everyday mind is the way."

(*Wu-Men-Kuan* case 19, in Pitken 1991)

When Hui-hai was asked about his practice, he replied: "When I'm hungry, I eat; when tired I sleep."

Q:        "And does everybody make the same efforts as you do, Master?"

Hui Hai:   "Not in the same way."

Q:        "Why not?"

Hui Hai:   "When they are eating, they think of a hundred kinds of necessities, and when they are going to sleep they ponder over affairs of a thousand different kinds. That is how they differ from me."

(Blofeld 1969, 95–96)

It would be easy to cite dozens of Chan and Zen texts emphasizing the above points. Familiarity with them tends to dull our appreciation of just how radical such claims are, from an Indian perspective as much as for a Western one. In European metaphysics "mind" evokes the Platonic *Nous* and Hegel's *Geist*, the latter cunningly employing historical development to realize itself. The Vedantic Brahman has different nuances, yet its famous identification with the *Atman* "Self" does not impede its transcendence. The contrast with Nan-chuan's quite ordinary mind (Ch. *xin*) is quite striking: chopping wood and drawing water, "just this!"

The Pali texts of early Buddhism do not emphasize "everyday mind" in the same way, for they often draw a strong contrast between the mind-consciousness of an ordinary worldling (*puthujjana*) and the liberated mind of an arhat. Yet there is a similar focus on not-clinging, especially in the *Salayatanavagga* "Book of the Six Sense Bases," the third collection of connected philosophical discourses in the *Samyutta Nikaya*, where the Buddha repeatedly teaches "the Dhamma for abandoning all." A noble disciple should develop dispassion toward the six senses and their objects (including the mind and mental phenomena) and abandon them, even feel revulsion for them, for that is the only way to end one's *dukkha* "suffering." "Through dispassion [his mind] is liberated. When it is liberated there comes the knowledge: 'It's liberated.' He understands: 'Destroyed is birth, the holy life has been lived,

what had to be done has been done, there is no more for this state of being.' "
Listening to this discourse, "the minds of the thousand bhikkhus were liberated from the taints by non-clinging" (Bhikkhu Bodhi 2000, 2:1143).[4] From a
Prajnaparamita and Zen perspective, all that is lacking in this passage is a clear
recognition that the *tathata* "thusness" of the "abandoned all" is the goal of
the spiritual quest. Such a conclusion may also be inferred from the emphasis
elsewhere in the Pali sutras on letting go of the five *skandhas*, "heaps," which,
like the twelve links of *pratitya-samutpada*, "dependent origination," are said
to encompass everything. The absence of grasping is what liberates.

## The Nonduality of Samsara and Nirvana

That the Pali emphasis on not-clinging and nonattachment does *not* include an
explicit recommendation of everyday mind is an important difference between
early Buddhism and Mahayana. Expressed another way, the issue at stake is how
we are to understand the relationship between samsara and nirvana. In early
Buddhism the nature of nirvana is notoriously, perhaps intentionally, obscure.
Few passages attempt to characterize it except negatively: the end of *dukkha*
"suffering," the end of *tanha* "craving," the end of *avidya* "ignorance." In short,
nirvana is the full negation of its opposite, the spiritual solution to samsara.
The main question is whether nirvana refers to attaining a different reality or
dimension of reality (e.g., experienced in meditative trance), or whether nirvana
refers to some different way of perceiving and living in this world.

This ambiguity is familiar to anyone who studies early Buddhist texts.
What has been less noticed is that the ambiguity of nirvana is ipso facto
shared by the ambiguity of samsara (literally, "going round and round," the
cycle of birth and death). Yes, we know that samsara is this world of *dukkha*,
and so on, but without a better understanding of nirvana—of the nature of
the alternative—it is not possible to be clear about what is negated and exactly
how it is negated. The basic difficulty is that nirvana and samsara form a
conceptual duality, in which the meaning of each is dependent on the other.
Neither can be understood on its own, without the other, which means that
we cannot really know what samsara is until we know what nirvana is. In
fact, preoccupation with such dualities is another example of how our attention gets stuck, how we bind ourselves without a rope.[5]

This has consequences for the entire Buddhist project, which relies upon
some version of that duality: the possibility of progressing from suffering to
liberation, from delusion to enlightenment. Does waking up mean that one
shifts from the former to the latter, or that we realize such dualistic thinking
is itself a conceptual trap?

"What do you think, Subhuti? In ancient times . . . did the Tathagata attain anything called the highest, most fulfilled, awakened
mind?"

"No, World-Honored One. According to what I understand
from the teachings of the Buddha, there is no attaining of anything
called the highest, most fulfilled, awakened mind."

The Buddha said, "Right you are, Subhuti. In fact, there
does not exist the so-called highest, most fulfilled, awakened mind
that the Tathagata attains. . . . Why? Tathagata means the suchness
[*tathata*] of all things." (Price and Wong 1974, 24)

This exchange from *The Diamond Sutra* supports an understanding of language that distinguishes Buddhism from "divine revelation" religions such
as the Abrahamic traditions, which are founded on the sacred word of God
(as recorded in the Bible and the Qur'an). For Buddhism any such linguistic
identification is attachment, and clinging is not the spiritual solution but part
of the problem. With language we construct the world, including ourselves,
and it is important to realize how we deceive ourselves when we identify with
any of those constructions, including Buddhist ones.

By no coincidence, the locus classicus for both denials—the denial
that samsara and nirvana are different, and the denial that the truth of Buddhism can be expressed in language—is the same: chapter 25 of Nagarjuna's
*Mulamadhyamakakarikas*, which deconstructs the concept of nirvana. It concludes with one of the most celebrated verses in Buddhism: "Ultimate serenity
[*shiva*] is the coming to rest of all ways of taking things, the repose of named
things; no truth has been taught by a Buddha for anyone, anywhere" (25:24,
in Candrakirti 1979, 262).[6] We are not saved by discovering any linguistic
truth, for there is no such liberating truth to identify with. This demotes all
Buddhist categories to *upaya* "skillful means," pointers that may be helpful
but not if we take the finger for the moon. What does that imply about the
distinction between samsara and nirvana?

There is no specifiable difference whatever between *nirvana* and
*samsara*; there is no specifiable difference whatever between
*samsara* and *nirvana*.

The limit [*koti*] of *nirvana* is the limit of *samsara*. There is
not even the subtlest difference between the two. (25:19–20, in
Candrakirti 1979, 259)[7]

Yet this perspective, by itself, may go too far to the other extreme, and end up
negating the spiritual path. If there is nowhere to go, there is no way to get

there, and thus no need for any spiritual practice, or for Buddhism at all. So in the same chapter Nagarjuna also distinguishes between them: "That which, taken as causal or dependent, is the process of being born and passing on, is, taken non-causally and beyond all dependence, declared to be *nirvana*" (25:9, in Candrakirti 1979, 255). There is no contradiction between this verse and verses 19–20. The key point is that samsara and nirvana are not different realms of existence (they share the same *koti*, "limits"), for the terms refer to different ways of experiencing or "taking" this world. What more can be said about that difference? Elsewhere I have tried to characterize the different ways of perceiving causality in verse 9.[8] The importance of Nagarjuna's position here is that it is consistent with the claim that samsara is awareness bound and nirvana is the "same" awareness liberated. Attention is liberated when it does not "stop at" or grasp at any particular thing, including any conceptual truth, including this one.

This also helps us understand the significance of the Madhyamaka distinction between two truths—*samvrti* the everyday transactional truth and *paramartha* the supreme truth—and why we need the lower truth to point to the higher truth. To claim, for example, that "nirvana is attention unbound" seems to invite our assent: "Yes, that's true!" But to commit ourselves to that proposition—to *identify* with it—would be self-contradictory and self-defeating insofar as such an identification binds our awareness to a particular set of concepts that we use to get a handle on the world, a worldview that thereby retains a grip on our awareness. Yet concepts and doctrines nonetheless retain their lower-truth value as teaching devices necessary to point to the higher "truth" that nonetheless always escapes their supervision.

## Attention Addicted

How is our awareness bound? According to the second noble truth, the cause of *dukkha* is *tanha* "craving," perhaps best understood as insatiability, when we can never get enough of what is sought. We often understand this as referring to physical urges—with sexuality as the archetype—but focusing on the body can be problematic for two reasons. First, emphasizing our physicality perpetuates the mind/body dualism that has haunted Western culture since long before Descartes. The danger is that we will understand the spiritual solution as mind (soul, rationality, etc.) transcending or dominating the body, which encourages the repressions and perversions that plague such a hierarchy. This hierarchy was also important in Shakyamuni's India (is it therefore an Indo-European or Axial Age problem?), for according to the traditional biographies his first spiritual practice was asceticism: starving the senses, in effect. Buddhism became a revolutionary "middle way" between sense indulgence and sense denial, because it emphasized attention-control (including *cetana* "intention-control") instead.

That brings us to the other reason for not focusing on the physical fixations. Buddhism also emphasizes another cause of our *dukkha*: conceptual proliferation (Pali *papanca*; Sanskrit *prapanca*), a linguistic process that is awkwardly subsumed within the *tanha* of the second noble truth. This world is samsara for us not only because we crave physically. *Prapancha* means that we live in a fantasy world of our own making, constructed out of our conceptualizing as well as our cravings. The relationship between desires and concepts becomes clearer when we see that the fundamental issue remains, again, our attention. Samsara is reified as awareness becomes preoccupied with pursuing certain desires (sex and food, but also money, fame, etc.) and fixated on certain ways of understanding and perceiving the (objectified) world. Both are types of clinging, and in both cases (really, different aspects of the same process) the solution involves nonattachment.

If getting stuck is the basic issue, neither desires nor concepts are problematical in themselves. We get into trouble not because we have concepts but because we "settle down" in particular ones—not only those that support a particular self-image, but also religious dogmas or political ideologies that offer us a secure fix on the world. The solution is not to get rid of all concepts, which would amount to a rather unpleasant type of mental retardation, but to *liberate* them, as Dogen seems to suggest in the *Sansuikyo* fascicle of his *Shobogenzo*: to be able to move freely from one concept to another, to play with different conceptual systems according to the situation, without becoming fixated on any of them. Conceptualizing, too, can be bound and unbound.

A similar point can be made about bodily desires, including sexuality. The importance of nonattachment does not mean recommending promiscuity over monogamy (or vice versa), for the issue is not the object(s) of our affection but the relationship between one's attention and sexual drive. Perhaps this helps us to understand tantric practices, which sometimes employ forbidden activities for spiritual purposes. The drive toward sexual union is often cited as the best example of craving, and Pali Buddhism strictly forbids monastics any genital contact, yet according to the tantric tradition the energy of that urge can be used in a liberatory way. Tantric accounts usually explain this practice physiologically—*prana* is redirected to the higher chakras—but there may be a simpler way to understand the process. Can attention retain or gain an awareness of its intrinsic nondwelling nature, even while engaged in coitus? The normal tendency, of course, involves a future-directed and increasingly urgent focus on the release of orgasm; yet nonattached, unbound attention is not driven to go anywhere or do anything, because it has nothing to gain or lose in itself. In the urge toward climax, can one become more aware of that which does not change, which does not get better or worse? Failure means becoming more enmeshed in the seductions of samsara, the craving for pleasure that leads to more *dukkha*. Success means freedom from addiction to pleasure, which is not the same as needing to avoid it.

Attention is normally *conditioned* by what it does, and especially by those things done intentionally. This points to the demythologized meaning of karma, including the Buddha's emphasis on *cetana*, which highlighted the role of intentions and volitions. The Buddha transformed earlier approaches emphasizing sacrifice and other rituals into an ethical principle by focusing on our motivations. "It is *cetana*, monks, that I declare to be *karma*. Having willed, one performs an action by body, speech and mind" (Nyanaponika and Bodhi 1999, 173). What distinguishes our actions from mere behavior, our responses from mere reactions, is that they are *intended*. Some such understanding of karma is implied by *anatta*, the denial that "I" am or have any unchanging core of substance or *svabhava*, "self-being." My subjective sense of self is a construct, and the most important components of that construction are *samskaras* "habitual tendencies," which mold character and constitute "my" karma.

According to this interpretation, karma is not an ineluctable law of the universe involving some precise calculus of cause and effect. The basic idea is simply that our actions have effects—more precisely, that our morally relevant actions and intentions have morally relevant effects that go beyond their utilitarian consequences. Shakyamuni "ethicized" karma into one of the keys to spiritual development: how one's life-situation can be transformed by transforming the motivations of one's actions right now. *Anatta* means that karma is not something I *have*, it is what "I" *am*, and what I am changes according to my conscious choices. "I" am (re)constructed by what "I" intentionally do, because "my" sense of self is a precipitate of habitual ways of thinking, feeling, and acting. Even as my body is composed of the food eaten, so my character is composed of conscious choices, constructed by my repeated mental attitudes.[9]

Buddhist teachings, however, distinguish good karma from awakening, which involves realizing the nondwelling nature of one's awareness. Beneficial karma may make it easier to practice, and insofar as one is awakened one is less motivated to create bad karma, yet the fundamental issue is not the quality of one's karma but freeing oneself from karmic conditioning.

According to Pali Buddhism, an enlightened person does not create any new karma but can still suffer the consequences of past karma. Moggallana, one of the Buddha's foremost disciples, is said to have endured a gruesome death for having murdered his parents in a previous lifetime. Less mysteriously, Angulimala renounced his career as a serial killer and quickly attained nirvana, yet was attacked and beaten by the townspeople he had terrified

(Bhikkhu Bodhi 1995, 710–17). These examples raise the question of what it means to be "unconditioned." The more objective issue concerns one's physical and social circumstances. Even when I realize that my attention is intrinsically free, I will still be "constrained" by my situation, including the images and expectations that others have of me. If I spiritually awaken in a prison, the cell doors will not magically open. One's attention, liberated or not, is always limited by the forms of awareness that circumstances make available. The paradox is that to be *one with* those conditions is to experience one's awareness and life as unconditioned. The explanation of that paradox is in the lacking-nothing nature of nonclinging attention.

Nevertheless, after awakening one's mental predispositions (*samskaras*) do not necessarily or immediately lose their attraction. A liberated smoker will not automatically lose the physical desire for a cigarette. A genuine awakening should make it much easier, of course, to ignore that urge, but the desire will arise. This point reflects on long-standing debates about whether enlightenment is instantaneous or gradual, all-or-nothing or in stages. Realizing the unbounded nature of one's attention may or may not be dramatic, but it happens suddenly. It is not something that *I do*, nor does it happen *to me*, for both of those ways of understanding are dualistic; rather, there is a *letting go*. Of what? Not simply of whatever I am grasping, but *of grasping*. Yet habitual tendencies do not simply evaporate. One's attention still tends to assume familiar forms, and this highlights the importance of continued practice: the more gradual process of making intrinsically free awareness more effectively free. This also touches on the problem with comprehending Buddhism philosophically, or taking it as a philosophy. I can understand (and write about?) all of this conceptually, without it making much difference in my daily life, in how my attention actually functions. Grasping the implications of these concepts is very different from letting go of grasping.

So far, I have made no reference to any "object of consciousness," preferring the notion of "attention or awareness taking form." Especially in a Mahayana context, any mention of form evokes the central claim of the *Heart Sutra* that "form (*rupa*) is no other than emptiness (*shunyata*), emptiness no other than form." So far, too, this chapter has not mentioned *shunyata*, largely because of the baggage that accompanies that overused term. For Madhyamaka *shunyata*, "the absence of self-existence," is a shorthand way of referring to the interconditionality of all phenomena, the fact that every phenomenon arises in dependence on others. In terms of my basic claim— delusion as attention bound, awakening as attention unbound—the *Heart Sutra's* famous equation gains a somewhat different significance. Awareness unbound is *shunya*, having no form or any other qualities of its own. More precisely, awareness whether bound or unbound is *shunya*, although bound awareness is unaware of its intrinsic nature because it is too busy grasping and too afraid to let go. Attention in itself can be characterized only by its characteristiclessness: being formless and colorless, "it" is no*thing*, which is why it can become any-thing, according to circumstances. Emptiness is not other than form, because no*thing*-in-itself attention is always assuming one or another form—not only visual and tactile ones, but sounds, tastes, smells, thoughts, and so on. Then perhaps the many statements in the *Heart Sutra* that "X (the five *skandhas*, the twelve *nidanas*, etc.) is *shunya*" are not making (or denying) an ontological claim about the nature of X-in-itself, but rather pointing out the nature of the relationship between empty-in-itself awareness and the various forms it assumes.[10]

Does this provide insight into some other basic claims? There is nothing whatsoever that needs to be attained. To be deluded is not to lack something; it is simply not to realize the nature of one's attention. This is consistent with *anatta*: the no-thing-ness of awareness is not a self. The *sense* of a self as separate from the rest of the world—the duality between subject and object—is a psychosocial construct composed of habituated ways of thinking, feeling, and acting. There is no need to get rid of the ego, because it has never existed. It is the self-image that persists because feelings, intentions, and actions refer to it. Buddhist emphasis on *anatta* implies that constant reference to this self-image is the foremost trap for our attention.

In place of the usual duality, in which consciousness becomes aware *of* some object or other, liberated awareness is nondual because it *becomes* one thing or another:

> There is a line a famous Zen master wrote at the time he became enlightened which reads: "When I heard the temple bell ring, suddenly there was no bell and no I, just sound." In other words, he no longer was aware of a distinction between himself, the bell, the sound, and the universe. This is the state you have to reach....
>
> Stated negatively, it is the realization that the universe is not external to you. Positively, it is experiencing the universe as yourself. (Kapleau 1966, 107, 137)

Compare the seventeenth-century Japanese Zen master Shido Bunan:

> The moon's the same old moon,
> The flowers exactly as they were,
> Yet I've become the thingness
> Of all the things I see.

As Dogen famously puts it at the beginning of *Genjo-koan*: "To study the Buddha way is to study the self. To study the self is to forget the self. To forget the self is to be actualized by myriad beings. When actualized by myriad things, your body and mind as well as the bodies and minds of others drop away" (Dogen 1985, 70).

If the self is a construct, so is the *external* world, for when there is no inside there is no outside. In the *Sokushinzebutsu*, "Our Mind Is the Buddha," fascicle of the *Shobogenzo*, Dogen described his own experience by quoting the Chinese master Yang-shan (d. 916): "I came to realize clearly that mind is nothing other than mountains, rivers and the great wide earth, the sun, the moon and the stars" (in Kapleau 1966, 205). If my usual sense of separation from mountains, and so on, is a delusion, then my nonduality with them is not something that needs to be attained. Instead, the delusion of a discrete self is to be dispelled by realizing the nondwelling nature of awareness.

According to the *Heart Sutra*, all dharmas are *shunya*. There is no birth and no cessation, no purity or impurity, no increase or decrease. Since awareness is literally a no-thing in itself, the categories of purity or impurity do not apply to it. Attention does not become purer when taking the form of a Buddha image, nor less pure when cleaning the toilet, or excreting into it. More controversially, it does not become better when I act compassionately, or worse when I murder someone in a fit of rage. But no birth and no death? Does that mean unbound awareness is immortal?

## The Anxiety of Awareness

Buddhist teachings contain many references to realizing "the Unborn," beginning with two well-known passages attributed to the Buddha in the *Udana*. In addition to such a claim in the *Heart Sutra* and other Prajnaparamita sutras and commentarial texts, similar statements are found in the records of many Chan/Zen adepts. None of them emphasized it more than the Japanese Zen master Bankei (1622–93), who used the concept as his central teaching. "Since the Buddha-mind takes care of everything by means of the Unborn [*fushou*], it has nothing to do with samsara or nirvana. Seen from the place of the Unborn, both of them are like the shadows in a dream" (Waddell 1984, 56). The Unborn, like the intrinsic nature of our attention, is not something that can be gained: "It's wrong for you to breed a second mind on top of the mind you already have by trying to *become* the Unborn. You're unborn right from the start. . . . The true Unborn has nothing to do with fundamental principles and it's beyond becoming or attaining. It's simply *being who you are*" (123). Simply realizing the nature of your awareness.

But how does simply *being who you are* escape birth and death? A monk asked Bankei: What happens when someone who believes in the Unborn dies? Is he born again or not? He responded: "At the place of the Unborn, there's no distinction between being born and not being born" (121).

Why not? Is the Unborn a transcendental consciousness that repeatedly takes on new bodies when previous ones die?[11] No, for the categories of life and death, like all other characteristics, simply have no purchase. Liberated awareness has no reason to fear death because no-thing has nothing to lose. We are reminded of Epictetus's classical argument in his *Letter to Menoeceus*: "When we are here, death is not, and when death is here, we are not." Nondwelling attention in itself lacks nothing, because there is nothing it could gain. With nothing to gain or lose, there are no "hindrances in the mind" and nothing to fear, as the *Heart Sutra* concludes.

The ego-self does have something to lose: itself, its self. The ego-self has nothing to lose, because it is a fictional construct. We suffer because awareness mistakenly identifies with (sense of) self, a construct that itself identifies with the body, which is subject to pain, illness, old age, and death. Bankei offered a curious "proof" of the Unborn to demonstrate that it is not the same as the self. "When you face me and listen to me say this, if somewhere a sparrow chirps, or a crow caws, or a man or woman says something, or the wind rustles the leaves, though you sit there without any intent to listen, you will hear and distinguish each sound. But it isn't your self that is doing the listening, it isn't self-power" (Waddell 1984, 58).[12] The point, apparently, is that our attention is not a function of self, not an act that the self *does*, because spontaneously hearing and identifying the sparrow is an unprompted act of perception that escapes its agency.

Whether or not we find this argument persuasive, the distinction between attention (awareness, mind, etc.) and sense of self remains basic to Buddhism. Awareness itself lacks nothing, but the sense of self lacks everything, because it is illusory, in the sense that it is nothing more substantial than an ever-changing network of mental and physical processes. Such an ungrounded and ungroundable *sense* of self can never become a *real* self. Nevertheless, the urge to become more real, and perpetual failure to achieve it, haunts the sense of self as a sense of lack. The "return of the repressed" in the distorted form of a symptom links this basic yet hopeless project with the symbolic ways we usually try to make ourselves real in the world. Groundlessness is experienced as the feeling that "there is something wrong with me," yet that feeling manifests, and we respond to it, in many different ways. The tragedy is that no amount of X can ever be enough if it is not really X that we want. When we do not understand what is actually motivating us—because what we *think* we need is a symptom of something else—we end up compulsive.

This applies not only to secular compulsions such as money, fame, and sexual gratification, but also to "spiritual" pursuits, insofar as we expect that religious practices will lead to an enlightenment that finally makes us (feel) more real. Enlightenment does not involve discovering a ground for our groundlessness, but realizing that our groundless awareness, "without a support or a basis," does not need any other ground. One's awareness cannot be secured, except in the realization that, being no-thing, there is nothing to secure.[13] Although a conditioned, impermanent sense of self cannot attain immortality, a nondwelling awareness can dwell in—or (better) *as*—an eternal present.

This implies that our fundamental problem is not fear of death but dread of our no-thing-ness. Solving the latter problem should also resolve the former, not because one realizes some transcendental consciousness that survives physical death to enter another body (what happens at death is not thereby determined), but because nonclinging awareness does not distinguish between being alive or not being alive, as Bankei puts it. Chopping wood, drawing water, eating when hungry, resting when weary—where is the birth and death in that?

Nevertheless, there is something fundamentally mysterious about the Unborn. I cannot comprehend it, cannot grasp its nature, because "I" *am* it. Our usual way of understanding attention and awareness assumes a tripartite epistemology: *I am aware of some thing. Anatta* implies that there is no such subject-predicate-object relationship, which means that "my" awareness is actually not "mine." Then whose awareness is it? It is easy to respond "no one's," yet that does not evade the deeper question: What does it mean for awareness not to be the consciousness *of* some agent? Why and how does liberated awareness assume the forms that it does? Some types of meditation (e.g., Zen *shikan-taza*) involve maintaining a "pure" attention that does not dwell on anything. Although thoughts and other mental phenomena continue to arise, the sky remains blue as such clouds drift through it. Where do they come from? Some such question likely prompted the Yogachara postulation of an *alaya-vijnana* unconscious, where karmic seeds dwell until conditions awaken them. A nondwelling, contemplative awareness allows those seeds to sprout, so they can be "roasted" by not identifying with them. Instead of responding to them, one lets them go.

Yet it is not only memories and affect traces from the past that arise unbidden into awareness. Our attention can take new, spontaneous, sometimes inexplicable forms, which is what we mean by creativity. How does that happen? Beethoven, Brahms, and Puccini believed that their compositions were dictated or assisted by God. Less explicitly religious composers (and artists, writers, etc.) have spoken of being "vessels"—for what? When awareness becomes liberated, something more is involved than what we normally understand as the everyday mind of chopping wood, and so on. In place of the Japanese term *kensho* for one's initial glimpse of enlightenment, some American Zen groups now refer to an "opening." *Opening* highlights another aspect of nondwelling, nongrasping attention: its noninstrumental responsiveness and sensitivity to what arises. To realize that my awareness is not mine is to discover that its no-thing-ness has infinite depths. When we think about nonclinging, we usually visualize external objects and sensory phenomena, but, when attention is not referring back to the self-image that is ego, there is also receptivity to what springs up from its own depths.[14]

## The Attention-Deficit Society

The earlier discussion of karma addressed only the individual aspects of moral cause and effect, yet we are social creatures subject to collective influences beyond personal agency. In other words, there is also collective karma. Traditional understandings of karma and rebirth, which can understand group karma only by bundling individual karmas, become implausible when applied to genocide, for example. To argue that all those who perished in Nazi concentration camps must have been reaping the karmic fruits of their evil deeds in previous lifetimes is fatuous, to say the least. There is, however, another way to approach the issue of collective karma: by considering what conditions our collective awareness. How has the development of the modern/postmodern world affected human attention—not only what we attend to, but how we attend to it? It is important to see the implications of the previous discussion for some of the social issues that concern us today. The constriction or liberation of awareness is not only a personal matter. What do societies do to encourage or discourage its emancipation?

Recent media coverage suggests that one of our major concerns about attention is the lack thereof. Attention-deficit disorder (ADD) and attention-deficit hyperactivity disorder (ADHD) have become serious medical issues in the United States, originally among schoolchildren but now among young adults as well.[15] What might be called the fragmentation of our attention is addressed in chapter 5. The present chapter concludes by noticing two other influences on our collective attention: its commodification and media/political manipulation.

### The Commodification of Attention

Although it is difficult to overemphasize the cumulative effects of television (including video and video games) on our collective attention habits, there is a more basic problem. For those of us in the developed (or "economized") world, the greatest "awareness trap" is consumerism, which involves sophisticated advertising that has become very good at manipulating our attention. Since production problems have become relatively easy to solve, today the bigger economic challenge is keeping us convinced that the solution to our *dukkha* is our next purchase. As the pioneering advertising executive Leo Burnett (1891–1971) put it, "Good advertising does not just circulate information. It penetrates the public mind with desire and belief." That penetration may have

been lucrative for his clients, yet it also has other, more problematic consequences: "[I]n a consumer society there are inevitably two kinds of slaves, the
prisoners of addiction and the prisoners of envy" (Illich 1973, 46).[16] Whether
or not one is able to afford the desired product, one's attention is captured.

Recently it has become more evident that attention is the basic commod-
ity to be exploited. "The new economy is not an information or a knowledge
economy. . . . It is an attention economy," according to a writer in South Africa's
*Financial Mail,* coining a meme that has proliferated in business circles.[17]
"The basic resource of this new economy is not something they provide us.
It's something we provide them—'mindshare,' in the charming idiom of the
trade. Now ask yourself this: What if there's only so much mind to share?
If you've wondered how people could feel so depleted in such a prosperous
economy, how stress could become the trademark affliction of the age, part
of the answer might be here" (Rowe 2001, unpaginated).[18]

Rowe is concerned about the commodification of what he terms *cognitive space,* the corporate response to the fact that people might sometimes be
concerned about something else besides buying and consuming. This has led to
"the ultimate enclosure—the enclosure of the cognitive commons, the ambient
mental atmosphere of daily life," a rapid development now so pervasive that
it has become like the air we breathe unnoticed. Time and space, he argues,
have already been reconstructed: holidays (including new commercialized
ones such as Mother's Day) into shopping days, the "civic commons of Main
Street" into shopping malls. Now advertising is infiltrating into every corner
of our conscious (and unconscious) awareness. Sports stadiums used to have
ads, but now renamed stadiums are themselves ads. Television shows used to
be supported by advertising; today insidious product placement makes the
whole show (and many films) an ad. The jewelry company Bulgari sponsored
a novel by Fay Weldon that included over three dozen references to its products. A 2005 issue of the *New Yorker* did not include any ads, because the
whole magazine was a promotion for the retail chain Target. Children are
especially vulnerable, of course, and two-thirds of three-year-olds recognize
the golden arches of McDonald's.[19]

In the past one could often ignore the ads, but enclosure of the cognitive commons now means that they confront us wherever our attention turns.
Unless we are meditating in a Himalayan cave, we end up having to process
thousands of commercial messages every day. And they do not just grab our
attention, they exploit it: "The attention economy mines us much the way
the industrial economy mines the earth. It mines us first for incapacities and
wants. Our capacity for interaction and reflection must become a need for
entertainment. Our capacity to deal with life's bumps and jolts becomes a
need for 'grief counselling' or Prozac. The progress of the consumer economy
has come to mean the diminution of ourselves" (Rowe 2001, unpaginated).[20]

Consumerism requires and reinforces a sense of our own impoverishment. By manipulating the gnawing sense of lack that haunts our insecure (because groundless) sense of self, the attention economy insinuates its basic message deep into our awareness: the solution is consumption.

## The Control of Attention

Dictatorships control people with violence and the threat of it, to restrain what they do. Modern democracies control people with sophisticated propaganda, by manipulating what they think. The title of one of Noam Chomsky's books sums it up well: *Manufacturing Consent*. We worry about weapons of mass destruction, but we should be as concerned about weapons of mass deception and weapons of mass distraction, which may be more insidious because more difficult to detect. To cite only the most obvious example, the disastrous 2003 invasion of Iraq would never have been possible without carefully orchestrated attempts to make the public anxious about something that did not exist. It was easy to do because September 11 has made us fearful, and fearful people are more susceptible to manipulation.

Traditionally, rulers and ruling classes used religious ideologies to justify their power. In premodern Europe the church supported the "divine right" of kings. In Asian Buddhist societies karma offered a convenient way to rationalize both the ruler's authority and the powerlessness of his oppressed subjects. It implied one should accept one's present social status because it is a consequence of one's past deeds. In more secular societies, however, acquiescence must be molded in different ways.

According to Alex Carey, "The twentieth century has been characterized by three developments of great political importance: the growth of democracy, the growth of corporate power, and the growth of corporate propaganda as a means of protecting corporate power against democracy" (Carey 1996, 18). Corporations are not mentioned in the United States Constitution—the founding fathers were wary of them and did not want to promote them—and corporate power only began to expand dramatically toward the end of the nineteenth century, so successfully that today there is little if any effective distinction between major corporations and the federal government. Both identify wholeheartedly with the goal of continuous economic growth, with less regard for its social or ecological effects. (We are repeatedly told that any unfortunate consequences from this growth obsession can be solved by more economic growth.) This often requires foreign intervention, for our access to resources and markets must be protected and expanded, usually under the guise of "defending ourselves."

Instead of raising questions about this orientation, the mainstream media—our collective nervous system—have become powerful profit-making corporations that serve to rationalize that belief system. Only a very narrow spectrum of opinion is considered acceptable or "realistic," and whatever problems arise require only a few minor adjustments here and there. As the earth begins to burn, as ecosystems start to collapse, the media focus our collective attention on the things that really matter: the Superbowl, the price of gas, the latest murder or sex scandal . . .

## *The Liberation of Collective Attention*

Who owns our attention, and who should have the right to decide what happens to it? Rowe concludes that we need a new freedom movement, to "battle for the cognitive commons. If we have no choice regarding what fills our attention, then we really have no choice at all." From a Buddhist perspective, however, it seems doubtful that any collective social protest movement could be successful without an alternative understanding of what awareness is and what alternative practices promote more liberated attention. It is not enough to fight against billboards and Internet banner ads without also considering what it might mean for awareness to be here and now, deconditioned from attention traps both individual and collective.

To conclude, let me emphasize that this chapter is a thought-experiment. Although I have tried to show that an understanding of the difference between bound and unbound awareness can be quite illuminating, I do not claim that this point by itself is enough to understand the liberation that the Buddhist path aims at. Buddhism includes many other related teachings: impermanence, nonself, interdependent origination (or nonorigination), and so on. Nevertheless, my argument implies that one of the most important issues, for each of us personally and also collectively as a society, is: What is our attitude toward attention/awareness? Is attention to be controlled and exploited, or cultivated and awakened? Is awareness to be valued as the means to some other end, or should we cherish and encourage its liberation as the most valuable goal to be sought? The Buddhist answer to such questions is clear. What is less clear is how much of a role that answer might play in the ways our society responds to that challenge.

# TWO

# Language Against Its Own Mystifications

## Deconstruction in Nagarjuna and Dogen

[W]e find ourselves in the midst of a rude fetishism when we call to mind the basic presuppositions of the metaphysics of language—which is to say, of reason. It is this which sees everywhere deed and doer; this which believes in will as cause in general; this which believes in the "ego," in the ego as being, in the ego and substance, and which projects its belief in the ego-substance on to all things—only thus does it create the concept "thing." . . . "Reason" in language: oh what a deceitful old woman! I fear we are not getting rid of God because we still believe in grammar. . . .

—Nietzsche, *Twilight of the Idols*

Why Nagarjuna and Dogen? Such a comparison is inviting because both obvious and difficult. On the one hand, they are two of the greatest Mahayana thinkers, linked by their commitment to its understanding of the world and (if we accept the traditional account) by a transmission lineage that extends from Shakyamuni through Nagarjuna to Dogen and his successors. On the other hand, however, there are vast cultural differences between them, due not only to geography and the millennium that separate them but just as much to the disparity between their very different languages, Sanskrit and Japanese.

These linguistic differences are further reflected in their extraordinarily different—I am tempted to say *opposite*—textual styles. Sanskrit has sometimes been considered the archetypal philosophical language, for its easily formed substantives encourage a preponderance of abstract universals. Certainly Nagarjuna is a philosopher's philosopher, notorious for a laconic, knife-edged logic wielding distinctions that no one had noticed before and that many since have been unable to see the point of. In contrast, Japanese, like Chinese, has a more concrete flavor, with a preponderance of simile and metaphor. Dogen's major work, the *Shobogenzo*, written in his own very idiosyncratic Japanese, is as poetical and allusive as Nagarjuna's *Mulamadhyamakakarikas* is dialectical and dry. Dogen's text is full of metaphors, and Nagarjuna's has very few. While Nagarjuna may seem preoccupied with splitting conceptual hairs, Dogen is concerned with exploring the semantic possibilities of Buddhist texts to discover new meanings, being willing and even eager to "misinterpret" certain passages to make his point.

What, then, can be gained from comparing them? My argument is, first, that Nagarjuna and Dogen nonetheless point to many of the same Buddhist insights, because they deconstruct the same type of dualities, most of which may be understood as versions of our commonsense but delusive distinction between substance and attribute, subject and predicate. This will be demonstrated by analyzing the enigmatic chapter 2 (on motion and rest) of the *Mulamadhyamakakarikas* and by examining Dogen's transgression of traditional Buddhist teachings in his *Shobogenzo*. The second part of this chapter, however, is concerned to determine the limits of this similarity: although both texts work to undermine our dualistic ways of understanding ourselves "in" the world, they reach quite different conclusions about the possibility of language expressing a "true" understanding of the world—a disagreement that may reflect something important about their different languages.

## What Does Nagarjuna Deconstruct?

> [W]e do not only designate things with them [words and concepts], we think originally that through them we grasp the true in things. Through words and concepts we are still continually misled into imagining things as being simpler than they are, separate from one another, indivisible, each existing in and for itself. A philosophical mythology lies concealed in language which breaks out again every moment, however careful one may be otherwise.
>
> —Nietzsche, *Human, All Too Human*

Few if any Buddhist scholars would dispute that Nagarjuna (second century CE?) is the most important Buddhist philosopher, and none of them would deny that the *Mulamadhyamakakarikas* (hereafter "the *Karikas*") is his most important work. It is something of a scandal, then, that the basic meaning of this difficult text remains so unclear and controversial. That is not for want of interpreters: no Buddhist thinker has received more attention recently, yet there is little agreement among his Western expositors. It is curious that Nagarjuna usually ends up expounding something quite similar to one's own favorite philosopher or philosophy: Shayer's Hegel, Stcherbatsky's Kant, Murti's Vedanta, Gudmundsen's Wittgenstein, Magliola's Derrida, Kalupahana's empiricism and pragmatism, and so forth. Does this mean that the *Karikas* is so foreign to our usual ways of understanding the world that it cannot be understood on its own terms?

The basic problem is not the nature of Nagarjuna's arguments themselves but their target. Despite (or because of) the various opinions of traditional and contemporary commentators on this matter, it remains unclear from Nagarjuna's texts precisely what or whom he is criticizing. Since we have no other reliable access to Nagarjuna's intentions, this is an issue that may never be settled. If, from a postmodern perspective, the opportunity this ambiguity provides is not entirely negative, then the onus falls upon each interpreter not only to offer a plausible account of Nagarjuna's motives but also to justify the continued importance of those motives for us.

For example, David Kalupahana has made a strong case that the opponent in Nagarjuna's chapter 2 is the atomic theory shared by the substantialist Sarvastivadins and the momentarist Sautrantikas (Kalupahana 1991, 35–36). This may well be true, yet that by itself does not go far enough to explain the significance of Nagarjuna's arguments today: for why we should be concerned about metaphysical debates between obscure Buddhist schools that thrived two thousand years ago?

The significance of those philosophical views increases for us, though, if they are attempts to resolve an inconsistency that plagues our ordinary "commonsense" way of understanding the world. In that case, however, it may not be necessary or even worth our while to devote time and energy expounding those particular metaphysical systems; it may be more useful for us to turn immediately to that commonsense understanding and address its supposed aporia more directly. In accordance with that, my target in this chapter is not any developed philosophical position (such as the atomic theory of Abhidharma Buddhism) but rather the more basic difficulties that plague our usual distinction between (what philosophers call) substance and attribute—which, Nietzsche would argue, may be traced back to our linguistic distinction between subject and predicate. In his chapter 2, Nagarjuna attacks this distinction in terms of the duality we ordinarily assume between a *goer* and his or her *going*.

By any standards, "the analysis of going and coming" is a peculiar and difficult text. Following the first chapter, which demonstrates our inability to understand the causal relationships among things, his chapter 2 is evidently meant to exemplify that general argument by offering a more concrete instance of Nagarjuna's deconstructive approach to the relationship between things (in this case, movers) and their predicates/attributes (moving). In the process, however, Nagarjuna seems to engage in a kind of logic-chopping that is difficult to follow and whose import is unclear. Exactly what is it that is being deconstructed? This chapter seems to exemplify Frederick Streng's objection to Nagarjuna's method, that it is "an analysis which appears to be rather arid and often simply a play on words" (Streng 1967, 181–82). L. Stafford Betty points particularly to the reification of *gamana*, "act of going": since the term is "empirically meaningless" and we do not need to grant that there is any such "thing" in the empirical world as a bare "act of going" without a goer, the argument fails (Betty 1983, 125–26). Yet is he looking in the wrong place? The *Karikas* does not offer an analysis of the world itself but analyzes our ways of understanding the world. It is these ways of thinking (which according to Nagarjuna are inconsistent) that make the world "empirical" for us. If so, we should look for a *gamana* in our categories of thought, and there we find it in our ingrained tendency to distinguish our experience into self-existing entities (subjects, nouns) and their activities (predicates, verbs). We do think of ourselves, for example, as persons distinguishable from our actions, and this implies some sort of reification not only of ourselves but also of the action, as the other substantives "act," "action," and "activity" also reveal.

The test of this approach is how much light it can shed on Nagarjuna's chapter 2, which may be summarized as follows:

(verses 1–7) Where does motion occur? Obviously not over the already-gone-over, nor over the not-yet-gone-over, but it cannot be on the being-gone-over, because that would imply that there is a *being-gone-over* distinct from *the goer that goes over it*.

(8–11) Who is going? We cannot say "the goer is going," because that would imply two goers: that the goer is a goer even without going.

(12–14) Where does going begin? Not on the already-gone-over, nor on the being-gone-over (in which case the going must already have begun). But it could not begin on the yet-to-be-gone-over (for beginning there would make it being-gone-over).

(15–17) Similar arguments are made about coming-to-rest (becoming stationary): Who comes to rest? Neither a goer (that would be a contradiction) nor a nongoer (who cannot *become* stationary). And where does coming-to-a-rest occur? Not on the already-gone-over, nor on the not-yet-gone-over, and it cannot happen on the being-gone-over (which would be a contradiction). So our usual understandings of going, beginning-to-go, and coming-to-rest have similar problems.

(18–21) It does not make sense to say that the goer is the same as the going, for then we could not distinguish (as we normally do) between the agent and the action. But neither can the goer be different from the going, for then each could exist without the other. In short, describing what happens in terms of some relationship between a goer and its going is unintelligible.

(22–25) (In summary:) A goer does not exist before going, for that would imply two goings. A goer cannot go on the three places of going (mentioned above), a nongoer cannot go on them, nor can someone who both is and is not a goer (a contradiction) go on them. "Therefore going, goer, and place of going do not exist."

Perhaps we can understand why some consider the above to be a "logical sleight-of-hand" which "resembles the shell game" (Betty 1983, 135), yet such a conclusion misses the point. The import of the above arguments is that our usual way of understanding motion—which distinguishes the goer from the going and from the place of going—does not really make sense when examined carefully, for the interdependence of the three shows that each is nonsensical when considered apart from the others. Nagarjuna's logic here (as in many other chapters) proceeds by demonstrating that once we have thus distinguished them—as ordinary language and "commonsense" do—then it becomes impossible to understand their relationship, a difficulty of the sort familiar to students of the mind-body problem. As Chandrakirti points out in his commentary to verse 23, the same argument also refutes our usual notions that a speaker speaks something and that an agent performs an action (the latter dualism being the topic of Nagarjuna's chapter 9). Very similar arguments are employed in his chapters 4, 5, and 8 to deconstruct our usual understanding of a perceiver perceiving a perceptual object; in chapter 6 to deconstruct the duality between persons and their feelings; and in chapter 5 to deconstruct the duality in its most general terms, between things and their attributes.

In Nagarjuna's chapter 2 we can see the problem most clearly by inquiring into the status of that-which-moves: in itself, is it a mover or not? Neither answer makes sense. For a mover to then be moving would be redundant ("a second motion"), and a nonmover moving is a contradiction. In contemporary analytic terms, we might say that Nagarjuna is pointing out a flaw in the ordinary language we use to describe (and hence our ways of thinking about) motion and rest: our ascription of motion predicates to substantive objects is actually unintelligible. In everyday life we constantly fudge this, sometimes assuming that things exist apart from their predicates, at other times identifying things and their predicates (a good example is the relationship between me and "my" body). Nagarjuna's dialectics demonstrate this inconsistency simply by distinguishing clearly between the possibilities. It may be that this tendency to distinguish substance from attribute reflects the inherent dualism of language. A linguistic statement typically predicates something about something: learning to speak a language is learning what things there *are* (nouns correspond to things) and what those things *do* (verbs correspond to actions and processes) or what those things *have* (adjectives correspond to attributes). Nevertheless, that such a dualism is widespread and even in a certain sense necessary (the "lower truth") does not make it a correct description of the way things really are ("the higher truth"), according to Nagarjuna.

This helps us to understand the general point of the Madhyamaka critique, by revealing what is being criticized: our usual, commonsense understanding of the world, which sees it as a collection of discrete entities (one of them myself) interacting causally "in" space and time. "Nagarjuna's rampage through the notions of the philosophers is directed at uncovering their ultimate nonsense with a view to releasing men from humiliating bondage to them" (Sprung, in Candrakirti 1979, 6).[1] Nagarjuna attacks more than the philosophical fancies of Indian metaphysicians, however, for there is a metaphysics, although an inconsistent one, inherent in our everyday view—most personally and painfully in the contradiction between my sense of myself as something nontemporal and unchanging (i.e., as distinct from my attributes, such as body), and the awareness that I am growing older and subject to death (indistinguishable from attributes such as "my" body). It is one or another aspect of this dualistic view that is made absolute in systematic metaphysics. This commonsense understanding is what makes the world samsara for us, and it is this samsara that Nagarjuna is concerned to deconstruct.

It is a consequence of our taken-for-granted distinction between things and their attributes that I now perceive the room in which I am writing as a collection of books and chairs and pens and paper . . . and me, each of which is unreflectively taken to be distinct from all the others and to persist unchanged until affected by something else. The causal relation (Nagarjuna's primary example of an attribute) is what we use to explain the interaction among things that are distinct from one another. If causality explains the interaction between things, then these things in themselves must be noncausal, and by no coincidence this is precisely our commonsense notion of what an object is: a thing whose continued existence does not need to be explained, for once created it "self-exists." The objectivity of the world (including the "subjectification" of myself as a thing in it but apart from it) depends upon this dualism between things and their attributes/causal relations. This constitutes samsara, because it is by hypostatizing such "thingness" out of the flux of experience that we become attached to things—again, the primal attachment being (to) the sense of self. Yet what we experience as such self-existing (*svabhava*) objects are thought-constructed reifications, a shorthand way of remembering that our perceptions tend to have a certain stability, which allows us to relate them together and form expectations about what they can do. This may be a necessary habit for us (which is why it is a lower *truth*), but such reifications create a delusive bifurcation between objects and their attributes (which is why it is a *lower* truth).

This point about the way we perceive the world is important, because without it one might conclude that Nagarjuna's critique of self-existence is a refutation of something no one believes in anyway. One does not escape his critique by defining entities in a more commonsense fashion as coming into and passing out of existence. The logic of the *Karikas* demonstrates that there is no tenable middle ground between self-existence independent of all conditions—an empty set—and the complete conditionality of *shunya*, "empty," phenomena. Nagarjuna's arguments against self-existence show the inconsistency in our everyday, taken-for-granted way of "taking" the world. While we accept that things change, we also assume that they remain the same—both of which are necessary if they are to be things that have causal relations. Recognizing this inconsistency, previous Indian philosophers tried to resolve it by absolutizing one of these two aspects at the price of the other. But the *satkaryavada* substance view of Advaita and Sankhya emphasizes permanence at the price of not being able to account for change, while the *asatkaryavada* modal view of Sautrantika Buddhism has the opposite problem of not being able to provide a connection between events. Chapter 1 of the *Karikas* argues, in effect, that any understanding of cause and effect that tries to combine these two separate views can be reduced to the contradiction of both asserting and denying identity. Nagarjuna concludes that their "relationship" is incomprehensible and therefore, from the highest point of view, unreal.

In sum, there is something confused and deluded about our ordinary understanding of the world, because it sees as dualities substance and attribute, subject and predicate, permanence and change. Instead of attempting to supply the "correct view," however, the Madhyamika simply deconstructs this commonsense understanding, a removal that allows something else—obvious but hitherto overlooked—to become manifest.

With the benefit of hindsight, however, we can notice that Nagarjuna's critique of such dualisms itself generates another dualism, one that during the following millennium would become increasingly problematical: that between language and silence. This dualism became so important because it reflects an essential and perhaps inescapable dualism at the heart of Buddhism, between delusion (of which language is a vehicle) and enlightenment (to which silence is believed to point).

Nagarjuna, of course, is very sensitive to the dualism of samsara and nirvana, and its deconstruction in his chapter 25 forms the climax of the *Karikas*. There is not the slightest difference between them, for the limits (*koti*) of the one are the limits of the other (verses 19–20). That which arises and passes away (i.e., samsara), when taken noncausally and without dependence, is nirvana (verse 9). Its beatitude (*shiva*) is the coming to rest of all ways of taking things (*sarvopalambhopasama*), the repose of named things (*prapancopasama*), which is why no truth has ever been taught by any Buddha to anyone, anywhere (verse 24).

The problem, however, is that this solution to the dualism of delusion and enlightenment resolves the tension between them only by displacing it onto another dualism between the manifold world of named things (*prapanca*) and its coming to rest in silence (*prapancopasama*). If nirvana involves realizing the *shunyata* of samsara, for Nagarjuna that "emptiness" involves the cessation of thought-construction. Some translations of 25:24 de-emphasize this cessation[2] but many other passages in the *Karikas* leave no doubt as to Nagarjuna's perspective on this matter: from the ultimate viewpoint no predication is possible. The dedicatory verses that begin the *Karikas* also emphasize that *prapancopasama* is the way things truly are (*pratitya-samutpada*), a claim echoed in 18:9 (where *tattva*, "suchness," is characterized by lack of mental fabrication), 13:8 (*shunyata* is *sarvadrstinam prokta nihsaranama*, "the relinquishing of all views"), and again even in the final verse of the *Karikas* (26:30), where the author bows to Gautama, whose compassion "taught the true doctrine which leads to the relinquishing of all views."[3]

Nagarjuna is well aware of the tension intrinsic to the claim that the true characterization of the nature of things is that things cannot be conceptually characterized. His solution is the two-truths doctrine. All predication is part of the lower truth. Chandrakirti's commentary on 13:8 quotes the *Ratnakuta Sutra* to make the point that *shunyata* is a medicine that must itself be expelled in order for the patient to recover fully. Since *shunyata* is itself *shunya*, one uses that lower truth to climb up a ladder that, finally, is kicked away. The Wittgenstein analogy is appropriate because Nagarjuna would also agree with the conclusion to the *Tractatus*: "What we cannot speak about we must pass over in silence."[4] However, this solution to the dualism of samsara and nirvana left a legacy that bifurcated too sharply between the lower and the higher truths, between means and ends, between thought/language and the peace that surpasses understanding. In the centuries that followed, these bifurcations reappeared in various doctrinal forms, especially in East Asian controversies about our "Buddha-nature." Significantly, the crux of these debates may also be expressed in terms of substance and attribute, subject and predicate: Is enlightened mind intrinsic or adventitious, something we already have or something we need to gain?

By no coincidence, this is precisely the issue in the dialectic between original enlightenment (*hongaku*) and acquired enlightenment (*shikaku*) that is said to have preoccupied the young Dogen. If we are endowed with the Dharma-nature by birth, why did all the Buddhas strive for enlightenment by engaging in spiritual practice? *Hongaku* seems to encourage a self-satisfied quietism complacent in its delusions, *shikaku* a self-stultifying split between means and ends, as we strive to become what we are. Dogen's solution to this dilemma not only transformed the understanding of the relationship between practice and enlightenment, but also led to a radically new appreciation of how language can combat its own mystifications.

## What Does Dogen Deconstruct?

> Language and symbols circumscribe; but, as living forces, they are dynamic enough to open up, constantly re-expressing, renewing, and casting-off, so as to unfold new horizons of their own life. In this way language and symbols know no limits with respect to how far they can penetrate both conceptually and symbolically. No Buddhist thinker was more intensely and meticulously involved with the exploration of each and every linguistic possibility of Buddhist concepts and symbols—even those forgotten, displaced ones—than Dogen who endeavored to appropriate them in the dynamic workings of the Way's realization.
>
> —Hee-jin Kim, "Method and Realization"

Nagarjuna's dialectical arguments are foreign to Dogen. In fact, the *Shobogenzo* is interested not in Buddhist philosophy as such, but in semantic analysis of passages from Buddhist sutras and Chan texts. These analyses are not inspired by any conventional piety toward such scriptures, for Dogen offers many deliberate, and often brilliant, "misinterpretations" of these passages. By transgressing the traditional readings and contradicting orthodox teachings, Dogen is able to challenge our usual understanding and generate a new way of "taking" the world freed from commonsense dualisms, including conventional Buddhist ones such as that between language and silence.

Hee-Jin Kim's exegesis of Dogen's analytical methods distinguishes seven different techniques in the *Shobogenzo*.[5] Although these overlap and are not exhaustive, let me begin by summarizing what Kim says about how each of these functions, and then attempt to understand what these techniques imply about how language can be used from the enlightened point of view. Following are a few of the many examples that could be cited for each technique.

1. *Transposition of lexical components.* A simple example is Dogen's discussion of *to-higan*, "reaching the other shore," in the *Bukkyo* fascicle, which transposes the two characters into *higan-to*, "the other shore's arrival" or "the other shore has arrived." The original meaning of *higan*, "the other shore" (i.e., nirvana), dualizes between a future event and one's present practice aimed at attaining that event. The transcribed term no longer refers to a future event but emphasizes the event of realization right here and now.

In the *Mujo-seppo* fascicle, *seppo* "preaching the Dharma" is reversed in the same way to become *ho-setsu* "the Dharma's preaching." This allows Dogen to say: "[T]his 'discourse on the Dharma' is 'the Dharma's discourse.'" There is no trifurcation between the speaker, the speaking, and the Dharma that is spoken.

2. *Semantic reconstruction through syntactic change.* Perhaps the best-known example is in the *Bussho* fascicle, which quotes from the *Nirvana Sutra*: "All sentient beings without exception have Buddha-nature" (*issai no shujo wa kotogotoku bussho ari*). Dogen rearranges the syntactical components to make them mean: all sentient beings—that is, all existence—is Buddha-nature (*issai shujo shitsuu-bussho*). Buddha-nature is no longer an attribute of sentient beings, something that needs to be actualized. Sentient beings and "their" Buddha-nature are nondual.

Another example of this reconstruction, to the same end, occurs in the *Juki* fascicle. *Juki* refers to the Buddha's prediction of a disciple's future enlightenment, but Dogen refigures the phrase *masani anokutara-sammyaku-sambodai o ubeshi*, "they shall attain supreme, perfect enlightenment," into *totoku anokutara-sammyaku-sambodai*, "they have certainly attained supreme, perfect enlightenment." The assurance of a future event is transformed into testimony to a present condition.

3. *Explication of semantic attributes.* In the *Uji* fascicle Dogen takes the common term *arutoki*, "at a certain time, sometimes, once," and reinterpets its components as *aru* or *u*, "to be," and *toki* or *ji*, "time, occasion," to make *uji*, "being-time," which he uses to signify the nonduality of existence and time, that is, of things and their temporal attributes. In other fascicles Dogen makes the same point by reducing each of these two concepts to the other: he says that objects are time (objects have no self-existence because they are necessarily temporal, in which case they are not objects in the usual sense) and, conversely, that time is objects (time manifests itself not in but as the ephemera we call objects, in which case time is different than usually understood). "The time we call spring blossoms directly as an existence called flowers. The flowers, in turn, express the time called spring. This is not existence within time; existence itself is time" (in Reiho 19058, 68). If there are no nouns, there are no referents for temporal predicates. When there are no things that have an existence apart from time, then it makes no sense to speak of things as being young or old. Nagarjuna had drawn the same conclusion: "Becoming other is not comprehensible either of the same thing [for then it is not the same thing] or of another thing [for then it is not the same thing]. So the young man does not grow old nor does the old man grow old" (13:5, in Candrakirti 1979, 147).

In a famous passage in the *Genjo-koan* fascicle of the *Shobogenzo*, the example of firewood and ashes is used to make the same point about things and "their" time:

Firewood becomes ash, and it does not become firewood again.
Yet, do not suppose that the ash is future and the firewood past.
You should understand that firewood abides in the phenomenal
expression of firewood, which fully includes past and future and
is independent of past and future. Ash abides in the phenomenal
expression of ash, which fully includes future and past. Just as
firewood does not become firewood again after it is ash, you do
not return to birth after death.

This being so, it is an established way in buddha-dharma
to deny that birth turns into death. Accordingly, birth is understood as no-birth. It is an unshakeable [sic] teaching in Buddha's
discourse that death does not turn into birth. Accordingly, death
is understood as no-death.

Birth is an expression complete this moment. Death is an
expression complete this moment. They are like winter and spring.
You do not call winter the beginning of spring, nor summer the
end of spring. (Dogen 1985, 70–71)

Although the beginning seems to echo Nagarjuna's deconstruction of the
duality between fire and fuel in chapter 10 of the *Karikas*, Dogen's explication
brings the issue home. Because life and death, like spring and summer, are
not in time, they are timeless. And if there is no one nontemporal who is
born and dies, then there are only the events of birth and death. But if there
are only those events, with no one *in* them, then there really is no birth or
death. Such is the consequence of the nonduality between me and that most
uncomfortable attribute of all, "my" birth/death.

4. *Reflexive, self-causative utterances.* Dogen uses repetition (*ji-ji* "time,"
*sho-sho* "birth," *butsu-butsu* "buddha," etc.) and identity statements ("mountains are mountains" and "emptiness is emptiness") for emphasis, and, taking
advantage of the facility with which the Japanese language allows nouns to
become verbs by adding the suffix *-su*, he delights in such Heideggerian-type
expressions as "the sky skys the sky." These techniques are used to exemplify
his notion of *ippo-gujin*, "the total exertion of a single dharma." This key term
embodies his dynamic understanding of interpenetration, according to which
each dharma in the universe is both cause and effect of all other dharmas.
This interfusion means that the life of one dharma becomes the life of all
dharmas, so that (as Zen masters like to say), *this* is the only thing in the
whole universe! The application of *ippo-gujin* to language allows words, too,
to transcend dualism.

5. *The upgrading of commonplace notions and use of neglected metaphors.*
By Dogen's time a number of metaphors had become traditional as ways to
contrast this world of suffering with the realm of enlightenment: for example,
*gabyo* "pictured cakes" (which cannot satisfy our hunger); *kuge* "sky-flowers"

(seen when the eye is defective, hence a metaphor for illusory perceptions); *katto* "entangling vines" (meaning worldly attachments); and *mu* "a dream" (as opposed to being awake). In such ways Buddhist teachings that had worked to deconstruct dualisms created new ones, and in the thousand years between Nagarjuna and Dogen these images had ossified to become more problematical. Here, too, Dogen's "misinterpretations" revitalize these depreciated terms by denying the dualism implicit in each. Instead of dismissing pictures (i.e., concepts), the *Gabyo* fascicle emphasizes their importance by transforming *gabyo wa ue ni mitazu*, "pictured cakes do not satisfy hunger," into *gabyo wa fu-ju-ki*, "pictured cakes are no-satisfaction-hunger," escaping the dualism of hunger and satisfaction into the nondualism of a hunger that, because it is itself ultimate reality, lacks nothing: "Because the entire world and all dharmas are unequivocally pictures, men and dharmas are actualized through pictures, and the buddhas and patriarchs are perfected through pictures." The *Kuge* fascicle revalorizes *kuge*, usually castigated as illusions, into "flowers of emptiness." In place of the typical Buddhist duality between reality and delusion, "all dharmas of the universe are the flowers of emptiness." Instead of the usual admonition to cut off all entangling vines, the *Katto* fascicle emphasizes the importance of worldly relationships such as the dharmic connection between teacher and student, which leads to ever-increasing understanding of the Dharma. And "all dharmas in the dream state as well as in the waking state are equally ultimate reality. . . . Dream and waking are equally ultimate reality: no largeness or smallness, no superiority or inferiority has anything to do with them."[6]

6. *The use of homophonous expressions.* In addition to employing associative techniques such as interweaving *shozan* "all the mountains" with *shosui* "all the waters," to vividly present the nonduality of mountain and water in the *Sansuikyo* fascicle, Dogen uses homophonous word pairs—puns—to reinforce his meaning. In the *Gabyo* fascicle, for example, the phrase *shobutsu kore sho naru yueni shobutsu kore sho nari*, "because all the Buddhas are verification, all things are verification," identifies *shobutsu* "all the Buddhas" with *shobutsu* "all things."

7. *Reinterpretation based on the principle of absolute emptiness.* Dogen "misinterprets" some of the most famous Zen stories to give them a radically different meaning—often one diametrically opposed to the traditional understanding. In the *Katto* fascicle, for example, Dogen challenges the traditional view of Bodhidharma's Dharma transmission to his four disciples Tao-fu, Tsung-chih, Tao-yu, and Hui-k'o. According to their different responses to his challenge, Bodhidharma says that they have attained his skin, flesh, bones, and marrow, respectively—the last because Hui-k'o demonstrates the highest attainment by saying nothing at all. Such, at least, is the usual view, which sees these four attainments as metaphors for progressively deeper stages of understanding, indicating a hierarchy of rank among the disciples. Dogen,

however, repudiates this common view by adopting the absolute standpoint: "We should know that the patriarch's saying 'skin, flesh, bones, and marrow' has no bearing on shallowness or deepness.... The patriarch's body-mind is such that the skin, flesh, bones, and marrow are all equally the patriarch himself: the marrow is not the deepest, the skin is not shallowest" (Kim 1981, 75). Kim cites many other instances to demonstrate these "transgressive" techniques, but what we now need to do is characterize their function. Two points stand out.

First, Dogen is doing more than twisting traditional texts to make them mean something clever. In the above examples he is using the freedom of a poet to conflate a problematic dualism—that is, a deluded way of thinking that causes problems for us. Despite the fact that this literary approach to language is so different from Nagarjuna's dialectical one, in each case there is a parallel with deconstructions in the *Karikas*. For example, *ho-setsu* denies any duality between the one who preaches the Dharma and the Dharma that is taught, even as many chapters of the *Karikas* challenge the duality between an agent and his or her action. *Uji* denies any duality between beings and their temporality, between springtime and its flowers, between us and our birth/death; this parallels Nagarjuna's deconstruction of the difference between time and things in his chapters 19 and 13. The *Bussho* fascicle denies any dualism between sentient beings and their Buddha-nature, which may be seen as another instance of Nagarjuna's repeated refutation of the duality between things and their attributes. *Higan-to* (like many other reconstructions) denies the usual duality between practice and realization (means and ends), even as Nagarjuna's nirvana chapter deconstructs the usual Buddhist duality between samsara and nirvana.

In each case Dogen, like Nagarjuna, does not allow himself to be limited by the usual dualisms of language. While Nagarjuna's dialectic exposes the unintelligibility of these dualisms by demonstrating that we cannot understand the relationship between the two terms, Dogen exploits the different resources of the Japanese language to concoct expressions that leap out of the bifurcations we get stuck in. For both thinkers, however, these deconstructions may be understood as conflating various recurrences of the subject-predicate dualism. Nirvana is not something I can attain. The Dharma is not something I can preach. Buddha-nature is not something I have (or do not have). "My" time is not something distinguishable from me. This is all the more striking because, although Dogen occasionally refers to Nagarjuna (Jap., Ryuju), these references are largely confined to quotations and passages from various Chinese collections, and so far as I know they do not reveal any familiarity with the arguments in primary texts such as the *Mulamadhyamakakarikas*.

This basic similiarity also serves to highlight the differences between them. Part of this difference is emphasis, a shift in focus necessary to respond to the historical development of Buddhist teachings in the thousand years between them—a development due in no small part to Nagarjuna's enormous influence. As we have seen, the dualisms that most preoccupy Dogen are versions of the practice/enlightenment, means/ends bifurcation. Granted, nirvana is not something that can be attained, but it still needs to be realized, and by his time many traditional Chan/Zen stories and metaphors designed to encourage this process had themselves become more problematical than helpful, in his view.

Dogen's revaluation of commonplace Buddhist metaphors, in particular, leaves us no doubt about his understanding of language, which is where the difference of emphasis between Nagarjuna and Dogen becomes a more significant difference of perspective. Concepts, metaphors, parables, and so forth are not just instrumental, convenient means to communicate truth, for they themselves manifest the truth—or rather, since that is still too dualistic, they themselves are the truth that we need to realize. "Metaphor in Dogen's sense is not that which points to something other than itself, but that in which something realizes itself," summarizes Kim. "In short, the symbol is not a means to edification but an end in itself—the workings of ultimate truth" (Kim 1975, 110). As Dogen himself puts it in the *Muchu-setsumu* fascicle: "[T]he Buddha-dharma, even if it is a metaphor, is ultimate reality." If one does not try to get some graspable truth from the metaphor, it can be a way one's mind consummates itself: although symbols can be redeemed only by mind, the mind does not function in a vacuum but is activated by—or as—symbols.

In an important essay on language in the Chan/Zen experience, Dale Wright has argued that such awakening is not from language but to language. As in Gadamer's hermeneutic, language is less an obstructing barrier than a reservoir of possibilities becoming available to those not trapped within its dualistic categories; it is not a clothing that hides truth but a medium that manifests it—in short, not a veil but a window. "Far from being a transcendence of language," concludes Wright, "this process would consist in a fundamental reorientation within language [that] would require training to a level of fluency in distinctive, nonobjectifying, rhetorical practices" (Wright 1992, 125, 131–33).

Within the Buddhist tradition, this move from transcendence of language to reorientation within it is perhaps best exemplified by the difference between Nagarjuna and Dogen. The latter shows us that words and metaphors can be understood not merely as instrumentally trying to grasp and convey truth (and therefore dualistically interfering with our realization of some truth that transcends words), but as being the truth—that is, as being one of the many ways that Buddha-nature *is*. To the many dualisms that Nagarjuna deconstructs, then, Dogen explicitly adds one more: he denies the dualism between language and the world. If we are the ones who dualize, why blame the victims? A birdsong, a temple bell ringing, a flower blooming, and Dogen's transpositions, too, blossoming for us as we read them . . . if we do not dualize between world and word, then we can experience the Buddha-dharma—our own "empty" nature—presencing and playing in each.

## A Scheme We Cannot Throw Off?

> Now we read disharmonies and problems into things because we think only in the form of language—and thus believe in the "eternal truth" of "reason" (e.g., subject, attribute, etc.) . . . Rational thought is interpretation according to a scheme that we cannot throw off.
>
> —Nietzsche, *Will to Power*

Both Buddhist thinkers exploit the very different strengths of their respective languages. The complex syntax of Nagarjuna's sophisticated Sanskrit permits precise and terse philosophical analysis. The looser syntax of Dogen's Japanese, due to the greater ambiguity of its Chinese ideographs, allows a poetic allusiveness that lends itself to his semantic transpositions. We have seen that this difference is further reflected in their respective attitudes toward language. To Nagarjuna it seems to be fundamentally problematical, for he limits himself to employing it negatively to deconstruct the dualities that are delusive (from the ultimate point of view) although necessary in daily life (from the conventional point of view). In contrast, Dogen views and uses language more positively by emphasizing the innovative possibilities that Chinese and Japanese encourage but Nagarjuna's philosophical Sanskrit apparently did not.

I wonder how much the languages themselves contribute to this difference. Do Nagarjuna's and Dogen's different approaches perhaps reflect different "mental spaces" created in employing the different types of script? The meaning of an alphabetic script is more indirect (or representational) because letters must first be converted into sounds, while Chinese and Japanese ideographs express their meaning more directly, without speech. How such a non-oral/aural meaning could arise is suggested by the peculiar origin of Chinese characters. According to Simon Leys, the earliest Chinese inscriptions "did not record language, but meanings—directly, and speechlessly: they transcended language" (Leys 1996, 29).

> This Chinese emblematic meta-language developed independently from contemporary speech. For convenience, however, the written characters were progressively given conventional sounds; thus, eventually the inscriptions did not merely convey silent meanings, they could also be read aloud. In the end, they themselves

generated a language—monosyllabic and non-inflected (features
that remain as the special marks of its artificial origin)—and
since this language carried all the prestige of magic and power,
it gradually supplanted the vernacular originally spoken. (Leys
1996, 29–30)

Perhaps an alphabetic script is more likely to suggest a representational
understanding of meaning and truth: as letters represent sounds, so words
re-present things, implying that language is something superimposed on the
world. In contrast, does an ideographic script de-emphasize such a duality
between meaning and reality, encouraging instead the view that thought is
(part of) reality?

In either case, what was more important for Buddhism is that the very
different resources of these different languages—Nagarjuna's alphabetic Sanskrit and Dogen's ideographic Japanese—could be tapped for the same end:
deconstructing the delusive dualisms implicit in our usual ways of "taking"
the world, most of them variations of the fundamental ones between subject
and predicate, substance and attribute. By dividing up the world into things
and their relations, and most of all by distinguishing my sense of self from
the world I live and act "in," I overlook something important about the actual
nature of that world, including myself.

This parallel suggests Nietzsche was wrong when he reflected that "rational thought is interpretation according to a scheme that we cannot throw off."
Nagarjuna and Dogen both demonstrate, in their different ways, that language
at its best can work against its own mystifications. However, neither of them
believed that such conceptual deconstructions are, in themselves, sufficient
to escape the dis-ease that plagues us insofar as we feel separate from the
world (from our bodies, our activities, our death). Both took for granted a
religious tradition that provided the context for their philosophical enterprises,
a rich heritage of ethical and meditative practices provided by Buddhism to
help us transform our ways of experiencing the world. They knew that the
most important deconstruction extends beyond language to deconstruct the
delusive duality between my sense of self and the world.

# THREE

# Dead Words, Living Words, and Healing Words

## *The Disseminations of Dogen and Eckhart*

What does Derrida's type of deconstruction imply about religion and for religion? Toward the end of his life this issue became more important to him and to many of those influenced by his work.[1] In one of his most protracted discussions on the relationship between deconstruction and religion, "Comment ne pas parler: Dénégations" (translated as "How to Avoid Speaking: Denials"), Derrida is primarily concerned to distinguish deconstruction from negative theology. The apophatic language of negative theology suggests a project similar to his, yet the uses to which that language is put have been quite different. Negative theologies tend to conclude that, since all predicative language is inadequate to express the nature of God, only a negative attribution can approach him. This denies God any attributable essence, but merely to reserve a "hyperessentiality," a being beyond Being. Derrida refers specifically to Meister Eckhart, and we can see his point in Eckhart's great sermon on the text "Blessed are the poor," where Eckhart prays to God to rid him of God, for his own real being is above God. Reference to any such unconditioned being is incompatible with Derrida's argument that there is no "transcendental signified," since every process of signification, including all supposed self-presence, is an economy of differences. "There are only, everywhere, differences and traces of differences" (Derrida 1981, 26).

Even if this point about hyperessentiality is accepted, however, a great deal remains to be said about the apophatic language of negative theology. One place to start—or rather (since we never begin at the beginning) one textual strand I would like to continue spinning—is a fine paper by John D. Caputo entitled "Mysticism and Transgression: Derrida and Meister Eckhart."[2] In this essay Caputo is concerned that Derrida's deconstruction has been too easily tied with the familiar death-of-God scenario and used to refute the possibility of God or the sacred. Criticizing this as reductionist, Caputo argues for what he calls the "armed neutrality" of Derrida's *différance*: armed because it holds all existence claims suspect, yet ontologically neutral because it does not imply the existence or nonexistence of any entity. *Différance* establishes the possibility of a language that addresses God just as much as a discourse that denies God, for it does not settle the God question one way or another. "In fact, it *un*settles it, by showing that any debate about the existence of God is beset by the difficulties which typically inhabit such debates, by their inevitable recourse to binary pairs which cannot be made to stick" (Caputo 1989, 28; his emphasis).

It is easy to see why many deconstructionists might be uncomfortable with this conclusion, since the God-quest has usually been our search for an Unconditioned that grounds us. Nonetheless, I think Caputo is correct, and perhaps more than he realizes. It may be easier to see this if we shift from God-talk to Buddha-talk, for the point I want to make has been expressed more clearly in the Buddhist tradition. According to Buddhism, what needs to be *un*settled is neither the God-question nor the Buddha-question but most of all the "commonsense" everyday world, riddled as it is with unconscious, because automatized, ontological committments. Madhyamaka can argue that the limits (*koti*) of this world are the same as the limits of nirvana because our everyday world has been mentally conditioned and socially constructed by attributing self-existence to the objects within it. We experience the world as a collection of discrete, self-existing things that interact causally *in* objective space and time, which leads to suffering insofar as we understand ourselves, too, to be such self-existing things nonetheless subject to the ravages of time and change: beings that are born only to become ill, grow old, and die.

This implies a more radical possibility for the *un*settling that Caputo refers to and that *différance* implies. Merely by subverting such ontological claims, and without making any metaphysical claims of its own, the Buddhist deconstruction of all self-existence (especially our own) can allow something else to manifest—something that has always been there/here yet has been overlooked in our concern to reify (objectify) things in order to fixate on them. Such deconstruction can heal us by revealing a less dualistic way of understanding and experiencing the relation between us and the supposedly objective world we suppose ourselves to be "in."

For Buddhism this sense of separation between me and the world lies at the heart of our notorious inability to be happy. Buddhism relates our dis-ease to the delusive nature of the ego-self, which like everything else is a manifestation of the universe *yet feels separate from it*. The basic difficulty is that insofar as "I" feel separate (i.e., feel myself to be an autonomous, self-existing consciousness), I also feel uncomfortable, because an *illusory* sense of separateness is inevitably insecure. The unavoidable trace of nothingness in my fictitious (constructed rather than self-existing) sense of self is therefore experienced as a sense of lack. In reaction, the sense of self becomes preoc-cupied with trying to make itself—its self—self-existing, in one or another symbolic fashion. The tragic irony is that the ways we attempt to do this cannot succeed, for a sense of self can never expel the trace of lack that always shadows it insofar as it is constructed, while in the most important sense we are already self-existing, since *the infinite set of differential traces that constitutes each of us is nothing less than the whole universe.* "The self-existence of a Buddha is the self-existence of this very cosmos. The Buddha is without a self-existent nature; the cosmos too is without a self-existent nature" (*Karikas* 22:16 in Candrakirti 1979). What Nagarjuna says here about the Buddha is equally true for each of us, and for that matter everything in the universe, the difference being that a Buddha knows it. I think this touches on the enduring attraction of what Heidegger calls onto-theology and what Derrida calls logocentrism, not just in the West but everywhere. Being/being means security to us because it means a ground for the self, whether that is understood as experiencing Transcendence or intellectually sublimated into a metaphysical principle underlying everything. We want to meet God face-to-face, or gain enlightenment, but the fact that everything is *shunya* means we can never attain that. We can, however, realize what we have always been—and never been.[3]

In accordance with this, Madhyamaka and Chan/Zen Buddhism have no teaching to transmit, no doctrine that must be believed or grasped in order to be saved. If our ways of living in the world are what need to be unsettled, what is to be taught will vary according to the person and the situation, because people fixate on different things. "If I tell you that I have a system of *dharma* [teaching] to transmit to others, I am cheating you," declared the sixth Ch'an patriarch, Hui-neng. "What I do to my disciples is to liberate them from their own bondage with such devices as the case may need" (Price and Wong 1974, 132).

This type of unsettling does not give us an answer to the God-question or the Buddha-question in the place we look for it, but provides a different way of experiencing by deconstructing our everyday world into a different one. At the same time (and this reappropriates Caputo's point), from another perspective this nondual way of experiencing nonetheless deepens the reli-gious question, because it leaves the resacralized world *essentially* mysterious in a fashion that cannot be resolved and does not need to be resolved. Every nondual "thing" or event acquires a numinous quality that cannot be fully understood causally or reductively.

What does this Buddhist deconstruction imply about language? How does it affect the ways we hear and speak, read and write? There is some support in the Buddhist tradition, as in negative theology generally, for denying or at least depreciating the value of language. The implication is that linguistic meaning is so inevitably dualistic that it can never adequately describe or express reality; therefore a wise person speaks seldom and little. Nagarjuna denied that he had any views of his own. "If I had a position, no doubt fault could be found with it. Since I have no position, that problem does not arise" (*Vigrahavyavartani* 29). How could he avoid taking a position? "Ultimate serenity is the coming to rest of all ways of taking things, the repose of named things; no truth has been taught by a Buddha for anyone, anywhere" (*Karikas* 25:24, in Candrakirti 1979, 262). This "coming to rest of all ways of taking things" is also found in Chan—for example, in the way that Tung-shan Shou-ch'u (d. 990) distinguished between dead words and living words: "If there is any rational intention manifested in the words, then they are dead words; if there is no rational intention manifested in the words, then they are living words" (C.-Y. Chang 1971, 271). Tung-shan does not deny the usefulness of language but does question its "rational" function—which seems to mean, he denies its validity as a way to understand or "take" things. More recently, the Japanese Zen scholar and popularizer D. T. Suzuki perpetuated a similar distinction in the way he explains the process of working on a koan. The purpose of a koan is to subvert all rational attempts to solve it, he claimed, whereupon we may be transported into a different and nonrational way of experiencing it and the world, including language.

There is a problem with this understanding of "enlightened language," and it is a mistake to conclude that Tung-shan's or Suzuki's view is *the* Buddhist or *the* Mahayana view of language—even if we ignore the obvious contradiction that that would seem to involve! The difficulty with denigrating "rational intentions" and trying to "end all ways of taking things" is that this tends to reinforce the deluded dualism we already make between words and things, between thought and world. The danger is that we will now "take" language/thought as a filter that should be eliminated in order to experience things/the world more immediately—an approach that reconstitutes the problem of dualism in the means chosen to overcome it. An alternative approach was hinted at by Chan master Yun-men Wen-yen (d. 949): "There are words which go beyond words. This is like eating rice every day without any attachment to a grain of rice" (C.-Y. Chang 1971, 271). Hui-neng tells us how words can go beyond words, in the process of explaining why he has no dharma to transmit to others:

> Only those who do not possess a single system of *dharma* can formulate all systems of *dharma*, and only those who can understand the meaning [of this paradox] may use such terms. It makes no difference to those who have realized the essence of mind whether they formulate all systems of *dharma* or dispense with all of them. They are at liberty to come or to go. They are free from obstacles

or impediments. They take appropriate actions as circumstances require. They give suitable answers according to the temperament of the inquirer. (Price and Wong 1971, 132)

For Caputo, following Derrida, Eckhart's "godhead beyond god" is another signifier with transcendental pretensions (Caputo 1989, 33), which needs to be deconstructed and shown to be the function of a network of differences (the sort of deconstruction that Nagarjuna, for example, performs on nirvana in chapter 25 of the *Mulamadhyamakakarikas*). For Derrida no words go beyond words, yet these words of the sixth patriarch imply that for Buddhism there is another perspective where one signifier does not necessarily equal another or simply reduce to being a function of others. I think there is no better way to gain an appreciation of how words can go beyond words than by considering how Hui-neng, Dogen, and Eckhart understood language. And the best way to understand their understanding of language is, of course, to look at how they actually used words.

## Playing with Words

Hui-neng, Dogen, and Eckhart: arguably the greatest Chinese Chan master, the greatest Japanese Zen master, and the greatest medieval Christian mystical writer. They are so elevated in our pantheon of religious heroes that we are apt to overlook how opportunistic—indeed, how thoroughly unscrupulous[4]—they were in the ways they employed language.

Hui-neng's opportunism is obvious in the two passages from his *Platform Sutra* already quoted above. His own words provide some excellent instances of language "free from obstacles or impediments," of teachings that "give suitable answers according to the temperament of the inquirer" and that do not hesitate to contradict received Buddhist teachings. Consider his response to the question of a monk, Chang Hsing-ch'ang, who could not understand the usage of the terms "eternal" and "not eternal" in the *Mahaparinirvana Sutra*:

> "What is not eternal is the buddha-nature," replied the patriarch, "and what is eternal is the discriminating mind together with all meritorious and demeritorious dharmas." "Your explanation, sir, contradicts the sutra," said Chang. "I dare not, since I inherit the heart seal of Lord Buddha. . . . If buddha-nature is eternal, it would be of no use to talk about meritorious and demeritorious dharmas; and until the end of a *kalpa* no one would arouse the *bodhicitta*. Therefore, *when I say 'not eternal' it is exactly what Lord Buddha meant for 'eternal.'* Again, if all dharmas are not eternal,

then every thing or object would have a nature of its own [i.e., self-existence or essence] to suffer death and birth. In that case, it would mean that the essence of mind, which is truly eternal, does not pervade everywhere. *Therefore when I say 'eternal' it is exactly what Lord Buddha meant by 'not eternal.'* . . . In following slavishly the wording of the sutra, you have ignored the spirit of the text." (Price and Wong 1971, 134–35)

From this passage alone it is difficult to understand why Hui-neng reversed the meaning of the two terms. We would need to know more about the situation within which this dialogue took place, the con-text of the text. But apparently it worked: "All of a sudden Chang awoke to full enlightenment." Whether we find Hui-neng's explanation helpful or not, the important point here is that, by his own criterion, there is no arguing with such success.

In his final instructions to his successors before passing away, Hui-neng taught more about how to teach: "Whenever a man puts a question to you, answer him in antonyms, so that a pair of opposites will be formed, such as coming and going. When the interdependence of the two is entirely done away with there would be, in the absolute sense, neither coming nor going" (Price and Wong 1971, 142). If someone is fixated on one view, challenge her with the opposite view—not to convert her to that view but to unsettle her about all views, so that one might slip out between them.

> Language and symbols circumscribe; but, as living forces, they are dynamic enough to open up, constantly re-expressing, renewing, and casting-off, so as to unfold new horizons of their own life. In this way language and symbols know no limits with respect to how far they can penetrate both conceptually and symbolically. No Buddhist thinker was more intensely and meticulously involved with the exploration of each and every linguistic possibility of Buddhist concepts and symbols—even those forgotten, displaced ones—than Dogen who endeavored to appropriate them in the dynamic workings of the Way's realization. (Kim 1981, 9)

Many Buddhists believe that concepts are inherently delusive, and that they should be eliminated in order to realize our true nature. Dogen's approach was very different, and he devoted much energy to demonstrating the importance of language and its possibilities. Before discussing his understanding of language, however, let us notice how he used it.

> Throughout the *Shobogenzo,* Dogen painstakingly dissects a given passage and explores its semantic possibilities at every turn, liter-

ally turning conventional diction upside down and inside out. The result is a dramatic shift in our perception and understanding of the original passage. One of the most rewarding aspects of translating Dogen's *Shobogenzo* is his radical challenge to ordinary language. To Dogen the manner of expression is as important as the substance of thought; in fact, the experimentation with language is equivalent to the making of reality. Furthermore, Dogen frequently puts forth deliberate, often brilliant, "misinterpretations" of certain notions and passages of Buddhism. This distortion of original meaning is not due to any ignorance of Chinese or Japanese (indeed, it testifies to a unique mastery of both) but rather to a different kind of thinking—the logic of the Buddha-dharma. (Kim 1985, 60)

Among the many examples that may be cited, here are a few of the most interesting[5]:

- Dogen's discussion of *to-higan*, "reaching the other shore," transposes the two characters into *higan-to*, "the other shore's arrival," or "the other shore has arrived." The transcribed term no longer refers to a future event but emphasizes the event of realization here and now.

- *Seppo* "preaching the dharma," is reversed in the same way to become *ho-setsu* "the dharma's preaching." This allows Dogen to say: "This 'discourse on the Dharma' is 'the Dharma's discourse.' "

- Dogen takes the term *arutoki*, "at a certain time, sometimes, once," and recombines its components *u*, "to be, to have," and *ji*, "time, occasion" to make *uji*, "being-time," which he uses to signify the nonduality of existence and time.

- The *Bussho* fascicle quotes from the *Nirvana Sutra*: "All sentient beings without exception have Buddha-nature." Dogen rearranges the syntactical components to make them mean: All sentient beings *are* Buddha-nature. As Kim points out, this changes potentiality into actuality, and it liberates us from anthropocentrism. Sentient beings, everything that exists, and Buddha-nature all become nondual.

- Like Heidegger, Dogen converts nouns into verbs and uses them to predicate the same noun, in order to say, for example, "the sky skys the sky." This allows him to escape the subject-predicate dualism of language and point out that, for example, spring "passes without anything outside itself."

- The *Zazenshin* fascicle of the *Shobogenzo* reinterprets a koan about thinking (*shiryo*), not-thinking (*fu-shiryo*), and nonthinking (*hi-shiryo*). The original koan, which Dogen quotes, reads as follows: "After sitting, a monk asked Great Master Yueh-shan Hung-tao: 'What are you thinking in the immobile state of sitting?' The master answered: 'I think of not-thinking.' The monk asked: 'How can one think of not-thinking?' The master said: 'Nonthinking.'" Dogen transforms Yueh-shan's "I think of not-thinking" into "Thinking is not-thinking." *Fu-shiryo* becomes *fu no shiryo*: the not's, or (as Kim puts it) the absolute emptiness's, thinking. That is, *fu-shiryo* no longer refers to the absence or denial of thinking, but suggests instead that authentic thinking is when "the not" is thinking.

What ties together all these remarkable examples is not merely that Dogen unscrupulously twists traditional texts to make them mean whatever he wants them to say. In each case Dogen is conflating a problematic dualism—that is, a deluded way of thinking that causes problems for us. *Higan-to* denies the usual duality between practice and realization. *Ho-setsu* denies any duality between the one who preaches the Dharma and the Dharma that is taught. The *Bussho* fascicle denies the duality between sentient beings and their Buddha-nature. *Uji* denies any duality between beings and their temporality; converting nouns into verbs allows Dogen to deny, for example, the duality between springtime and things in springtime. *Fu no shiryo* denies the especially dangerous dualism (for Buddhist practitioners) between thinking and not-thinking (as it occurs in zazen); practice is not a matter of getting rid of thinking but of realizing the "emptiness" of thinking. *In each instance Dogen does not allow himself to be limited by the usual dualisms of our language, and of our thought, but concocts expressions that leap out of the bifurcations we get stuck in.* For Kim it is "abundantly clear that in these linguistic and symbolic transformations Dogen acts as a magician or an alchemist of language conjuring up an infinity of symbolic universes freely and selflessly as the self-expressions of Buddha-nature" (Kim 1985, 63).

These examples, along with others discussed in the previous chapter, clarify Dogen's understanding of language. Concepts, metaphors, parables, and so forth are not just instrumental, convenient means to communicate truth, for they themselves manifest the truth—or rather, since that way of putting it is still too dualistic, they themselves are the truth that we need to realize. "Words are no longer just something that the intellect manipulates abstractly and impersonally but something that works intimately in the existential metabolism of one who uses them philosophically and religiously in a special manner and with a special attitude. They are no longer mere means or symbols that point to realities other than themselves but are themselves the realities of original enlightenment and the Buddha-nature" (Kim 1975, 110).

In the *Sansuikyo* fascicle Dogen criticizes those who have only an instrumentalist view of language, and who think that koans are simply nonsensical ways to cut off thought: "How pitiable are they who are unaware that discriminating thought is words and phrases, and that words and phrases liberate discriminating thought." What a challenge to the traditional Buddhist dualism between language and reality: the goal is not to eliminate thinking but to liberate it! Despite their problematical aspects, "words are not essentially different from things, events, or beings—all 'alive' in Dogen's thought" (Kim 1985, 57, 58).

"Alive," because language, like any other thing or event, is (and must be realized to be) *ippo-gujin*, "the total exertion of a single dharma." *Ippo-gujin*, a key term for Dogen, embodies his dynamic understanding of the Hua-yen doctrine of interpenetration. According to Hua-yen, each dharma (here meaning any thing or event, and for Dogen this explicitly includes linguistic expressions) is both the cause of and the effect of all other dharmas in the universe. This interfusion means that the life of one dharma becomes the life of all dharmas, there being nothing but that dharma in the whole universe. Since no dharma interferes with any other dharma—because each is nothing other than an expression of all the others—dharmas transcend all dualism. In this way they are both harmonious with all other dharmas yet function as if independent of them.[6]

If we apply this Hua-yen view of dharmas to language, words and metaphors can be understood not just as instrumentally trying to grasp and convey truth (and thereby dualistically interfering with our realization of some truth that transcends words) but as being the truth—that is, as one of the many ways that Buddha-nature *is*.

Dogen is more literary than Hui-neng, yet I do not see any fundamental difference in their teachings and in their views of language. Like Beethoven and the romantic tradition that followed him, Hui-neng opened the door to a path that others explored, in this case by developing the Chan tradition. Is there anyone comparable to Hui-neng and Dogen in Christianity?

> He is a master of life *and* a master of the letter who plays with the syntax and semantics of the scriptural texts and the texts of the masters before him in order to tease out of them ever new senses. He is a master of repetition who knew well that his commentary was not to be a simple reproduction but a new production, a new

rendering which made the old text speak anew and say what had
not been heard. He was constantly altering the syntax of a text,
rewriting it so that it said something new. He would fuss with
trivial features of a text to which no attention at all had been
paid and make everything turn on them, even to the point of
reversing their traditional meaning. . . . He would invert sayings
to see what fruit they would yield.

Is this more of Kim on Dogen? It could be, but in fact it is Caputo on
Eckhart. Let us let him finish his point.

There is no better example, to my knowledge, of a certain mystical dissemination and a religiously joyful wisdom than the bril-
liantly, playful virtuosity of Eckhart's German sermons and Latin
treatises. He rewrites the words of Scripture, turns and twists the
most familiar sacred stories, reinterprets the oldest teachings in
the most innovative and shocking ways. . . . And always with the
same effect: to prod the life of the spirit, to promote its vitality,
to raise its pitch, to enhance its energy. Like a religious answer
to Nietzsche six centuries before the fact, Eckhart engages with
Dionysian productivity in a multiplication of religious fictions
which serve the interests of a "life" which lives out of its own
superabundance, without why or wherefore, for the sake of life
itself. . . . (Caputo 1989, 35)

"There is a grammatological exuberance, a transgressive energy, in Eckhart,"
summarizes Caputo, and because of his own exuberance we can readily for-
give the trendy vocabulary (today we are so eager to transgress!). However,
we need some examples.

Eckhart reads *mutuo*, "reciprocal" as *meo tuo et tuo meo*, "mine yours
and yours mine." He plays with the name of his own religious order (*ordo
praedicatorum*, "order of preachers") to make it an "order of praisers"—that
is, those who offer divine predicates. In the Vulgate version of Romans 6:22,
*Nun vero liberati a peccato*, "Now, however, you have been liberated from sin,"
Eckhart discovers eight different grammatical functions in *vero*, including:
truly (*vere*) delivered from sin; delivered from sin by truth (*vero*, the dative
of *verum*), and so forth. At the beginning of the Gospel of John, *In principio
erat verbum*, "In the beginning was the Word," the words *principium*, *erat*,
and *verbum* are submitted to similar readings, multiplying and disseminating their meanings. Perhaps the most shocking of all, Eckhart presumes to
change the opening lines of the Pater Noster (believed to be the only prayer
we have from Jesus) so that "thy will be done" becomes "will, be thine [i.e.,

God's]," because he believed that willing to do God's will is not as good as getting beyond willing altogether (Caputo 1989, 37).[7]

In the famous story where Jesus says that Mary has chosen the better part (namely, the *vita contemplativa*), Eckhart reverses the traditional understanding by explaining that the repetition of Martha's name ("Martha, Martha, you worry and fret about so many things") means that she had two gifts, the *vita activa* as well as the *vita contemplativa*, and therefore Martha had chosen the better part! This follows from Eckhart's emphasis on spiritual vitality, his teaching that true thankfulness is fruitfulness (i.e., to be made fruitful by the gift one receives, to give birth from it in return). Caputo concludes his article by praising this typical "mystical perversity" whereby Eckhart argues that the better part belongs not to Mary "languishing dreamily at the feet of Jesus, trying to be one with the One" but to Martha who rushes here and there preparing for Jesus's visit "with all the energy and robustness of life."

Perhaps the most significant instance of Eckhart's unscrupulous use of language is the way he plays with the binary terms "Being" and "Nonbeing" (or "Nothing") by nonchalantly reversing their meaning. Sometimes he refers to the being of creatures and describes God as a nothing without the slightest bit of existence. At other times he contrasts the "nullity" of all creatures with the being of God, in which case it is not that God has being, or even that God is being, but that being is God (*esse est deus*). Caputo says that Eckhart "understands quite well that the terms 'Being' and 'Nothing' are functions of each other, that each is inscribed in the other, marked and traced by the other, and that neither gets the job done, alone or together" (Caputo 1989, 31).

Well put, yet Eckhart, like Dogen, plays with syntax and semantics not just to tease out ever new senses, not just to see how many meanings he can make dance on the head of a pin, but to develop some special types of expression, particularly those that can help us to see through the duality between ourselves and God. In the *Bussho* fascicle Dogen reorders syntax to make "All beings have Buddha-nature" into "All beings are Buddha-nature," and Eckhart is happy to reverse the referents of Being and Nothingness to the same end, without ever asserting that both God and creatures have being, for that would involve a dualism between the two: if God is nothing it is because he is our nothingness, and if we are nothing it is because all our being is actually God's. Another denial of that same duality occurs in reading "thy will be done" as "will, be thine [God's]." And Eckhart uses the story of Mary and Martha to deny a derivative dualism between the contemplative life and the active life.

Caputo does not deny a more orthodox side to Eckhart, which denies God (*Deus*) the better to assert the Godhead (*Deitas*) and which understands that Godhead as a superessentiality more real than reality. That is one tendency in Eckhart's writings, yet it is not the only aspect or for us the most significant aspect. " 'I pray God that he may make me free of God' is an ongoing prayer which keeps the discourse open. This is a prayer against closure, against turning the latest and best creations of discourse into idols. It arises from an ongoing distrust of our ineradicable desire for presence, of our insidious tendency to arrest the play and build an altar to a produced effect" (Caputo 1989, 34). This is so well expressed that I hesitate to quibble; yet I think that Eckhart is concerned with more than resisting conceptual closure. Although he does not want to build altars to the products of his originality, his linguistic play is happy to produce them, because he wants to do something more than keep the conversation going. Like Hui-neng and Dogen, he wants us to change the ways we experience and live "in" the world.

This brings us to a crucial question that can no longer be avoided. If, as I have been trying to show, Hui-neng, Dogen, and Eckhart exemplify a freedom with language that Derrida has more recently celebrated; if their writings contain some of the best examples of the liberated kind of dissemination that Derrida's deconstruction implies, which is not pious about any produced effects but is ready to challenge them all; then what is the difference, if any, between what Derrida is doing and what they are doing? What makes their deconstructive disseminations "religious" and Derrida's not?

## The Total Exertion of a Single Word

The answer to this question is most evident in Dogen, although a similar response is implicit in Hui-neng's and Eckhart's writings.

Earlier, in a discussion of *ippo-gujin* ("the total exertion of a single dharma") aspect of language, I emphasized that for Dogen language does not just instrumentally attempt to grasp and convey truth, it *is* truth—that is, one of the ways that Buddha-nature *is*. But of course that is not to deny that language is instrumental as well. The point of the Hua-yen doctrine of interpenetration is that each dharma is both the cause and the effect of all other dharmas. One way to understand this is that linguistic expressions are at the same time both means—they refer to other things—and ends in themselves. This dual function is even embodied in the term "dharma," which (as already noticed) for Buddhism means both things themselves (what really is) and Buddhist teachings (what Buddhism says about what is). Both meanings are necessary. To dwell only on the instrumental and referential aspect of language overlooks the *ippo-gujin* of words, yet to emphasize only *ippo-gujin* ignores the ability of words to affect the ways we perceive things "in" the world. That latter function is also crucial for Buddhism insofar as Buddhism is primarily concerned with helping us transform the way we live in the world: Shakyamuni Buddha said that he taught only *dukkha* and how to end *dukkha*.

Distinguishing these two inseparable aspects of language enables us to clarify the differences between Buddhism and Derrida. On the one side, it seems to me that Derrida's writings do not reveal awareness of the *ippo-gujin* aspect of language. From a Hua-yen perspective, it may be said that Derrida demonstrates how each linguistic-dharma is an effect of all other dharmas, but he overlooks the other aspect equally essential for Mahayana: that each linguistic-dharma is at the same time the only dharma in the whole universe. Yes, every signification is a function of a network of differences, yet for that very reason each transient produced effect is also an end in itself—in fact, the *only* end in itself, the sole reason that the cosmos exists.[8]

Perhaps a favorite metaphor may be used to illustrate this point. The musicological analysis of a score may reveal interesting and important things about the text, but that analysis can never convey the living experience of listening to that music, of actually hearing (for example) that climactic moment in classical sonata form when the key returns to the dominant and the tension that has been building up is resolved harmonically. While that harmonic resolution has meaning only in relation to earlier developments in the music, there are different ways of hearing it. Although we usually retain a sense of ourselves as enjoying the music, there are those all-too-rare moments when we forget ourselves and *become* the music, when we forget past and future to regain an "eternal now" no longer falling away, in which notes no longer succeed each other but the same one dances up and down. This reveals the nondual *ippo-gujin* of music, which at that moment is not different from our own "empty" nature.

Words and symbols can be *ippo-gujin* as well, because besides being instrumental they are, like music and everything else, groundless—that is, without any self-nature or self-presence, which fact Mahayana expresses with the term *shunya*, "empty." From a Buddhist perspective, our intellectual quest may be seen to derive from a sublimated version of the same *dukkha* that haunts the rest of our lives. In response, we try to fixate ourselves somewhere, if only (for intellectuals like me and those likely to read this) on some produced linguistic effect. But as all our various searches for unconditioned grounds and origins are doomed to fail, our philosophizing too sails on an unfathomable ocean without any permanent harbors to cast anchor in. It is only when language is not used as a way to compensate for one's own groundlessness—which makes one grasp at it in order to try to get some truth from it—that language can become a way the mind consummates itself.

We might want to say that this epiphany involves more than a dance with words, but we can just as well call it a special kind of dance. The playfulness of Hui-neng, Dogen, and Eckhart is an end in itself, yet it also embodies an understanding of our *dukkha* and is a considered response to our *dukkha*. The deconstructions of dualisms that we find in these religious innovators can help to free us from our own "mind-forg'd manacles" (as William Blake put it), from chains of our own making (the Zen metaphor).

Their projects are religious, and Derrida's is not, because this other aspect of language—which works to deconstruct the *dukkha* of our lives—is also lacking in Derrida. Derrida in effect deconstructs the subject-object opposition by disseminating it, because he does not believe that it can be recuperated or regathered. That is because we have no access to any nonduality prior to that duality.[9] As a consequence, his deconstruction is more focused on the *dukkha* that operates in language, which is the place we intellectuals search for a truth to fixate on; his philosophical critique does not address the role of grasping and fixation in the rest of our lives.

Dogen's Buddhism and Eckhart's Christianity offer broader critiques of attachment intended to inform and alter the ways we live "in" the world. Buddhist usage of language and claims about language are part of a larger, holistic practice—including moral precepts, ritual, meditation exercises, and so on—that develops nonattachment in all our activities and is therefore able to discover and liberate the *ippo-gujin* in all of them. The deconstructions and disseminations we find in Hui-neng, Dogen, and Eckhart gain their force—a power that survives through the centuries to touch us today—from their challenge to the deadened categories and automatized dualisms that structure the ways we live and suffer in the world.

FOUR

# Zhuangzi and Nagarjuna
# on the Truth of No Truth

To know how to stay within the sphere of our ignorance is to attain the highest. Who knows an unspoken discrimination, an untold Way? It is this, if any is able to know it, which is called the Treasury of Heaven.

—Zhuangzi

Ultimate serenity is the coming to rest of all ways of taking things, the repose of named things; no truth has been taught by a Buddha for anyone, anywhere.

—Nagarjuna

A Chinese legend has it that when old Laozi disappeared into the western frontier he journeyed to India and became Shakyamuni Buddha. I am not in a position to confirm or refute that story, but I enjoy speculating about another: Zhuangzi (often romanized as "Chuang-tzu"), the greatest Daoist philosopher, followed in the footsteps of his predecessor (whom he never mentions) by also traveling to India, where he . . . became Nagarjuna, the greatest of the Buddhist philosophers.

Unfortunately for me, this second possibility is even less likely. One problem is the deathbed story in chapter 32 of the *Zhuangzi* (book and presumed author share the same name), where Zhuangzi declines the lavish funeral his disciples want to give him. There is also a worrisome historical discrepancy: Zhuangzi lived in the fourth century BCE, while most scholars place Nagarjuna in the second century CE. No less troublesome, perhaps, is the radical difference in their philosophical styles. Zhuangzi is unparalleled in Chinese literature for his mocking and satirical tone, and his prose directs its most acid humor at the pretensions of logic. Nagarjuna is unparalleled in Indian thought for his laconic logic, which wields abstract distinctions that no one had noticed before and many since have been unable to see the point of.

61

Despite these formidable objections, Zhuangzi and Nagarjuna share something even more important: the targets and conclusions of their philosophies are remarkably similar, as I will try to show. For a start, both are antirationalists who present us with strong reasons for not believing in reason. According to A. C. Graham, "For Zhuangzi the fundamental error is to suppose that life presents itself with issues which must be formulated in words so that we can envision alternatives and find reasons for preferring one to the other" (Graham 1981, 6).[1] This error is also a pretty good characterization of what Nagarjuna does, except that Nagarjuna uses his dry distinctions to perform a self-deconstruction refuting the possibility of logic to re-present the world conceptually. His magnum opus, the *Mulamadhyamakakarikas* addresses the major philosophical problems of his day, not to determine a definitive position but to demonstrate that no conceptual solutions to them are tenable. Like Zhuangzi, who "temporarily 'lodges' at the other man's standpoint" (Graham 1981, 24) the better to show what is wrong with that standpoint, Nagarjuna adopts his contemporaries' terminology in order to show what is wrong with that terminology.

On the surface, though, the *Zhuangzi* could hardly be more dissimilar. It offers a bewildering succession of anecdotes and arguments whose shifting tone makes it difficult and sometimes impossible to determine which voice represents the author. "Where then is the real *Zhuangzi?* . . . the text turns into a hall of mirrors where a frightening succession of images recedes into infinity and illusion becomes indistinguishable from reality" (Watson, in Mair 1983, x). This postmodernist playfulness, which prefers posing questions to drawing conclusions, functions quite differently from Nagarjuna's univocal dissection of this and that alternative. It subverts our need for a master discourse, for that text which subsumes and unifies others into the truth—that Truth our philosophical labors stake out and lay claim to, the perfectly reasonable position that Zhuangzi loves to mock.[2]

What if there is no such Truth? Or is this insight itself the Truth? Is that a contradiction (and therefore impossible) or a paradox (which encourages a leap to a different level of understanding)? These questions will be addressed by considering what Zhuangzi and Nagarjuna have to say about them. Zhuangzi has been labeled a relativist and/or a skeptic and Nagarjuna a skeptic and/or a nihilist, but in their cases such bald designations put the cart before the horse. We cannot understand whether Zhuangzi is a relativist without first considering what the rest of us expect from the truth. We cannot appreciate their skepticism without considering what motivates the commonsense belief in objective knowledge. Instead of inquiring into what kind of a skeptic or relativist Zhuangzi is—that is, which of our boxes he would fit into (and what fun he would have with that!)—it will be more fruitful to inquire into the relationship between knowledge and his other important themes: no-self, mind-fasting, and dreaming. By no coincidence, these themes are just as important for Buddhism.

## The Illusion of Self and Things

Daoism and Buddhism are unique among the major religions in denying the ontological self. *Anatta* "nonself," is one of the three "basic facts" taught by Shakyamuni Buddha, along with *anicca* "impermanence," and *dukkha* "dissatisfaction." Two of his central teachings deconstruct the self synchronically into *skandhas* "heaps," and diachronically into *pratitya-samutpada* "dependent origination." These doctrines explain how the illusion of self is constituted and maintained. All experiences associated with the illusory sense of self can be analyzed into one of five impersonal *skandhas* (form, sensation, perception, volitional tendencies, and conditioned consciousness), with no remainder. There is no transcendental soul or persisting self to be found over and above their functioning.

This *skandha* analysis has been overshadowed and even subsumed into *pratitya-samutpada*, perhaps the most important Buddhist doctrine of all. Dependent origination explains "our" experience by locating all phenomena within an interacting set of twelve factors (ignorance, volitional tendencies, conditioned consciousness, the fetus, sense organs, contact, sensation, craving, grasping, becoming, new birth, suffering and death), each conditioning and conditioned by all the others. In response to the question of how rebirth can occur without a self that is reborn, rebirth is explained as one in a series of impersonal processes that occur without there being any self that is doing them or experiencing them. When asked to whom belong, and for whom occur, the phenomena described in *pratitya-samutpada*, the Buddha explained that each factor arises from the preconditions created by the other factors; that's all. The karmic results of action are experienced without there being anyone who created the karma or anyone who receives its fruit, although there is a causal connection between the act and its result.

As one would expect from its very different literary style, the *Zhuangzi* is less systematic in its critique of the self, yet the rejection is no less clear. Chapter 1 declares that "the utmost man is selfless" and chapter 17 that "the great man has no self" (Graham 1981, 45, 150). Chapter 2, the most philosophical, begins with Ziqi in a trance, and he says afterward, "[T]his time I had lost my self, didn't you know?" Like other Daoist anecdotes about mindfasting, which explain how to lose one's self, these passages are not concerned to philosophically deconstruct the self into its elements, but they emphasize or presuppose the need for us to get beyond self.

Why is that so important? One problem with the self is its supposed identity: it provides the continuity that persists through change. Insofar as we value the self-identical, the world as a locus of transformation—which threatens the self—tends to be devalued. Yet Daoism and Buddhism agree that there is no such ontological identity or continuity, which means that we are, in effect, depreciating everything that exists in order to cherish something illusory. Daoist emphasis on the ceaseless transformation of things does not reserve a corner for the self to watch from or hide away in, for it is the transformation of that "self" the Zhuangzi celebrates the most. On his deathbed, Master Lai looks upon heaven and earth as a vast foundry and looks forward to being refashioned by the Master Smith. Will he be made into a rat's liver, or a fly's egg (Graham 1981, 88–89)?

Since self does not provide the desired identity, perhaps the most important of those interests is finding or constructing some such identity. Insofar as we have a sense of self, we also feel a need to fixate it or stabilize it—a need that can never be fulfilled if the self is indeed fictional. To have a sense of self without being able to know what one's self is, to be preoccupied with something that cannot be secured because it does not exist—these are formulas for dis-ease (*dukkha*). The implications of this for our understanding of truth will become important later when we consider the intellectual ways our minds seek a stable dwelling-place.

The other way to express the problem with self is its separation from other things. The subject that observes and manipulates objects becomes alienated from its world. To experience oneself as one of many things in the world is to experience the world as a collection of separate things, which according to Daoism and Buddhism is a serious error.

Nagarjuna emphasized that the Buddhist deconstruction of self is just as much a critique of thingness, of the self-existence of things. The first verse of his *Karikas* asserts its thoroughgoing deconstruction of all self-being: "No things whatsoever exist, at any time or place, having risen by themselves, from another, from both or without cause" (Candrakiriti 1979, 36). Paralleling the contemporary poststructural radicalization of structuralist claims about language, Nagarjuna's argument merely brings out more fully the implications of *pratitya-samutpada*. Dependent origination is not a doctrine about causal relations among things, because the mutual interdependence of phenomena means there are really no things.

The importance of this move becomes clearer when we realize that, although Nagarjuna addresses the philosophical controversies of his time, his main target is the unconscious "metaphysics" disguised as the world we live in. If philosophy were merely the preoccupation of some academics, we could ignore it, but we are all philosophers. The fundamental categories of our everyday, commonsense metaphysics are the self-existing things we interact with all the time—chairs, doors, cups, cars, trees, and so on—that originate, change, and eventually cease to be. In order to explain the relations among these objects the categories of space, time, and causality are also necessary. So we experience the world as a collection of discrete things, each of which has its own being (self) yet interacts causally with others in objective space and time. The problem with this understanding of the world is not simply that it is erroneous but that this error causes us to suffer, for we understand ourselves in the same way, as special instances of self-existing things that are nonetheless subject to the ravages of time and change.

If I self-exist, how can I change? How could I die? For that matter, how could I have been born? This is the simple contradiction that Nagarjuna uses to deconstruct self-being. That all phenomena appear and disappear according to conditions means that our usual way of perceiving the world as a collection of separately existing things is a delusion. Nagarjuna does not follow this critique by presenting the "correct" Buddhist metaphysics, for merely by subverting such ontological claims the Buddhist deconstruction of self-existence (especially our own) can allow something else to become apparent—something that has always been apparent yet is overlooked in our preoccupation with satisfying desires and trying to make ourselves more real (self-existent). For Nagarjuna this is the everyday world experienced as nirvana, since there is no specifiable difference whatever between them except for our deluded way of "taking" the world. For Zhuangzi, too, the reason we experience this world as a collection of discrete things rather than as the Dao is that we misperceive it.

I have ignored chronology to discuss Nagarjuna first, because his analysis is more focused and easier to explicate, which means it can help us with some of the obscure passages in the *Zhuangzi*, such as the following: "The men of old, their knowledge had arrived at something: at what had it arrived? There were some who thought there had not yet begun to be things—the utmost, the exhaustive, there is no more to add. The next thought there were things but there had not yet begun to be borders. The next thought there were borders to them but there had not yet begun to be 'That's it, that's not.' The lighting up of 'That's it, that's not' is the reason why the Way is flawed" (Graham 1981, 54).

Instead of offering an account of social development or evolution, Daoist history is the story of a progressive decline in our understanding of the Way. Some of the old sages knew the ultimate, which is that there are no self-existing things, everything being a manifestation of the Dao. Later, people perceived the world as made up of things, but these things were not seen as separate from one another (no borders); their interrelationships and transformations meant the world was still experienced as a whole. Still later, people came to see things as truly discrete, and the world became a collection of objects, yet even they did not use discriminative thinking to understand the world. Once people became trapped in their own dualistic concepts, the Dao was lost.

Zhuangzi often refers to the problem of "That's it, that's not." When that way of thinking lights up, the Dao is obscured. What is he criticizing? One target is the logical analysis that philosophers employ, particularly the Chinese sophists and Mohists of Zhuangzi's time. Yet this by itself is too narrow, for (like the position of Madhyamika scholars who think Nagarjuna's analyses are aimed only at certain Indian philosophical positions) it overlooks the discriminations that we have all learned to make in the process of coming to experience the world in the "ordinary" way. Chapter 2 of the *Daodejing* (a text the inner chapters of the *Zhuangzi* never refer to) discusses and by implication criticizes the conceptual dualisms that bifurcate into opposed categories: "When the world knows beauty as beauty, ugliness arises. When it knows good as good, evil arises. Thus being and nonbeing produce each other," and the same is true for difficult and easy, long and short, and so on (Lin 2006, 4). Nagarjuna is less poetical and more explicit about the problem with such bifurcations. "Without relation to 'good' there is no 'bad,' in dependence on which we form the idea of 'good.' Therefore 'good' [by itself] is unintelligible." For the same reason the concept "bad" is also unintelligible by itself (*Karikas* 23:10–11, in Candrakirti 1979, 213). We distinguish between good and bad because we want to affirm one and reject the other, but their interdependence means we have both or neither. Since the meaning of each is the negation of the other, one can consciously be "good" only by consciously avoiding "bad." In the same way, my love of life is haunted by my dread of death, hope for success is equaled by fear of failure, and so forth.

Insofar as all thinking tends to alternate between "That's it" and "That's not," between assertion and negation, this type of critique tends to end up incorporating all conceptual thinking, including everything that we usually identify as knowledge. This general understanding is consistent with Buddhist emphasis on the letting go of all concepts and with the *Zhuangzi* passages on mind-fasting, which negates such thinking. Yan Hui "expels knowledge" by learning to "just sit and forget" (Graham 1981, 92), and Old Dan teaches Confucius to practice fasting and austerities to "smash to pieces [Confucius's] knowledge" (Graham 1981, 132). Perhaps we can see how such a radical mental cleansing might also wash away the self, but what would that leave behind? Is there an alternative type of thinking that does not fixate on "That's it" and "That's not"?

Other important passages in the *Zhuangzi* explain how "That's it" thinking divides up the world into discrete things, for example:

[When a "That's it" that "deems" picks out things,] the Way interchanges them and deems them one. Their dividing is formation,

their formation is dissolution; all things whether forming or dis-
solving in reverting interchange and are deemed to be one. Only
the man who sees right through knows how to interchange and
deem them one; the "That's it" which deems he does not use,
but finds for them lodging-places in the usual. The "usual" is the
usable, the "usable" is the interchangeable, to see as "interchangeable" is to grasp; and once you grasp them you are almost there.
The "That's it" which goes by circumstance comes to an end; and
when it is at an end, that of which you do not know what is so
of it you call the "Way." (Graham 1981, 53–54)[3]

Although our dualistic ways of thinking cause us to discriminate between things
in the world and to see them as separate from one another, the Dao does not
discriminate between things but treats them as nondual, for it transforms them
into one another. The next sentence is more obscure. Burton Watson translates
it as "Their dividedness is their completeness; their completeness is their impair-
ment" (Watson 1996, 36). This seems to be making a point consistent with the
alternation of yin and yang in the *I Ching*: things take form (yang movement)
by individuating, yet with the completion of that movement (e.g., maturity)
the yang principle is fulfilled and begins to yield to yin dissolution; however,
the Dao transforms them into one another, at whatever stage, because they are
not separate from one another. Likewise, those who understand this clearly do
not treat things as separate from one another. Such people are not trapped by
discriminative concepts that fixate things into this or that, for their more fluid
thinking is aware that designations are always tentative, appropriate only for
particular situations and purposes. Such tentative judgments are made because
they are useful. Realizing that judgments are to be made according to their
usefulness frees one from rigid discriminations and enables us to perceive how
things change into one another—and realizing that is close to realizing the Dao.
The discriminations that are made according to particular circumstances cease
when those circumstances change. What remains then is the world experienced
as it is before our conceptual thinking divides it up: what is called the Dao.[3]

According to this passage, the best judgments ("truths") are tentative,
because they are appropriate only for particular situations and different judgments are needed when those situations change. This perspective is expressed
more clearly in the third Daoist classic, the *Liezi*: "Nowhere is there a principle
that is right in all circumstances or an action that is wrong in all circumstances. The method we use yesterday we may discard today and use again
in the future; there are no fixed right and wrong to decide whether we use it
or not. The capacity to pick times and snatch opportunities, and be never at
a loss to answer events belongs to the wise" (in Graham 1990, 163–64).

If ethical relativism means denying a fixed moral standard by which to
evaluate situations, one could hardly find a better formulation, yet the last

sentence seems to confuse the issue again, by emphasizing a distinction that most relativisms do not reserve a place for. There is an important difference between the sage and the rest of us. Evidently it is not enough to defend such a relativistic position, or to be a relativist in practice, for those philosophers who accept relativism do not thereby become wise, and those who live relativistically do not necessarily live wisely. Mahayana Buddhism makes a similar point with its doctrine of *upaya*, the "skillful means" with which the bodhisattva works for the liberation of all sentient beings, adopting and adapting whatever devices are suitable to the immediate task at hand, disregarding conventional moral codes and even the Buddhist precepts when necessary. This type of relativism, too, is reserved for beings who have attained a high level of spiritual development—the Buddhist equivalent of a Daoist sage.

The difference is that sages are liberated by relativism, or into relativism, while the rest of us are more likely to become its victims, since the freedom it encourages panders to our preoccupation with satisfying insatiable cravings and trying to secure a sense of self that can never be secured. In other words, the difference is self. Those deluded by a sense of self are trapped in their own self-preoccupation, in which case ethical relativism rationalizes doing whatever is necessary to get what one wants. Since sages and bodhisattvas are liberated from self-preoccupation, and because they do not experience others as objects whose well-being is distinct from their own, relativism frees them from the formal constraints that the rest of us seem to need and allows them to get on with the task of saving all sentient beings while actually doing nothing at all (a paradox embraced by both traditions).

If the issue of ethical relativism in the *Zhuangzi* cannot be understood without also considering the role of self, what about other types of relativism, such as knowledge?

## Being No-thing

Much of our problem with understanding the Daoist and Buddhist critiques of self comes down to envisioning an alternative. What can it mean, not to have or not to *be* a self? In both traditions the answer is: to become no-thing. The way to transcend this world is to forget oneself, which is also to become nondual with the world. To become so completely "empty" of any fixed form is to be able to become any-thing. That the Buddha (and our own Buddha-nature) has no fixed form by which he can be recognized is emphasized in Mahayana, especially in the Prajnaparamita literature, whose teachings are very similar to Nagarjuna's. The *Heart Sutra* asserts that all form is emptiness (*shunyata*), and in the *Diamond Sutra* the Buddha says that those who attempt to see him by form or sound cannot see him, for he is not to be recognized by any material characteristic (Price and Wong 1974, 21).

For Zhuangzi also no-thingness characterizes the Dao itself, and becoming no-thing is a return to the source from which things including us arise: "There is somewhere from which we are born, into which we die, from which we come forth, through which we go in; it is this that is called the Gate of Heaven. The Gate of Heaven is that which is without anything; the myriad things go on coming forth from that which is without anything. Something cannot become something by means of something, it necessarily goes on coming forth from that which is without anything; but that which is without anything is for ever without anything. The sage stores away in *it*"(Graham 1981, 103; translator's emphasis).

Having achieved this, the sage can "let the heart [*xin*] roam with other things as its chariot" (Graham 1981, 71). A later chapter quotes the bodhisattva Guanyin:

> Within yourself, no fixed positions:
> Things as they take shape disclose themselves.
> Moving, be like water,
> Still, be like a mirror,
> Respond like an echo.
> Blank! as though absent:
> Quiescent! as though transparent.
> Be assimilated to them and you harmonize,
> Take hold of any of them and you lose.
> (Graham 1981, 281)

The mind as a mirror is perhaps the most important metaphor in the *Zhuangzi* and provides one of its most-quoted passages, from the very end of the inner chapters: "Hold on to all that you have received from Heaven but do not think you have gotten anything. Be empty, that is all. The Perfect Man uses his mind [*xin*] as a mirror—going after nothing, welcoming nothing, responding but not storing" (Watson 1996, 95).

In terms of the image, self-forgetting or mind-losing (*wang xin*) is the practice of polishing one's mind-mirror and keeping it free of impurities. Needless to say, such meditative techniques are also important in Buddhism. Although Nagarjuna does not discuss such practices, as a monastic he was doubtless familiar with them, and they provide the context within which his work must be situated, especially its emphasis on *prapancopasama*, "the cessation of conceptual ways of understanding," which is necessary if one is to experience things as they are. Burton Watson suspects that the *Zhuangzi* must originally have been accompanied by similar practices to help students realize what it describes, yet all that survives in the text are some references to controlled breathing (Watson, in Mair 1983, xiii).[4]

By such practices the *xin* of the sage becomes "the reflector of heaven and earth, the mirror of the myriad things" (Graham 1981, 259). Nonetheless, the mirror metaphor, like all metaphors, has its limitations. To be a perfectly polished mirror is not quite the same as being no-thing at all. There is still a dualism between reflector and reflected. This may encourage the tendency of contemplative types to stand back from the world, but Zhuangzi will have none of that. "To be transformed day by day with other things is to be untransformed once and for all. Why not try to let them go? For the sage, there has never yet begun to be Heaven, never yet begun to be man, never yet begun to be a Beginning, never yet begun to be things" (Graham 1981, 110–11). To forget oneself completely, truly to become no-thing, means more than to reflect the transformations of things: it is to be wholly identified with them, to be them—in which case there are really no things and no transformations, since "that which is without anything is for ever without anything" (quoted above, p. 69). Such a world is not a collection of things but composed of events and processes. Evidently someone who realizes he or she is no-thing remains no-thing even as he or she playfully assumes this or that form. When there is no thing or self that exerts itself to do things, there is the spontaneity (*ziran*, "so of itself") of actions that are experienced as no actions (*wu wei*), of transformations that are just as much nontransformations.

When I forget my-self I fall into the world, I become its manifold of interdependent phenomena transforming into one another. What does this mean for language and truth? Do they too become such a transformative manifold?

## The Ignorance of Truth and the Truth of Ignorance

To realize that there are no things is not to float in a porridge where each spoonful is indistinguishable from the next. It is to store away in the Gate of Heaven, which remains no-thing even as all things arise from it and transform into one another.

If we replace "things" in the previous paragraph with "words," what would that imply about language?

According to A. C. Graham (in Mair 1983, 8), grasping the Dao is a matter not of "knowing that" but of "knowing how," as shown by the many craftsmen Zhuangzi is fond of citing.[5] What would "knowing how" with words be like? It is no coincidence that Zhuangzi himself provides one of the greatest examples, and not only for Chinese literature.[6] Clearly there is a special art to this as well, which is not completely indifferent to logic and reasoning as we have come to understand them in the West, yet which is not to be identified with them, either. One of the delights of the *Zhuangzi* for Western readers is the way its many different voices disrupt our distinctions between form and content, rhetoric and logic—bifurcations that may be questionable legacies of the Western intellectual tradition.

What is the knowing how with words that Zhuangzi shows? "The Way has never had borders, saying has never had norms. It is by a 'That's it' which deems that a boundary is marked" (Graham 1981, 57). A *"That's it!" which deems* is speech that fixates things and becomes fixated itself, which Zhuangzi repeatedly contrasts with the more fluid *"That's it!" which goes by circumstances*, speech that changes when circumstances change. The parallel here between things and words is so close that it is more than a parallel. Our language fixates the world into things, and once they are fixated the words that fixate them are also fixated—into "the truth." In contrast to the everyday world of differentiated objects, the Dao is not an otherworldly denial of things nor their transcendence, but their no-thingness, which enables their interpenetration and incessant transformation into one another.

In contrast to the everyday use of words that fixates things by fixating categories, the Dao does not involve an ineffable rejection of language as inevitably dualistic and delusive, but celebrates language such as we find in the *Zhuangzi*, a playfulness possible when we are no longer trapped by and in our own words. "Words exist because of meaning; once you've got the meaning you can forget the words. Where can I find a man who has forgotten words so I can have a word with him?" (Watson 1996, 118). Here we are delighted by the tension between wanting to escape words (that "deem") and delighting in words (that do not deem).

Why do we cling to words that deem? As one would expect, here too the problem is self. "Saying is not blowing breath, saying says something; the only trouble is that what it says is never fixed" (Graham 1981, 52). That is no trouble at all if we do not need to fixate on words, but the problem is we do. The transformation of words, like the transformation of things, is terrifying to an insecure (because illusory) self that is always seeking to secure itself. How uncomfortable it is to realize that one's opinion of something is wrong and needs to be changed. How much more anxious does one become when one starts letting go of all one's opinions about the world and, most of all, one's opinions about oneself—to let go of the self-image whereby one's self is fixated. If the self is that which needs to settle on "That's it" or "That's not," without such a self there is no need to dwell on only one perch: "What is It is also Other, what is Other is also It. There they say 'That's it, that's not' from one point of view, here we say 'That's it, that's not' from another point of view. Are there really It and Other? Or really no It and Other? Where neither

It nor Other finds its opposite is called the axis of the Way. When once the axis is found at the center of the circle there is no limit to responding with either, on the one hand no limit to what is it, on the other no limit to what is not" (Graham 1981, 53).

"It is easy to keep from walking; the hard thing is to walk without touching the ground" (58). And it is easy to keep from talking; the hard thing is to talk without needing a ground. According to Graham's gloss, it is easy to withdraw from the world and live as a hermit; it is harder to remain above the world while living in it. Yet without a self we float quite easily, if its need to ground itself is what weighs us down.

In place of our usual distinction between knowledge and ignorance, this yields a knowing that becomes indistinguishable from a kind of ignorance. "How do I know that what I call knowing is not ignorance? How do I know that what I call ignorance is not knowing?" (58). What we usually consider knowing—deeming that something "is *this*"—can reveal our ignorance about the transforming nature of language and things. What is often understood as ignorance—not settling finally on "It's this" or "It's that"—can reflect insight into that nature. If "we have the axis on which things turn, and to start from have that which is other than ourselves, then our unraveling will resemble failing to unravel, our knowing will resemble ignorance" (63). This "ignorance" of the sage allows her to play with truths freely insofar as she feels no need to fixate herself by fixating on any particular one.

The exception will be when we want to accomplish something, yet that is no problem for the sage, whose free roaming harbors no such schemes. "Since the sage does not plan, what use has he for knowledge?" For him our usual "knowledge is a curse," whereas "utmost knowledge doesn't plan" (82).

As this last quotation suggests, Zhuangzi's understanding of knowledge and ignorance can be formulated into two levels of truth. Such a two-truths doctrine is also essential to Buddhism, especially Mahayana, and its paradigmatic formulation is by Nagarjuna: "The teaching of the Buddhas is wholly based on there being two truths: that of a personal everyday world and a higher truth which surpasses it. Those who do not clearly know the true distinction between the two truths cannot clearly know the hidden depths of the Buddha's teaching. Unless the transactional realm is accepted as a base, the surpassing sense cannot be pointed out; if the surpassing sense is not comprehended nirvana cannot be attained" (*Karikas* 24:8–10, in Candrakirti 1979, 230–32).

Shakyamuni himself made an implicit distinction between words that deem and words that change with circumstances when he compared his own teachings to a raft that may be used to cross the river (of samsara) to the other shore (nirvana) and then should be abandoned, not carried around on one's back. Nagarjuna also did not understand his own writings as committing him to a particular view: There is no position to be taught because there is no truth that needs to be attained; all we need to do is to let go of delusion. In the *Diamond Sutra* Subhuti asks the Buddha if his realization of supreme enlightenment means that he has not acquired anything. "Just so, Subhuti. I have not acquired even the least thing from the consummation of incomparable enlightenment, and that is called the consummation of incomparable enlightenment" (Price and Wong 1974, 21). Then it could just as well be called supreme ignorance—something not to be confused with ordinary ignorance.

How does this reconcile with the two-truths doctrine enunciated by Nagarjuna, which emphasizes the importance of the higher truth in attaining nirvana? Any insight identified as the higher truth becomes the lower truth. Does this make no-truth the higher truth? Describing no-truth makes it part of the lower truth. We need to realize the contextual, "upayic" function of all truth. That makes it sound easy, yet the rub is that such a realization requires a letting go of oneself, which is seldom if ever easy. The basic problem, again, is that discriminating between ignorance and truth—rejecting the one, grasping the other—is an intellectual way (is especially the intellectual's way) the self tries to find some secure ground for itself. With such discriminations we tame the mystery and terror of the world into the truths we deem necessary because they teach us what the world is, who we are, and why we are here. Untold millions have killed and died defending such truths. In politics it is the ideology that will usher us into the promised land. In religion it is faith in the doctrine that can save us and that therefore needs to be defended at all costs against heretics. It can also be the "liberating insights" of psychoanalysis and deconstruction, or the "enlightening" Asian wisdom of Buddhism and Daoism. This is not to deny that they can be liberating and enlightening, but only when we do not need to secure our-selves can we become comfortable with the lack of such a higher truth to identify with.

Then the truth of no-truth must always self-deconstruct. On the one hand, it needs to be expressed somehow, for without that there is no Daoist or Buddhist teaching and no help for the benighted. As Nagarjuna puts it, the transactional realm—our everyday use of language and usual understanding of truth—is necessary to point out the surpassing sense of truth, that there is no higher truth whose understanding liberates us. Yet what one hand offers the other must take away. No statement of this paradox can be final, pretending to offer a definitive understanding. Trying to do so makes us like the would-be sage who realized that no one should have disciples and then promptly organized a group of disciples to disseminate this teaching. Does intellectual understanding of these issues make us into converts who, in effect, join that band of disciples?

## Dreaming of Waking Up

Last night Zhuang Zhou dreamed he was a butterfly, spirits soaring he was a butterfly (is it that in showing what he was he suited his own fancy?), and did not know about Zhou. When all of a sudden he awoke, he was Zhou with all his wits about him. He does not know whether he is Zhou who dreams he is a butterfly or a butterfly who dreams he is Zhou. Between Zhou and the butterfly there was necessarily a dividing; just this is what is meant by the transformation of things.

—Zhuangzi

Everything in this world can be taken as real or not real; or both real and not real; or neither real nor not real. This is the Buddha's teaching.

—Nagarjuna

The meaning of Zhuangzi's celebrated butterfly dream has been much debated and always will be, since clearly the ambivalence of its meaning is as much Zhuangzi's intention as the ambivalence of the dream. The central tension of the story is between Zhuang Zhou waking up and Zhuang Zhou wondering whether he has indeed awakened. What is the difference? The story does not want to persuade us that this world is a dream, but to raise doubts about whether this world might be a dream. Evidently ignorance on this matter is more valuable than knowing the answer. Is that because ignorance is preferable, if we want to truly wake up and experience things as they really are? Or is there a kind of ignorance that is itself waking up?

Insofar as we want to understand Zhuang Zhou's dream, it is helpful to place it in context by considering the two other important passages on dreaming in the inner chapters of the *Zhuangzi*.

> How do I know that the dead do not regret that they ever had an urge to life? . . . While we dream we do not know we are dreaming, and in the middle of a dream interpret a dream within it; not until we wake do we know that we were dreaming. Only at the ultimate awakening shall we know that this is the ultimate dream. Yet fools think they are awake, so confident that they know what they are, princes, herdsmen, incorrigible! You and Confucius are both dreams, and I who call you a dream am also a dream. (Graham 1981, 59–60)

This dreaming is less ambiguous than Zhuang Zhou's butterfly one. We are all dreaming, which we will realize when we finally awaken. This assertion must be understood in its wider context, which wonders whether we are wrong to love life and fear death. Perhaps those who do so are exiles who have forgotten the way home. If so, life itself is the ultimate dream and death the ultimate awakening.

Despite Nagarjuna's unwillingness in the epigraph above to commit himself to one view at the cost of the other, there are prominent passages in the Mahayana scriptures that unambiguously assert that this world is unreal and dreamlike. In chapter 2 of the *Ashtasahasrika Prajnaparamita*, for example, Subhuti declares that beings, all objective facts, and even the Buddha and nirvana itself are like an illusion and a dream (Conze 1973, 98–99). The *Diamond Sutra* concludes that we should view things as like a bubble, a lightning flash, a dream (Price and Wong 1974, 53).

There is one more important dream in the inner chapters of the *Zhuangzi*: "You dream that you are a bird and fly away into the sky, dream that you are a fish and plunge into the deep. There's no telling whether the man who speaks now is the waker or the dreamer. Rather than go toward what suits you, laugh: rather than acknowledge it with your laughter, shove it from you. Shove it from you and leave the transformations behind; then you will enter the oneness of the featureless sky" (Graham 1981, 91).

This dream is more like the butterfly dream. The speaker does not know whether he is awake or dreaming. But why is it so important for us to know that? What in us needs to know which is which? Instead of dreaming about waking up, perhaps we should consider why we are so wary of dreams. What makes a dream a dream? Things in a dream are unreal in the sense that they do not have any objective stability or self-existence. They are constantly appearing, disappearing, and transforming into something else. Yet that is also true for this world, according to Zhuangzi and Nagarjuna! In which case the distinction between the two realms becomes less important. To wake up, then, is to realize there is only the dream. To dream of waking up from that dream is to fantasize about attaining a Reality that will save me from my empty, unfixed, transforming nature, which makes me uneasy because I want to remain self-identical as the rest of the world changes. If so, to "wake up" from my constantly changing nature (in which I become, say, a butterfly) is actually to fall asleep into the ignorance that thinks "I" am this body and this particular self among a collection of other discrete things. To dream I am a butterfly, and so forth, is to wake up to my self-less, endlessly transforming nature.

As with other dualistic categories, however, the concept of dreaming has meaning only in relation to the concept of waking up and leaving dream transformations behind. If there is only the dream, there is no dream. Yet the *Zhuangzi* says that the alternative to dreaming is not another world or higher dimension but "the oneness of the featureless sky." Such a featureless oneness is indistinguishable from no-thing-ness. It is important to forget oneself and experience this no-thing-ness—to become no-thing—because that extinguishes the self. It is just as important not to remain in that featureless oneness, because, in Buddhist terms, that is "clinging to emptiness." Although form is not other than emptiness, emptiness is not other than form. Their nonduality is the great dream that we awaken not from but to.

# FIVE

# CyberBabel

There will be a road. It will not connect two points. It will connect all points. It will not go from here to there. There will be no there. We will all only be here.

—MCI television advertisement

To be only *here,* and for here to be always *now*: Would that be the technological fulfillment of our dreams, or a dystopian nightmare? Or both? Our new cyberenvironments have begun to compress space and time so radically that we cannot help wondering if, or how, they are also altering consciousness itself. Are we on the cusp of some kind of profound transformation of the human condition?

If so, not everyone is looking forward to it. According to one of the sharpest critics of cybertime, Paul Virilio, instantaneous communication and almost-as-fast transportation are creating the "desert" of a global endless-day time. His main concern is that remote control and long-distance telepresence technologies are producing an "ultimate state of sedentariness," both terminal and final, opening up "the incredible possibility of a 'civilization of forgetting,' a *live* (live-coverage) society that has no future and no past, since it has no extension and no duration, a society intensely present here and there at once—in other words, *telepresent to the whole world.*" Virilio believes that, instead of augmenting our awareness, such a telepresent society degrades the life of subjects and the mobility of objects by "atrophying the *journey* to the point where it becomes needless" (Virilio 1997, 33).

Why should we make the effort to go anywhere or do anything if everywhere is already here, if everytime is now? The differences between here and there, now and then, become so vitiated that they also become meaningless. Our relationships are constructed of encounters and departures, people (and things) who were *there* coming *here,* and then going *somewhere else*—in short, a dialectic of presence and absence. Because we cannot relate to everything and everyone at the same time, we take for granted the spatiotemporal schema that meetings and farewells presuppose. Virilio is concerned that cybertimelessness is eroding that schema. Without such a dialectic, continuous telepresence tends to become indistinguishable from continuous loneliness. "The resistance of distances having ceased, the lost world will send us back to our solitude, a multiple solitude of some billions of individuals whom the multimedia are preparing to organize in quasi-cybernetic fashion" (Virilio 1997, 128).

In a 2004 *Washington Post* article, Catie Getches seems to be describing what this actually means:

> All it takes is a little time alone, especially late at night, to confirm how much technology has transformed culture and how it has changed the way we relate to each other. That's because being alone is not what it used to be. These days, even momentary solitude seems like something to be avoided at all cost. And technology makes it possible: Thanks to cell phones, no one has to face that stroll down the street, the five-minute commute or the lunch line without companionship. . . .
>
> So it seems as if it should be easier for everyone to connect, late at night or whenever. But the more technology we turn on, the more relationships we have to manage simultaneously—and the more likely we are to ask our best friends if they can hold. I have programmable phone lists and speed dial at my fingertips, and yet I feel more disconnected than ever—somehow, it's easier than ever to be two places at once but nearly impossible to, as my mom says, just "be here now." Yet being in two places at once has become strangely familiar: You don't just go out to lunch with a friend anymore. You go out to lunch with the friend and the friend's cell phone book. . . .
>
> It's so common now to correspond by e-mail alone, it's easy to go for days without actually interacting with a real live human. . . . (Getches 2004)

Getches's insight does not stand alone. Repeated studies have shown, for example, that increased Internet usage is associated with less family communication and a reduced social circle.[1] The more time people spend online, the higher their rates of loneliness and depression. "The frequency of contact and volume of contact does not necessarily translate into the quality of contact," according to John Powell, a counselor at the University of Illinois. "All the students I work with have incredibly many pseudo-intimate relationships online—but without the kind of risk and vulnerability that goes with sitting across a café booth from another person." The result is that students are having increasing difficulty "maintaining really satisfying connections."[2]

Getches expresses the paradox: to be connected to everyone is to be disconnected, to relate to everyone is to lose the ability to relate deeply. Is that because of an "economy" to our relationships? If interacting with an actual physical presence is what might be called a "very high-context information medium," telecommunication is a low-context medium that sustains lower-context interpersonal meaning—that is, lower-context relationships. When we communicate with so many more people, we tend to find ourselves communicating less with the people most important to us. Given that we have a limited amount of attention and energy for relating to others, a profusion of low-context cybercommunications will have to be at the price of our most important high-context relationships.

Can this point be extrapolated? To be *attentive* to everything telepresent would spread one's awareness so thinly that it would amount to *ignore*-ance. In terms of my *responsiveness* to that infinity of information, doesn't infinite possibility likewise imply paralytic indecision? How do I decide what to do, what should have priority, when nothing is more present than anything else, physically or temporally?

Of course, we are not yet in that situation, and may never be, but we are getting close enough to appreciate the problem. For a minor example, consider how compact disc players and iPods have changed the ways we listen to music. Today, when I happen to hear some interesting composition by someone hitherto unknown to me, I usually—often immediately—go online to check it out, to find out what other CDs are available from that performer or composer, and what other listeners think about those CDs. Instead of focusing on the CD I have been listening to, I want to acquire more of the same. I can order other CDs instantly and sometimes do. What happens to those CDs when they arrive? To tell the truth, they tend to pile up unheard for a while, because although there is time to buy them (that does not take long, with one-click ordering) there seems to be less time to listen to them. My desire to hear them becomes internalized as another, if pleasant, aspect of the time compression that increasingly squeezes my life. A decade or so ago, my attention would have been focused on appreciating that particular CD for several days or weeks, but now it is almost as easy to explore related possibilities. In other words, my interests and desires can propagate effortlessly. The *increasing choice* that has been identified as central to modernity[3] has become closer to *infinite choice* today, for many of us. Thanks to Amazon and other online services, my problem is not obtaining the CDs I want, but finding or making the time to listen to them with the attention they deserve.

In *The Paradox of Choice: Why More Is Less,* Barry Schwartz argues that, instead of making us happier, ever-increasing choice is linked to decreasing well-being, by making it more difficult for us to decide among so many options. Along with several other psychologists recently, he emphasizes that what does enhance our well-being is close personal relationships such as family and church communities. Social *ties*—spouse and children being the obvious example—actually limit our freedom, which implies that freedom in itself might not be as important as we usually think.[4]

What does the paradox of choice mean for *how* I listen to all my CDs? When I do have the time to hear one of them, often downloaded into my iPod, I am constantly aware, at some level of consciousness, that if I am not completely satisfied with what I am hearing, there are a thousand other CDs on that iPod I could be listening to right now. A century ago, someone who loved Beethoven's music might have only a few opportunities, or maybe none at all, to hear some of his piano sonatas, even if the ticket price of a live performance were not a factor. I can listen to any of those thirty-two sonatas anytime I want. A century ago, one was part of a live audience, each member having made efforts to obtain a ticket and gather for that specific event, and once there you were *there,* so you settled down *then* and focused on the music being performed. For me, the decision to listen to any particular *selection* is never completely settled in the sense that I can immediately change it if I become dissatisfied with it, for any reason at any time. Awareness of these other possibilities tends to distract me from the music I am actually hearing. I must, in effect, *continually decide* to listen to this particular piece.

What gives this rather trivial example some significance, of course, is that the point applies just as much to so many other aspects of our lives: books, TV channel-surfing, DVDs, video games, surfing the Net, and so on. Needless to say, this near-infinite choice is not all bad. I have enjoyed exploring the classical repertoire, discovering obscure composers and new performers. I am far from suggesting that we should give all this up, even if that were possible. Nonetheless, how all these options are affecting our attention spans is an important issue. Lately I seem to be listening to fewer symphonies and more short, simple pieces; am I the only one?

The Norwegian scholar Thomas Eriksen has distilled this phenomenon into a temporal principle. As he sees it, what we lack most now is lack of information: we are drowning in an info-glut (Eriksen 2001, 19). Our old time habits were based on info-scarcity, hence the traditional importance placed on learning how to forage for the facts we needed. Suddenly, like the sorcerer's apprentice, we find ourselves trying to survive an information tsunami, and our scarcest resources have become *attention* and *control over our own time.* Eriksen formalizes this relationship into a general law of the information revolution: "When an ever increasing amount of information has to be squeezed into the relatively constant amount of time each of us has at our disposal, the span of attention necessarily decreases" (Eriksen 2001, 21–22, 69).[5]

I think Eriksen's insight can be extrapolated to include the near-infinite range of consumption possibilities that also besiege our attention and proliferate our cravings. That gives us the following reformulation:

$$\frac{\text{same (limited) amount of time}}{\text{more possibilities (info-glut + digital shopping mall)}} = \text{shorter attention span}$$

Even without the omnipresent seduction of near-infinite consumer alternatives, such an avalanche of information (and therefore shorter attention spans) challenges our ability to construct narratives and logical sequences. Info-excess puts pressure on traditional, more complexly structured ways of thinking that emphasized cause/effect and organic development. In their place, "the World Wide Web inculcates a strong and almost reflex-like preference for heightened visual stimuli, rapid changes of subject matter, and diversity, combined with simplicity of presentation" (Dawson 2001, 7). Sherry Turkle has noticed that some of her MIT students now reason and arrange their ideas differently. "There is this sense that the world is out there to be Googled," she says, "and there is this associative glut. But linking from one thing to another is not the same as having something to say. A structured thought is more than a link."[6] Has linking replaced thinking?

A cascading glut of decontextualized signs (Eriksen 2001, 109), with an inelastic amount of attention to make them meaningful, results in link-glut, association-glut. Does infinite linking become equivalent to no links at all? This may be a new problem, but it is not a new metaphor, for it was developed in Jorge Luis Borges's prescient 1941 short story "The Library of Babel."[7] In this fable Borges's narrator describes a world consisting only of a boundless library with endless shelves of books containing nothing but line after line of apparently random letters and punctuation.

> In all the Library, there are no two identical books. From these incontrovertible premises, the librarian deduced that the Library is "total"—perfect, complete, and whole—and that its bookshelves contain all possible combinations of the twenty-two orthographic symbols (a number which, though unimaginably vast, is not infinite)—that is, all that is able to be expressed, in every language.

If they exhaust all orthographic possibilities, the library's books must encompass all (linguistic) truth and wisdom, including the correct answer to every conceivable question. But at a price. "When it was announced that the Library contained all books, the first reaction was unbounded joy. All men felt themselves the possessors of an intact and secret treasure. There was no personal problem, no world problem, whose eloquent solution did not exist—somewhere in the hexagon. . . ." We rejoice in having so much information at our fingertips. "At that same period there was also hope that the fundamental mysteries of mankind—the origin of the Library and of time—might be revealed. . . ."

Might such a Library transform the human condition, perhaps even alter our consciousness? "That unbridled hopefulness was succeeded, naturally enough, by a similarly disproportionate depression. The certainty that some bookshelf in some hexagon contained precious books, yet that those precious books were forever out of reach, was almost unbearable."

Out of reach, because an all-inclusive data-glut turns out to be equivalent to no data at all, if it is impossible to locate texts providing the information one seeks. This is a problem that could not be solved even if the Library had a Google-like search engine, because the basic issue is not how to find the right books, but rather the meaningless (because completely decontextualized) nature of the infinite data that the Library's books contain. Eriksen reflects on how our own data-glut affects the way we experience the present: "The moment, or instant, is ephemeral, superficial and intense. When the moment (or even the *next*) *moment* dominates our being in time, we no longer have space for building blocks that can only be used for one or a few configurations with other blocks. Everything must be interchangeable with everything else *now*. The entry ticket has to be cheap, the initial investment modest. Swift changes and unlimited flexibility are main assets. In the last instance, everything that is left is a single, overfilled, compressed, eternal moment" (Eriksen 2001, 119; his emphasis).

## An Eternal Present?

Is Eriksen's eternal moment the *eternal now* that religious mystics yearn for? Not quite. What makes the mystic's *now* eternal is that it is not ephemeral nor superficial. According to the Neoplatonist philosopher Plotinus, "There is all one day, series has no place; no yesterday and no tomorrow." Nicholas of Cusa made the same point: "All temporal succession coincides in one and the same Eternal Now. So there is nothing past or future." The Chan (Zen) master Huang-po: "Beginningless time and the present moment are the same. . . . You have only to understand that time has no existence."[8] Instead of repeatedly falling away, replaced by a different *now*, the eternal presence that these mystics claim to have experienced does not exclude past and future but encompasses them. Cybertime, however, aspires to a different timelessness.

"*When time is chopped up into sufficiently small units,* ... it ceases to exist as duration (which presupposes that events take a certain time) but continues to exist as *moments about to be overtaken by the next moment*" (Wilber 1977, 123; his emphasis).

What is the difference between these two types of eternal presence? The cyberpresent results from slicing time ever more thinly until sense of duration disappears, replaced by accelerating speed. Our awareness usually hops from one perch to the other, yet now it hops more and more quickly because we are running on an accelerating treadmill. Eriksen's point is that this is possible only because now-moments—our treadmill steps—are denuded of meaningful content. Each step tends to become interchangeable with the previous step, or the next one. Whatever content there is is immediately replaced by different content. Without a relationship to previous and following moments, the present becomes dehistoricized, autonomous, and fungible with the next moment. "To define the present in isolation is to kill it" (Paul Klee, quoted in Virilio 1997, 10).

This point may seem abstract, but aren't we already experiencing the psychological implications? As Margaret Gibbs, a psychologist at Fairleigh Dickinson University, points out: "We've become a society where we expect things instantly, and don't spend the time it takes to have real intimacy with another person."[9]

From a Buddhist perspective, accelerating cybertime still perpetuates the dualism that we experience between things (including ourselves) and the time they are "in." The sense of a self *within* (and therefore *distinguishable from*) time is a delusion that causes suffering. This perceived split between things and their temporality is not something real or objective but mentally constructed—which opens up the possibility that it can be deconstructed.

According to Buddhism, to end our *dukkha*, "suffering," we must realize *anatta*, "not-self." This does not mean getting rid of the self (since there never has been a self) but rather realizing that one's sense of self is *shunya*, "empty"—in modern terms, a psychological and social construct. Existential psychology emphasizes the consequences of repressing our fear of death, but from a Buddhist perspective dread of death still projects our main problem into the future. The Buddhist emphasis on *anatta* implies that our worst *dukkha*, and therefore our most troublesome repression, is our groundlessness right now. We never feel real enough because there is an emptiness at the core of our being. In other words, the *sense* of self is haunted by a sense of lack, which it vainly tries to resolve or escape.

What does this have to do with cybertime? Norman O. Brown gives us a good hint: time is "a schema for the expiation of guilt" (Brown 1961, 277). If "guilt" is replaced with "lack," we can say that our usual ways of experiencing and understanding time are tied up with our ways of trying to resolve or evade our sense of lack. That is why we are usually uncomfort-able with the *eternal present* of the mystics: to really live in the *now* exposes our groundlessness.

In contrast to premodern preoccupation with finding security by repeating the past, modernity emphasizes the future in the belief that our lack will be resolved and we will become more fulfilled (grounded) if and when our projects have been successfully completed. In sociological terms, Western cultures emphasize achievement more than affiliation; tradition is less important than the freedom to change and improve our situation. The psychoanalyst Neil Altman realized this when he was a Peace Corps volunteer in India: "It took a year for me to shed my American, culturally based feeling that I had to make something happen . . . Being an American, and a relatively obsessional American, my first strategy was to find security through getting something done, through feeling worthwhile accomplishing something. My time was something that had to be filled up with progress toward that goal" (Altman, in Levine 1997, 204–5).

Since the goals we accomplish bring no satisfaction (our sense of lack still itches), we always need more ambitious projects. Unfortunately, this same dynamic also seems to be operating collectively, in our preoccupation with never-enough economic growth and never-ending technological development. As Max Weber pointed out, this historical process has become all the more obsessive because it has no teleological end-point.[10] We feel compelled to grow ever faster because there is nowhere in particular that we are trying to get to. Such a future-orientation, however, no more reflects the "true" nature of time than does the Mayan obsession with keeping the sun on its course by ritual sacrifice. Like the Mayas, our modern orientation remains motivated by an individual and collective groundlessness that has not been understood.

To become comfortable with that groundlessness—to transform it—the sense of a self that is distinct from the time it is "in" must be deconstructed. The rest of this essay adumbrates the Buddhist solution, which provides an expe-rience very different from the durationless, disconnected cybertime(lessness) that Virilio fears and Getches laments.

In his *Shobogenzo* the thirteenth-century Japanese Zen master Dogen Kigen conflated the usual dualism between time and the things "in" it by reduc-ing each pole to the other. *Objects are time* because they lack any nontemporal existence. Things like apples and cups have no atemporal essence outside of time, because their impermanent "being" is actually a temporal *process* (an apple is eaten or rots, a ceramic cup eventually cracks). This point may seem rather abstract, but the same is true, of course, for the temporal processes that are you and I. In other words, it is not quite right to say that "I" am "in" time, because I am *essentially* temporal.

Conversely, Dogen also demonstrates that *time is objects*, for our aware-ness of time depends on the way things change (for example, the way the hands circle around the face of a clock). This too conflates the usual duality of things "in" time. Time is not an objectively existing "container" of self-existent things; rather, it manifests *as* the temporal processes we experience as objects—in which case time, too, is quite different from how it is usually understood. "The time we call spring blossoms directly expresses an existence called flowers. The flowers, in turn, express the time called spring. This is not existence within time; existence itself is time" (in Matsunaga 1972, 68). In short, time is not something objective, just "out there." Time *is* flowers, apples, and cups—and you and I.[11] Dogen devised a new term to designate such nondual process-things: *uji*, literally "being-time":

> "Being-time" here means that time itself is being . . . and all being is time. . . .
>
> Time is not separate from you, and as you are present, time does not go away. . . .
>
> Do not think that time merely flies away. Do not see flying away as the only function of time. If time merely flies away, you would be separated from time. The reason you do not clearly understand being-time is that you think of time as only passing. . . . People only see time's coming and going, and do not thoroughly understand that being-time abides in each moment. . . .
>
> Being-time has the quality of flowing. . . . Because flowing is a quality of time, moments of past and present do not overlap or line up side-by-side. . . . Do not think flowing is like wind and rain moving from east to west. The entire world is not unchangeable, is not immovable. It flows. Flowing is like spring. Spring with all its numerous aspects is called flowing. When spring flows there is nothing outside of spring. (Dogen 1985, 76–80; trans. altered)

Paradoxically, however, if there is *only* time, there is *no* time. I am "being-time" when I no longer situate my activities within a clock-time understood as external to me. Then, in place of the fungible cyberpresent as an ever-thinner line moving between the infinities of past and future, I live in (or *as*) an eternal now whenever I *become* what I am doing. Ironically, to *be* time is also to *be free from* time. If every thing already *is* time—if, for example, the "being" of a flower *is* its gesture of blossoming—then we are freed from the delusion that time is something external to the flower, an outside "container" that the flower is "in." The same is true for our own lives, of course. This experience is something that professional musicians and athletes are often familiar with, as "being in the flow." When I "forget myself" as someone who is *doing* the dancing and become *one with* the dancing, I am living in what might be called *timeless time*. Or rather, "I" am not "in" it, but life is experienced as an eternal present, which in fact it has always been.

In contrast to such a nondual resolution of our problem with time, the space-time compression of cybertechnologies merely aggravates the delusive split between time and the things "in" it, because all it does is enable us to quantify objectified time more minutely and coordinate our schedules more precisely. Cybertime achieves near instantaneity by speeding us up, but it still presupposes the basic, problematic duality between objectified time and the supposedly separate things (most problematically, us) that are *in* it. It celebrates that so many more things can happen so much more quickly, yet we remain ungrounded, lack-ridden beings subject to all the *dukkha* inherent in the delusion of a self trapped in an external, objective temporality.

As clock-time became central to modern social organization, life became "centered around the emptying out of time (and space) and the development of an abstract, divisible and universally measurable calculation of time" (Aveni 1991, 135). Cybertime does not provide an alternative to this historical development; it completes it. We experience time as increasingly dominating our lives. Despite all our "time-saving" technologies, we must run faster and faster (trying) to do everything that needs to be done.

The collective objectification of clock-time means that now, insofar as we are social beings, we must live according to this commonly agreed standard. The complexities of social interaction require such a mechanism for their coordination, though it alienates us from natural temporal rhythms, including the biorhythms of our own bodies. In order to get to work (or class) by 9:00 AM, one has to catch the 8:22 bus. But to live *only* according to that collective construct is to "bind ourselves without a rope," to use the Zen metaphor again. In contrast, with Dogen's *uji* "being-time," the temporality of an activity is intrinsic to the activity itself. We can sometimes notice this difference in, for example, the way music is played. Often the notes march along precisely following the time signature of the score, but sometimes we become so absorbed in those notes that we do not notice the time signature at all because the music embodies its own time. According to Buddhism, *anatta* opens up the same possibility for us. Awakening to my nonduality with the world frees me from the self-preoccupation involved in always trying to ground myself. There is no separate self that needs to become real, and therefore no need to use time efficiently to do so. To experience Dogen's "being-time" is to become aware of a present that does not change, which is not gained or lost, although its content constantly transforms.

If Dogen is correct, our technological preoccupation with ever-increasing speed is the problem, not the solution. There is no technological solution, because what is required is a transformation in the ways our minds work. To counteract Eriksen's law (more information means decreasing attention span), Buddhism and other spiritual paths offer meditation practices that can change us. Such practices increase our attention span by slowing us down, which enables us to "forget ourselves" so that we can become one with whatever we do.

# SIX

# Dying to the Self that Never Was

Buddhist "awakening" (nirvana, satori) includes realizing that there is no ontological self and never was. Although this is quite a remarkable claim, there are provocative similarities in the way that some other religions (for example, Daoism, discussed in chapter 4) emphasize the importance of overcoming the delusion of self. Christianity, for example, urges a change of heart (*metanoia*) so drastic that it involves a kenosis (Phil. 2:6), a total emptying of the self so that "not I but Christ lives in me" (Gal. 2:20). Christ's own death and resurrection are not enough: we ourselves must be crucified and resurrected in order to realize that "the Kingdom of God is at hand" right here and now.

Does this mean that Christian "dying to the self" is in some sense equivalent to the Buddhist understanding of *anatta*? Or are they better understood as competing descriptions of the (not-)self? These are intriguing questions but impossibly broad, of course. As soon as we try to answer them, we realize that one cannot generalize about *the* Christian tradition or *the* Buddhist tradition in this way. Both religions are rich in a great variety of schools, texts, and practices, and the differences between them have been just as important in developing the tradition as their agreements have been in maintaining it. Meister Eckhart's statements about the self in his treatises and sermons cannot be equated with the viewpoint(s) on the self in the recorded sayings of the desert fathers, and the eighth-century Tibetan debate at bSam-yas between Chan and Vajrayana representatives warns us not to try the same thing with Buddhism. Perhaps even more important, a comparison or contrast between Buddhist *anatta* and Christian kenosis may be less a doctrinal issue than a *practical* one—that is to say, a matter of differing or congruent spiritual practices.

Rather than presuming to address such a general question, then, this chapter will attempt to make a much more limited contribution by comparing two specific contemplative practices. It considers the similarities and differences between one method of koan meditation in contemporary Zen Buddhism, as I understand it, with the technique of meditative prayer recommended in

*The Cloud of Unknowing*, a well-known fourteenth-century English manual of Christian practice.[1] The koan technique that I will describe is so distinctive that one might expect it to be unique. That *The Cloud* espouses such a similar technique is very suggestive.

## Mu

We begin with a summary of the koan (Chinese, *kung-an*) method. Yet we cannot assume that there is a single koan method, for the reasons already mentioned. Chinese Chan / Korean Son / Japanese Zen themselves comprise a set of related traditions, incorporating various schools and developments, and there are also different types of koan that are used in different ways. So it must be emphasized that what follows is my own interpretation of Mu koan practice as used by a contemporary Zen master, Koun Yamada (1906–88), former director of the Sanbo Kyodan school of Japanese Zen. An advantage of this focus is that it concerns a method of meditation I have practiced myself, which requires me to add the caveat that the way of Zen is actually to practice and not to reflect on how that practice works, for the latter may hamper the former. Rather than subvert our comparison, however, this initiates it, for *The Cloud of Unknowing* also urges us to immerse ourselves completely in the practice and not to try to understand what is happening: "Be blind in this time and shear away desire of knowing, for it will hinder thee more than help thee" (McCann 1952, 50).[2]

Essentially, a koan is a paradoxical problem that in principle cannot be solved rationally. In order to answer a koan, the student must bypass his or her usual ways of thinking and "leap" to another type of understanding, which constitutes a nonconceptual insight into one's Buddha-nature or "true nature." Most koan are derived from dialogues between Zen masters or between master and student. For example: "A monk asked Joshu: 'Why did Bodhidharma come from the West?' Joshu said: 'The oak tree in the garden' " (*Mumonkan* case 37, in Aitken 1991).

This *mondo* (the record of a dialogue) becomes a koan when a student is asked: What is the meaning of Joshu's reply? The student might answer, for example, that there was no reason why Bodhidharma came from the West; just as a tree has no meaning but *is*, so Bodhidharma just *came*. Such a reply would normally be rejected. The only way a student can come to understand Joshu's reply is with a state of mind similar to Joshu's when Joshu made his remark—that is, by having a similar awakening. The koan helps him or her to do this because no logically derived answer is acceptable. The principle of koan practice is that, if the questioning process is continued in the proper way, the conceptualizing function of the mind becomes paralyzed and eventually bypassed.

Traditionally, three requirements or factors are said to be essential to Zen practice, and especially for koan work: great faith, great determination, and great doubt.[3] The great (literally, "deep-rooted") faith necessary is not belief in any being or doctrine that can "save" anyone but rather the confidence that is necessary in order to practice: faith that the enlightenment of the Buddha (and Zen masters) is genuine, not a delusion or a hoax, and faith that we too can realize this same thing since we are of the same Buddha-nature. Great determination is the resolve that I too will become enlightened and devote all of my energy to that end.

The most interesting for our purposes is great doubt, which refers to the state of perplexity generated when one works on a koan. "Doubt" here is not to be understood in the ordinary sense, for it refers to a particular state of "doubting," experienced both mentally and physically, that blocks conceptualizing:

> When working on Zen, the most important thing is to generate the *I chin* [doubt-sensation]. What is this doubt-sensation? For instance: Where did I come from before my birth, and where shall I go after my death? Since one does not know the answer to either question, a strong feeling of "doubt" arises in the mind. Stick this "doubt-mass" onto your forehead [and keep it there] all the time until you can neither drive it away nor put it down, even if you want to. Then suddenly you will discover that the doubt-mass has been crushed, that you have broken it into pieces. The masters of old said:
> The greater the doubt, the greater the awakening.
> The smaller the doubt, the smaller the awakening.
> No doubt, no awakening. (Po-shan, in Chang 1970, 94–95)

It is important to devote oneself completely to the search for a solution to one's koan. "A Zen yogi should resolutely vow that he will never stop working until the doubt mass is broken up," Po-shan said. "This is the most crucial point" (in G. Chang 1970, 95). Shoichi Kokushi, the Japanese founder of Tofukuji temple, advised students, "[T]hink yourself to be down an old deep well; the only thought you then have will be to get out of it, and you will be desperately engaged in finding a way of escape; from morning to evening this one thought will occupy the entire field of your consciousness" (Suzuki 1950, 71–72).

This may be illustrated by considering what is perhaps the best known of all koans, "Joshu's Mu," which is the first case of the *Mumonkan*, a well-known collection of forty-eight koans assembled by the thirteenth-century Chinese master known in Japanese as Mumon Ekai: "A monk in all seriousness asked Joshu: 'Has a dog Buddha-nature, or not?' Joshu retorted 'Mu!' " The koan point—the problem to be solved—is: What is "Mu"?

The monk of the story seems to have heard that, according to Mahayana teachings, all sentient beings have (or, as Dogen would put it, are) Buddha-nature, yet evidently he could not understand how a half-starved mongrel could have the same nature as Shakyamuni Buddha. Literally, *mu,* like the Chinese original term *wu,* is a negative somewhat similar to the English "un-" or "non-." In Chinese philosophy it sometimes refers to the Void from which the universe originates. But it is a mistake to take Joshu's cryptic answer as denying the Buddha-nature of a dog, or as making any doctrinal statement about Buddha-nature or the origin of the universe or anything else. The value of this short interchange as a koan is that, once this point is understood, little room is left for speculation. There is not much of a handle left for the conceptualizing mind to (try to) grasp.

The importance of the doubt-sensation is evident in Mumon's commentary on this koan: "You must concentrate day and night, questioning yourself through every one of your 360 bones and 84,000 pores" (Kapleau 1966, 79). But how is one to do that? In the traditional way of working on this koan, the Zen master would repeatedly press the student for the correct answer, while rejecting all of his or her responses. Eventually the student would run out of replies, and then he or she might be encouraged simply to repeat the sound "Muuu..." over and over again. Nowadays the process is usually shortened. Students are informed at the beginning that all conceptual answers are unsatisfactory, and they are instructed to treat "Mu" as a kind of mantra, to be repeated not aloud but mentally in coordination with breath exhalations. The thought or rather the internal sound of "Mu" is focused on in order to let go of all other thoughts. In his commentary on this case, Hakuun Yasutani (Koun Yamada's teacher) elaborates:

> Let all of you become one mass of doubt and questioning. Concentrate on and penetrate fully into Mu. To penetrate into Mu means to achieve absolute unity with it. How can you achieve this unity? By holding to Mu tenaciously day and night! Do not separate yourself from it under any circumstances! Focus your mind on it constantly.... You must not, in other words, think of Mu as a problem involving the existence or non-existence of Buddha-nature. Then what must you do? You stop speculating and concentrate wholly on Mu—just Mu!...
>
> ... At first you will not be able to pour yourself wholeheartedly into Mu. It will escape you quickly because your mind will start to wander. You will have to concentrate harder—just "Mu! Mu! Mu!" Again it will elude you. Once more you attempt to focus on it and again you fail. This is the usually pattern in the early stages of practice.... Upon your attainment to this [later]

stage of purity, both inside and outside naturally fuse.... When
you fully absorb yourself in Mu, the external and internal merge
into a single unity. (Kapleau 1966, 79–80)

Notice what is *not* encouraged here. One should not cultivate blankness of
mind, which is quietism, nor should one try to push thoughts away, which
creates a mental division between that which is pushing away and the thoughts
that are pushed away. Po-shan writes: "Some who suppress distracted thought
and stop its arising consider this to be Buddhism. They, however, are going
astray by using delusory thought to suppress delusory thought. It is like trying
to press down the grass with a rock or to peel the leaves of a plantain, one
after another—there is no end" (in G. Chang 1970, 99). Instead, the principle
is to concentrate on one thing—in this case, repeating "Muuu . . ." endlessly—in
order to become absorbed into it and literally *become* it.

This process was also described by the thirteenth-century Japanese Zen
master Dogen: "To study Buddhism is to study yourself. To study yourself is
to forget yourself. To forget yourself is to perceive your intimacy [nonduality]
with all things. To realize this is to cast off the mind and body of self and
others."[4] Putting all one's mental energy into "Mu" and cutting off all thoughts
with "Mu" undermines the sense of self, which is a mental construct sustained
by our usual ways of thinking. At the beginning of my practice, I attempt to
concentrate on "Mu" but am distracted by other thoughts and mental processes.
Later I am able to focus on "Mu" and not wander away from it. The stage of
ripeness and purity, when "both inside and outside naturally fuse," is when there
is no longer a sense of an "I" that is repeating the sound; there is only "Mu."[5]
This stage is sometimes described by saying that now Mu is doing mu: it is Mu
that sits, Mu that walks, Mu that eats, Mu that is doing everything.

If one perseveres, there may arise the sensation of hanging over a
precipice, dangling by a single thread. The eighteenth-century Japanese Rinzai
reformer Hakuin wrote that "Except for occasional feelings of uneasiness and
despair, it is like death itself" (Suzuki 1956, 148). The solution is to throw
oneself completely into Mu:

> Bravely let go
> On the edge of the cliff
> Throw yourself into the Abyss
> With decision and courage.
> You only revive after death.
> (Po-shan in G. Chang 1970, 103)

At this point, one's teacher can help by cutting the last thread: an unexpected
action, such as a blow or shout or even a few quiet words, may startle the

student into letting go. "All of a sudden he finds his mind and body wiped out of existence, together with the koan. This is what is known as 'letting go your hold' " (Hakuin, in Suzuki 1956, 148). Many of the classical Zen stories tell of how a student was enlightened by some sudden action or perception. In one famous instance, a student was enlightened by the sound of a pebble striking bamboo. What happens in such cases is that the shock of the unexpected sensation causes it to penetrate to the very core of one's being—in other words, it is experienced nondually. One lets go and dies "the Great [Ego] Death." "It is as though an explosion has occurred. When this happens you will experience so much!" says Yasutani. "With enlightenment you see the world as Buddha-nature, but this does not mean that all becomes as radiant as a halo. Rather, each thing *just as it is* takes on an entirely new significance or worth. Miraculously, everything is radically transformed though remaining just as it is" (in Kapleau 1966, 80).

From a Buddhist perspective, it is important to remember that this transformation does not involve something like "the death of the self." This experience is possible only because there is no self and never has been. The point of the process is for the sense of self to realize that it is not self-existing or self-sufficient—in short, that it is not a self. One way to express it is that the sense of self is actually a manifestation of something that cannot be grasped or understood and therefore can only be experienced as a *nothing*. Our consciousness is a spring bubbling up from an unfathomable source. Awakening happens when the bottom of the bucket drops out, to use the Zen metaphor.

## Wrapping Oneself in a Cloud

The anonymous *Cloud of Unknowing* is the product of a very different tradition, medieval Christianity. Needless to say, the theological gap is considerable. In place of the Buddha-nature that all sentient beings *are* and that the Buddha merely shows us how to realize, Christianity usually emphasizes the vast difference between the creator God and his sinful creatures. Salvation is achieved through Christ, God's incarnation on earth. Yet *The Cloud* contains few references to Christ. The goal of the method described is to attain "with a loving stirring and a blind beholding unto the naked being of God himself only" (McCann 1952, 19). What is remarkable is that the Zen koan process described above and *The Cloud* method of experiencing "the naked being of God" are so similar.

*The Cloud of Unknowing* takes its title from the meditation method that it recommends. Those who want to experience God should wrap themselves in "a darkness or a cloud" that "treads down" all thinking.

Lift up thine heart unto God with a meek stirring of love; and mean himself and none of his goods. And thereto look that thou loathe to think on aught but himself, so that nought work in thy mind nor in thy will but only himself.

Cease not, therefore, but travail therein till thou feel list. For at the first time when thou dost it, thou findest but a darkness, and as it were a *cloud of unknowing*, thou knowest not what, saving that thou feelest in thy will a naked intent unto God. This darkness and this could, however, howsoever thou dost, is betwixt thee and thy God, and hindereth thee, so that thou mayest neither see him clearly by light of understanding in thy reason, nor feel him in sweetness of love in thine affection. And therefore shape thee to bide in this darkness as long as thou mayest, evermore crying after him whom thou lovest. For if ever thou shalt see him or feel him, as it may be here, it must always be in this cloud and in this darkness. (McCann 1952, 12)

A later passage clarifies what the term "cloud" means:

When I say darkness, I mean a lack of knowing: as all thing that thou knowest not, or hast forgotten, is dark to thee; for thou seest it not with thy ghostly [spiritual] eye. And for this reason it is called, not a cloud of the air, but a *cloud of unknowing*, which is betwixt thee and thy God.

And if ever thou shalt come to this cloud and dwell and work therein as I bid thee, thou must, as this *cloud of unknowing* is above thee, betwixt thee and thy God, right so put *a cloud of forgetting* beneath thee, betwixt thee and all the creatures that ever be made . . . also all the works and conditions of the same creatures. I except not one creature, whether they be bodily creatures or ghostly; nor yet any condition or work of any creature, whether they be good or evil. But, to speak shortly, all should be hid under the *cloud of forgetting* in this case.

Yea, . . . in this work it profiteth little or nought to think of the kindness or the worthiness of God, nor on our Lady, nor on the saints or angels in heaven, nor yet on the joys of heaven. . . . For although it be good to think upon the kindness of God, and to love him and praise him for it: yet it is better to think upon the naked being of him, and to love him and praise him for himself. (12–13)

Most of us are familiar with such Zen admonitions as "If you meet the Buddha on the way, kill him!" It is quite remarkable to find a Christian text that urges us, in effect, not to waste time thinking about Jesus, nor Mary, nor the angels and saints in heaven.

> But now thou askest me and sayest: "How shall I think on himself [God], and what is he?" Unto this I cannot answer thee, except to say: "I know not."
>
> For thou hast brought me with thy question into that same darkness, and into that same *cloud of unknowing*, that I would thou wert in thyself. For of all other creatures and thy works—yea, and of the works of God himself—may a man through grace have fullness of knowing, and well can he think of them; but of God himself can no man think. And therefore I would leave all that thing that I can think, and choose to my love that thing that I cannot think. For why, he may well be loved, but not thought. By love may he be gotten and holden; but by thought neither. And therefore, although it be good sometime to think on the kindness and the worthiness of God in special, and although it be a light and a part of contemplation: nevertheless in this work it shall be cast down and covered with a *cloud of forgetting*. And thou shalt step above it stalwartly, but listily, with a devout and a pleasing stirring of love, and try to pierce that darkness above thee. And smite upon that thick *cloud of unknowing* with a sharp dart of longing love; and go not thence for aught that befalleth. (14)

*The Cloud* is fond of quoting St. Denis: "The most godly knowing of God is that which is known by unknowing" (93). Many Zen koans emphasize the same point, for example *Mumonkan* case 34: "Mind is not the Buddha, knowing is not the Way."

The method recommended in these extraordinary passages suggests comparison with the Zen "doubt-sensation," which is used in a similar fashion to halt and bypass conceptual thinking: "When working on Zen, one does not see the sky when he lifts his head, nor the earth when he lowers it. To him a mountain is not a mountain and water is not water. While walking or sitting he is not aware of doing so. Though among a hundred thousand people, he sees no one. Without and within his body and mind nothing exists but the burden of his doubt-sensation. This feeling can be described as 'turning the whole world into a muddy vortex'" (Po-shan in G. Chang 1970, 95).

Turning the world into a muddy vortex sounds less elegant than "wrapping oneself in a cloud of unknowing" (presumably the former sounds better in Chinese), but the function appears to be similar. If so, the "doubt-block" evidently incorporates *both* the cloud of unknowing and the cloud of forgetting, since no distinction is made between them in Zen. Perhaps the difference is due to the Christian dualism between God and his creatures: creatures *below* God must be forgotten if we are to experience the God *above* us. Zen teachings make no such separation. Because we normally perceive things through a fog of our delusions about them, we do not realize their (or our) Buddha-nature, and to experience their Buddha-nature is to realize that there are actually no sentient beings—one way to express this being that there is *only* Buddha-nature. To awaken is to realize that the limits of samsara are not different from the limits of nirvana. So the Zen goal is to experience the true nature of this world, including its creatures, not to rise above the world in order to experience a God that created it.

There is, however, a more significant difference between the *clouds* and the doubt-sensation. The doubt sensation arises in trying to solve one's koan. "Let all of you become one mass of doubt and questioning." The Christian experience of the *clouds* seems to involve no such questioning. Instead, *The Cloud* espouses *love*: "By love may he [God] be gotten and holden; but by thought neither . . ."

We might conclude that this difference reflects a general difference between Christianity and Buddhism, but of course there are many devotional elements and practices within Buddhism, especially in Mahayana. Instead, let us notice what seems to be a significant difference between the paths of theistic bhakti and nondualistic *jnana*, "knowledge" or "wisdom." Theism, which conceives of the absolute/ultimate as a personality, seems to involve a more affective (in the sense of emotional) spiritual path than those nondualisms that understand the absolute/ultimate to be impersonal and emphasize achieving a new *understanding*. The theistic mystic conceives of Christ, Krishna, Amida, and so on, as personalities with whom he or she can unite in a loving relationship. The Buddhist or Vedantic nondualist wants to realize his or her Buddha-nature, Brahman, One Mind, and so on. This difference appears to be rooted in a divergent understanding of human faculties. *The Cloud* exemplifies much of theistic mysticism in giving humans "two principal working powers": "All reasonable creatures, angel and man, have in them, each one by himself, one principal working power, which is called a knowing power, and another principal working power, the which is called a loving power. Of the which two powers, to the first . . . God who is the maker of them is evermore incomprehensible; but to the second . . . he is, in every man diversely, all comprehensible to the full. Insomuch, that one loving soul alone in itself, by virtue of love, may comprehend in itself him who is sufficient to the full . . ." (McCann 1952, 9–10).

According to this, the knowing power can only be an obstacle, for God can be known only through love. One must therefore reject the first faculty and work with the second. Buddhism offers a different understanding of the intellect. Granted, conceptualization is a problem, perhaps the root of our delusions, but our usual conceptualizing is not the only way the intellect can work. There is another, more nondual functioning, which in Mahayana is often called *prajnaparamita*, "transcendental wisdom."

It is interesting to speculate further about the differences between a spiritual path that works with the emotions and one that works on the intellect. Love as ordinarily experienced is dualistic in distinguishing the lover from the beloved. The emotions require a personalized other on which to focus. The intellect, in contrast, seems to imply a qualityless impersonality because samadhi involves "letting go" of all mental phenomena, emotions as well as concepts. Can we then understand the difference in *goals* as due to the difference in *paths*, rather than vice versa?

What Zen koan practice and *The Cloud* do have in common—where they intersect again—is in the longing and the intensity of practice. The desperate need of the Zen student to solve his or her koan is matched by the intense desire of the *Cloud* practitioner to experience "the naked being of God." "All thy life now must always stand in desire if thou shalt advance in degree of perfection" (McCann 1952, 7). In both cases, it is this longing that generates the mental energy necessary to cut through the deluding web of dualistic thoughts and feelings. Zen stresses the intensity with which one must try to unite with Mu. "When working on Zen, it is important not to lose the right thought. This is the thought of *tsen*, meaning 'to bore into.' If one loses the thought of *tsen*, he has no alternative but to go astray" (Po-shan, in G. Chang 1970, 99). The Japanese equivalent, *zan-zen*, means "to bore into the work of zen."

With "Mu" too there is a significant parallel in *The Cloud*:

And if thou desirest to have this intent lapped and folden in one word, so that thou mayest have better hold thereupon, take thee but a little word of one syllable, for so it is better than two; for the shorter the word, the better it accordeth with the word of the spirit. And such a word is this word GOD and this word LOVE. Choose whichever thou wilt, or another: whatever word thou likest best of one syllable. And fasten this word to thine heart, so that it may never go thence for anything that befalleth.

This word shall be thy shield and thy spear, whether thou ridest in peace or in war. With this word, thou shalt smite down all manner of thought under the *cloud of forgetting*. Insomuch, that if any thought press upon thee to ask thee what thou wouldst have, answer with no more words but this one word. (McCann 1952, 16)

"Mu" is used in precisely the same way: to smite down all other thoughts as they arise. I have read that Tennyson claimed to have induced mystical experiences by reciting his own name: "Tennyson, Tennyson, Tennyson." Other, more historically important parallels are found in the Vedic "Om" chant and the Prayer of the Heart used in Eastern Orthodox Christianity. *The Cloud* abounds in similar admonitions against entertaining thoughts:

> And therefore the sharp stirring of thine understanding, that will always press upon thee when thou settest thee to this blind work, must always be borne down; and unless thou bear him down, he will bear thee down. (McCann 1952, 20)

> Therefore say: "Go thou down again"; and tread him [any thought] fast down with a stirring of love, although he seem to thee right holy, and seem to thee as if he would help thee to seek him [God]. (15)[6]

Compare the following, from Yasutani's "Commentary on Mu":

> You must melt down your delusions with the red-hot iron ball of Mu stuck in your throat. The opinions you hold and your worldly knowledge are your delusions. Included also are philosophical and moral concepts, no matter how lofty, as well as religious beliefs and dogmas, not to mention innocent, commonplace thoughts. In short, all conceivable ideas are embraced within the term "delusions" and as such are a hindrance to the realization of your Essential-nature. So dissolve them with the fireball of Mu! (Kapleau 1966, 79–80)

"Delusions" here encompass all mental phenomena, emotional as well as intellectual, including visions and hallucinations. As the mind ripens through such meditation practice, one may experience *makyo* (Jap., literally "devil world"), which is a general term for various types of illusions and other psychosomatic phenomena, whether blissful, frightful, or indifferent. It is emphasized in Zen that such transient experiences are neither good nor bad in themselves and are not significant unless one clings to them, in which case they become an obstacle (Kapleau 1966, 38–41). Although theistic mystics have often valued such experiences highly, *The Cloud* is aware of this danger too: "Such a blind stirring of love unto God for himself, and such a secret setting upon this *cloud of unknowing* . . . thou wert better to have it and to feel it in thine affection ghostly, than to have the eye of thy soul opened in contemplation of beholding of all the angels and saints in heaven, or in hearing of all the mirth and melody that is among them in bliss" (McCann 1952, 20–21).

In wrapping oneself in the cloud, one should abandon all desire to understand what is happening. Instead of trying to control the process, one should lose oneself in it: "Let that thing do with thee and lead thee wheresoever it willeth. Let it be the worker, and thou but the sufferer; do but look upon it and let it alone. Meddle thee not therewith as though thou wouldst help it, for dread lest thou spill all. Be thou but the tree, and let it be the carpenter.... Be blind in this time and shear away desire of knowing, for it will more hinder thee than help thee" (49–50).

*The Cloud* urges complete devotion to this practice: "But although the shortness of prayer be greatly commended here, nevertheless the oftness of prayer is not therefore restrained ... if thou ask me what discretion thou shalt have in this work, then I shall answer thee and say, "Right none!" For in all thine other doings thou shalt have discretion, that they be neither too much nor too little. But in this work thou shalt hold no measure: for I would that thou shouldst never cease from this work the whiles thou livest" (56, 57–58). It is the same single-minded determination that Zen masters such as Yasutani encourage: "You will never succeed if you do *zazen* only when you have a whim to, and give up easily. You must carry on steadfastly for one, two, three, or even five years without remission, constantly vigilant" (Kapleau 1966, 80).

The purpose of the koan process is to undermine one's constructed sense of self in order to realize one's true nature. When I concentrate wholeheartedly on becoming one with Mu, "smiting down" all other thoughts, the habitual mental patterns that sustain my sense of self are gradually attenuated. *The Cloud* concurs: its forty-third chapter is entitled "That all knowing and feeling of a man's own being must needs be lost, if the perfection of this work shall verily be felt in any soul in this life." Although Buddhism views the basic problem as delusion (the distortion of human understanding), the Christian emphasis on sinfulness (the perversion of human will) gives a different slant. "Thou shalt loathe and be weary with all that thing that worketh in thy mind and in thy will, unless it be only God. For otherwise surely, whatsoever it be, it is betwixt thee and thy God. And no wonder if thou loathe and hate to think on thyself, when thou shalt always feel sin a foul stinking lump, thou knowest never what, betwixt thee and thy God: the which lump is none other thing than thyself" (McCann 1952, 60). In practice, however, it seems that these different problems tend to reduce to the same thing:

And therefore break down all knowing and feeling of all manner of creatures, but most busily of thyself. For on the knowing and the feeling of thyself hangeth the knowing and feeling of all other creatures; for in regard of it, all other creatures be lightly forgotten . . . thou shalt find, when thou has forgotten all other creatures and their works—yea! And also all thine own works—that there shall remain yet after, betwixt thee and thy God, a naked knowing and a feeling of thine own being: the which knowing and feeling must always be destroyed, ere the time be that thou mayest feel verily the perfection of this work. (60)

How may this "feeling of thine own being" be eliminated? The habitual thought patterns that sustain the sense of self are weakened by meditation practice, yet the ego-self persists, increasingly threatened and uncomfortable. The problem now is that the ego-self wants to be there to "become enlightened," or to observe and enjoy the presence of God. This is why the ego must be tricked or startled into "letting go" and being wiped out of existence. Letting go of itself is not something the ego-self can will to do, however much it may want to, any more than I can lift myself into the air by tugging on my shoestrings. Something else is necessary, which *The Cloud* calls "grace." "But now thou askest me how thou mayest destroy this naked knowing and feeling of thine own being. For peradventure thou thinkest that if it were destroyed, all other hindrances were destroyed: and if thou thinkest thus, thou thinkest right truly. But to this I answer thee and say, that without a full special grace full freely given by God, and also a full according ableness on thy part to receive this grace, this naked knowing and feeling of thine own being may in nowise be destroyed" (60).

The concept of grace is not common in Buddhism. Excepting the controversial "transfer of merit" that bodhisattvas are supposed to be able to effect, probably the closest equivalent in Mahayana is the conception of the Dharmakaya as radiating compassion to all beings. The Dharmakaya is impersonal and does not discriminate in its radiance (compare Matthew 5:45 and Luke 6:35). All beings share in it according to their receptivity, whereas the concept of grace seems dependent on that of a God who bestows it.[7] Yet, again, perhaps more significant than the doctrinal difference is the phenomenological similarity. Both experiences (of God and of Buddha-nature) are not subject to one's own will or understanding. Nor do they occur by passively sitting back and waiting for "it" to happen. *The Cloud* goes on to discuss what is necessary in order to develop a "full according ableness on thy part to receive this grace."

And this ableness is not else but a strong and a deep ghostly sorrow. But in this sorrow thou needest to have discretion, in this manner: thou shalt beware, in the time of this sorrow, that thou strain neither thy body nor thy spirit too rudely, but sit full still, as it were in a sleeping device, all forsobbed and forsunken in sorrow; and well were it to him that might win to this sorrow. All men have matter for sorrow; but most especially he feeleth matter of sorrow that knoweth and feeleth that he is. . . . And who has never felt this sorrow, let him make sorrow; for he hath never yet felt perfect sorrow. This sorrow, when it is had, cleanseth the soul, not only of sin, but also of pain that it hath deserved for sin; and also it maketh a soul able to receive that joy, the which reaveth from a man all knowing and feeling of his being. (McCann 1952, 60–61)

The reference to sitting "full still, as if in a sleeping device," is suggestive of *zazen* meditation, yet the sorrow that accompanies it is little discussed in Zen literature. That does not mean it is not experienced in Zen practice. Despair and tears are common during *sesshin* (group meditation retreats, during which intensive koan practice is conducted). Notice that the passage enjoins excesses of expression that might strain body or mind. One should sit still and simply endure the sorrow of realizing that one's ultimate problem is "the knowing and feeling of his own being." It is this suffering that somehow purifies and enables one to receive grace.

This invites comparison with more limited cases, in which the similarity to Buddhism is clearer. For example, accepting that I have character traits that I wish to correct, how do I change myself? The answer is that *I* usually cannot. Attempts to perfect oneself—"I *will* stop . . ."—are usually self-defeating, for in consciousness, too, actions tend to generate equal and opposite reactions. Deep character traits are such an integral part of the ego that the ego is unable to exclude them without some equally problematic compensation occurring. As with Jung's concept of the "shadow"—an autonomous splinter personality composed of everything the ego tries to exclude—to try to eliminate thoughts is to give them power over you. Nevertheless, people sometimes do change. How does that happen?

The implication is that it is not force of will but *awareness itself*, and the mental anguish we feel along with it (its emotional counterpart?), that eventually changes us. The effort necessary is directed toward gaining understanding, not forcefully overcoming some tendency. That is why we should appreciate our depressions as much as our joys. Such sorrows are often spiritual growing pains, due to noticing patterns of behavior and seeing through the corresponding rationalizations. The awareness of the fault is what changes us, yet the problem must be deeply felt, in which case it is accompanied by pain. It is as if the pain "burns up" the habit, finally freeing us from it. *The Cloud* describes this process on a larger scale, when the problem is no longer what I *do* but that I *am*—a process that is unmistakably Buddhist, too, given the *anatta* doctrine and emphasis on mindfulness. There is, however, a difference, to which we shall soon turn, for the goal in Zen is not so much to perfect ourselves as to realize that perfection which has always been and which we have always been. Once there is such awareness, change can occur more naturally and effortlessly.

One prepares for "the naked being of God himself" by following the path thus far outlined, yet the *Cloud* experience itself comes at the disposition of God, in various ways and degrees according to one's "ableness in soul":

> Some think this matter so hard and so fearful that they say that it may not be come to without much strong travail coming before, nor conceived but seldom, and that but in the time of ravishing. And to these men will I answer as feebly as I can, and say: that it is all at the ordinance and the disposition of God, according to their ableness in soul that this grace in contemplation and of ghostly working is given to.
>
> For some there be that without much and long ghostly exercise may not come thereto; and yet it shall be but full seldom and in special calling of our Lord that they shall feel the perfection of this work; the which calling is called ravishing. And some there be that be so subtle in grace and in spirit, and so homely with God in this grace of contemplation, that they may have it when they will in the common state of man's soul: as in sitting, going, standing or kneeling. And yet in this time they have full deliberation of all their wits bodily and ghostly, and may use them if they desire: not without some difficulty, but without great difficulty. (McCann 1952, 94)

The term "ravishing" expresses well not only its intimacy/nonduality but also the suddenness and even violence of the experience. "For if it be truly conceived, it is but a sudden stirring, and as it were unadvised, speedily springing unto God as a sparkle from the coal" (11).

Although there has been considerable controversy in Buddhism about whether the awakening experience is sudden or gradual, most Zen teachers emphasize that genuine enlightenment, in contrast to the arduous practice preparing for it, is instantaneous. " 'Bursting into enlightenment' requires but an instant. It is as though an explosion had occurred" (Yasutani, in Kapleau 1966, 80). Moreover, it can vary greatly in degree, from slight tip-of-the-tongue *kensho* to the great awakening of *daigo tettei*. The depth of one's experience usually accords with the length and intensity of one's practice, but not always. Some of the greatest Zen figures, such as the sixth Ch'an patriarch, Hui-neng, seem to have come to enlightenment almost without effort.[8]

## The Same Experience?

Our comparison of these two spiritual methods concludes by bringing us back to comparing their spiritual goals. We cannot avoid the obvious question: If these two spiritual techniques are indeed very similar, then are their results also similar? Are "God" and "Buddha-nature" different ways of describing the same nondual experience?

I shall not presume to answer that question, but end instead with two reflections that pertain to any answer. Both refer to aspects of the Zen enlightenment experience that seem to contrast with the theistic experience of God.

First, we should remember that the "true nature" that is realized in Zen is nondual in at least two ways: there is no duality between subject and object, nor between phenomena and Buddha-nature. My Buddha-nature is also the true nature of this world, when experienced as it really is, undistorted by delusion. Dogen expressed this beautifully: "I came to realize clearly that Mind is no other than mountains and rivers and the great wide earth, the sun and the moon and the stars" (in Kapleau 1966, 205).

*The Cloud* accepts our oneness with God in the mystical experience, but this is understood as grace overcoming our basically sinful nature:

> Beneath thy God thou art: for although it may be said in a manner that in this time God and thou be not two but one in spirit—insomuch that thou or another that feeleth the perfection of this work may, by reason of that oneness, truly be called a god, as scripture witnesseth—nevertheless thou art beneath him. For he is God by nature without beginning; and thou sometimes were nought in substance; and afterwards, when thou wert by his might and his love made aught, though wilfully with sin madest thyself worse than nought. And only by his mercy without thy dessert art thou made a god in grace, one with him in spirit without separation, both here and in the bliss of heaven without any end. So that, although thou be all one with him in grace, yet thou art full far beneath him in nature. (McCann 1952, 89–90)

This contrasts "the over-abundant love and worthiness of God in himself" with "the filth, the wretchedness, and the frailty of man, into the which he is fallen by sin, and the which he must always feel in some degree the whiles he liveth in this life, be he never so holy" (26). Zen, in contrast, teaches that our true Buddha-nature has always been pure. The "Great Cessation," a term for profound enlightenment, is a "designation for the state of mind flowing from the deep realization that, since inherently we suffer no lack, there is nothing to seek outside ourselves" (Kapleau 1996, 208 n.1).

Again, however, this presupposition of man's basically sinful nature—which would be considered a delusion in Zen—does not necessarily refer to a difference between the Christian and Buddhist nondual *experiences*. It may rather describe a difference in the way that the experience is conceptualized. Ironically, in recent Buddhist-Christian dialogue Zen proponents have often emphasized fundamental ignorance and karmic obstructions (requiring strenuous practice) more than Christians have. The latter have been more trustful of God's grace and the goodness of creation.[9] It may be that both aspects are needed for effective practice, and we should speak rather of a difference in emphasis, for until one realizes for oneself clearly that there is no lack, the sense of a lack is important in order to motivate the practice necessary to realize that intrinsically there is no lack.

The second reflection refers to another aspect of the Zen experience: that it reveals the "emptiness" (Sanskrit, *shunyata*; Japanese, *ku*) of phenomena—not only of the subject, but of everything that can be experienced. Koun Yamada, in an unpublished lecture entitled "Zen and Christianity," emphasized this. "The most important matter in Zen practice is to come to a clear and unmistakable *experience* of the fact that all things of the phenomenal world, myself included, are totally void. . . . This is *satori*."[10] Nagarjuna, the second-century Indian Buddhist philosopher, used *shunyata* not to characterize the true nature of reality but to deny that anything has any self-existence or reality of its own. Thus, in using terms like "Buddha-nature," we must be careful not to grab that snake by the wrong end, for referring to Buddha-nature is actually a way of denying that anything has any "own-nature," any permanent nature of its own—including God. One might argue, as Eckhart sometimes does, that this is equivalent to asserting that no created thing has a self-existing nature apart from God, but Nagarjuna's radical critique of self-existence leaves nothing to play that role. The only other alternative, it would seem, is to suggest that somehow emptiness *is* God.

In the same lecture Koun Yamada discusses the comments of several of his Christian Zen students on this matter. He asked one Catholic sister (now teaching Zen herself): "What is the relation between Emptiness and God?" Without any hesitation she answered, "Emptiness is God. God cannot be thought of as other than emptiness."

This may be a fruitful direction for Buddhist-Christian dialogue,[11] but in the interest of sharpening that encounter let me finish with a question about the practical—that is to say, the practice-oriented—differences between emptiness and God.

The "Great Death" necessary in Zen practice is to let go of all attachments and ego identifications, to which we cling for security, in order to realize the security of no-security in an "empty" world of radical impermanence that is *groundless*. I wonder, however, whether the *psychological* function of a personal God in theism is the opposite: God as the Great Security Blanket.

God is usually understood metaphorically as a stern yet loving parent, but even an Ultimate Reality toward which one is striving can serve the same reassuring role: it gives us an "emotional handle" to hold on to. Does faith in such a Reality make it easier to let go of everything else? Or does such a faith make it more difficult to let go of *every*thing? Is a Great Security Blanket also a great attachment, which we must eventually let go of?

SEVEN

# The Dharma of Emanuel Swedenborg

[H]idden under Judaic-Christian names, phrases, and symbols, and scattered throughout dreary, dogmatic, and soporific octavos, are pure, precious blessed truths of Buddhism.

—Philangi Dasa, *Swedenborg the Buddhist* (1887)

Revolutionary in theology, traveler of heaven and hell, great man of the spiritual world, great king of the mystical realm, clairvoyant unique in history, scholar of incomparable vigor, scientist of penetrating intellect, gentleman free of worldly taint: all of these combined into one make Swedenborg. . . . Those who wish to cultivate their spirit, those who bemoan the times, must absolutely know of this person.

—D. T. Suzuki, *Suedenborugu* (1913)

In January 1887 a former Swedenborgian minister named Carl Herman Vetterling, who now called himself Philangi Dasa, began publishing the first Buddhist journal in the United States. The inaugural issue of *The Buddhist Ray*, which he edited from his cabin in the mountains above Santa Cruz, proclaimed itself devoted to Buddhism in general, and to the Buddhism in Swedenborg in particular. The prospectus on the first page informed readers that it would "set forth the teachings imparted by the Mongolian Buddhists to Emanual Swedenborg, and published by him in his mystic writings." As this declaration suggests, Philangi Dasa was not afraid of controversy, and whatever the scholarly shortcomings of his journal it was not dull. "Delivering his unorthodox views with self-righteous conviction, he offended readers regularly but his outspoken brand of sincerity made *The Buddhist Ray* one of the liveliest Buddhist journals ever" (Tweed and Tworkov 1991, 6–7).

In the same year Philangi Dasa also published *Swedenborg the Buddhist; or The Higher Swedenborgianism, Its Secrets and Thibetan Origin*. Presented as a dream 322 pages long, it takes the form of a conversation among Swedenborg himself, a Buddhist monk, a Brahmin, a Parsi, a Chinese, an Aztec, an Icelander, and "a woman." The result is an amiable theosophical synthesis of religious beliefs and mythologies from many lands. As one would expect from his background and the texts available in his time, Philangi Dasa knew more about Swedenborg than about Buddhism, and his ostensible aim, to show that Swedenborg was really a Buddhist, is shadowed by another concern: to use Buddhism to reveal the shortcomings of Swedenborgianism. The tone is that of a disappointed lover: "Although I set much by Swedenborg, I would as soon put a razor in the hands of an infant as to put his theological writings into the hands of a man not versed in the spiritual teachings of Asia in general, and in the teachings of Buddhism in particular; for, he might embrace them and, with a large number of members of the 'New Church' society, die in doubt and despair."[1]

Philangi Dasa's journal and book have long been forgotten, yet he was not the only one to notice the similarities between Swedenborg and Buddhism. A few years later D. T. Suzuki, the Japanese scholar who would later become world-famous for his many books on Zen, was introduced to Swedenborg sometime during his years working with Paul Carus in Illinois (1897–1908).[2] A correspondence with Swedenborgians in the Philadelphia area led to an invitation to translate *Heaven and Hell* into Japanese, which was accomplished during a Christmastime visit to London. Upon returning to his homeland Suzuki introduced Swedenborg to Japan by publishing that translation in 1910, followed by translations of *Divine Love and Wisdom* and *The New Jerusalem and Its Heavenly Doctrine* (both 1914), and *Divine Providence* (1915). In addition, he published his own study in Japanese entitled, simply, *Suedenborugu* (1915). Much of this was compiled from English sources, but the introductory first chapter was original. It noted that

> [t]he theological doctrines presented by Swedenborg have some similarity to those of Buddhism.... True salvation rests upon a harmonious unity of what one believes with what one does. Wisdom and Love are the manifestation of the Divine, and Love has more depth and breadth than Wisdom. The Divine Providence reaches into the minutest things in the universe. There must not be any occurrences that happen by accident, but everything is conveyed by the Divine Providence through Wisdom and Love. The above are the very things which evoke the interest of scholars of religion and our Buddhists.[3]

In 1927 Suzuki published a nine-page article suggesting that Swedenborg's doctrine of correspondences may be compared with the Shingon doctrine that phenomena are aspects of Mahavairocana Buddha's ceaseless teaching. The last paragraph concludes: "There remains a great deal I wish to write about Swedenborg, but that remains for another day." Unfortunately, that day never came: except for this brief article, Suzuki's writings on Swedenborg ceased after 1915, when he was forty-five, although he continued writing for another fifty years, the majority of his books (totaling perhaps twenty thousand pages) being written after his mid-fifties. Curiously, these later Buddhist writings contain very few allusions to Swedenborg, despite the fact that there are references to, and sometimes detailed discussions of, many other Western writers, including Christian mystics such as Eckhart. It is not clear why Swedenborg figures so little in these many works, although evidently it was not due to any disaffection. All of Suzuki's published references to Swedenborg are positive, and he was fond of mentioning Swedenborg in conversation. According to his private secretary, Mihoko Bekku, as late as the 1950s he would sometimes remark, in response to an inquiry: "Well, Swedenborg would say . . ."[4] And when we consider the direction that Suzuki's life took after his encounter with Swedenborg, doesn't it suggest that the latter's personal example—Swedenborg's single-minded yet humble devotion to the task of recording his spiritual insights—may have served as an important model for Suzuki?

However influential Suzuki's translations may have been for the development of Japanese Swedenborgianism, his contribution to the dialogue between Buddhism and Swedenborg seems, like Philangi Dasa's, to have been forgotten, and I am not familiar with any more recent work on the topic. Nevertheless, I think their insight was not misplaced. This chapter will try to show that there indeed are profound similarities between what Swedenborg writes and what Buddhism teaches, and that today we have reached a point where we can appreciate them more fully. In recent years the dialogue between Buddhism and Christianity has become an important development in contemporary religious thought, yet as far as I know this dialogue has overlooked Swedenborg. If what follows is correct, however, Buddhists and Swedenborgians may have quite a bit to share and learn from each other.

Eschatologies tend to be so much a product of their particular time and place that few are credible today. Swedenborg's is the exception: in many respects what he describes is more meaningful to us today than it could have been to his contemporaries. One reason for this is that, despite its overtly Christian perspective, his religious understanding is largely nonsectarian and therefore attractive to spiritually inclined people of many different persuasions. This accords with the ecumenicism unavoidable in modern religious thought, and I believe it is particularly compatible with a Buddhist perspective. Their parallels are all the more interesting because reliable Buddhist teachings and texts were not available in Europe during his time.[5]

Swedenborg's views will be presented by focusing mainly on *Heaven and Hell*, his best-known work, which presents a summary of his purported visits to the afterworld. Since I would like to refer to more than one Buddhist tradition, my Buddhist citations will be more eclectic.

## The Concept of Self

*Heaven and Hell* presents a vision of human and postmortem existence contrasting sharply with our postmodernist suspicion of grand narratives that propose to explain everything. No narrative could be grander than Swedenborg's. Yet, like Buddhism with its doctrine of *anatta*, "not-self," his vision is postmodern insofar as it denies an ontological self. Swedenborg agrees that the self (his Latin term is *proprium*, literally "what belongs to oneself" is an illusion. In the twentieth century psychoanalytic and deconstructive ways of thinking have provided us with some homegrown handles to grasp what remains a very counterintuitive concept, the notion that our sense of self is not self-evident or self-present but a mental construction. For Swedenborg, too, the self is better understood as an economy of forces, although for him these forces are spiritual—more precisely, spirits. Good spirits (angels) and bad spirits (demons) are always with us, and their influence accounts for much of what we understand as our mental and emotional life. The evil spirits take up residence in our evil affections and bond there, as do the good spirits in our good affections. These spirits are of the same type as the affections or loves of the person they bond with (Swedenborg 1988, 295).[6] It is because their influence harmonizes with our own affections and tendencies that it enters our way of thinking and is accepted. In this way harmful spirits reinforce our bad character traits, and good spirits our better character traits. Some spirits are the source of our anxiety and depression (299). Even diseases (including the toothache that bothered Swedenborg!) and death can be caused by infernal spirits. Each of us has free will—that is, our ability to choose is preserved—because we are balanced between these two complexes of positive and negative spiritual forces.

The closest Buddhist parallel to this is the five *skandhas* "heaps, aggregates," whose interaction creates the illusion of self, according to the Pali Sutras. However, this similarity does not seem to be very deep, for within the Buddhist tradition (which, we must remember, originates in oral teachings over twenty-four hundred years old, creating textual quagmires that Swedenborgians do not need to worry about) it is not altogether clear what each *skandha* refers to (*rupa, vedana, samjña, sankhara,* and *vijñana* may each be translated in various ways) or how their interaction is to be understood (they are often taken ontologically, but they may refer to five different stages of cognition). So it is also unclear how "spiritual" each *skandha* is, although the earliest Pali commentaries seem to understand them more impersonally and mechanically as processes that lack a self that is doing them.

What remains important, however, is how both deconstructions of self flaunt the religious and philosophical climates of their own time by denying the existence of a Cartesian-type soul, defined by its self-consciousness. To the Buddhist critique of mental/physical and subject/object dualisms, Swedenborg adds a new and very significant dimension: each individual *is* one's inmost affection or ruling love (1988, 58). Just as Buddhism contradicts the Vedantic notion of a pure soul or consciousness covered with karmic impurities, so Swedenborg contradicts the long Western tradition (going back at least as far as Plato) of a sinful or confused psyche that needs to be purified so it can shine forth in its uncorrupted glory. In place of such a pristine self-consciousness, Swedenborg emphasizes that what I love is what I am. Whatever we do motivated by such love seems free to us. The religious task is not to discover what resides behind this love—some pure consciousness that is supposedly doing the loving—but to transform oneself by changing one's ruling love (from love of self to love of God and neighbor).

This understanding of our mental life is consistent with the Mahayana Buddhist denial of the dualism between subject and object, self and world. In this context I like to quote the Japanese Zen master Dogen: "I came to realize that mind is no other than mountains and rivers and the great wide earth, the sun and the moon and the stars."[7] If there is no self inside, it makes no sense to talk about the world as being "outside" one's mind. Inasmuch as this understanding transforms observed objects into manifestations of mind, it "animates" not only the so-called material world but also the events of "my" mental activity, which gain more of a life of their own independent of being thought by "me." And this is precisely what Swedenborg says: "Those things of wisdom and love which are called thoughts, perceptions, and affections, are substances and forms, and not entities flying and flowing out of nothing. . . . The affections, perceptions and thoughts there [in the brain] are not exhalations but are all actually and really subjects, which do not emit anything from themselves, but merely undergo changes according to whatever flows against and affects them" (Swedenborg 2003a, 42). Such mental phenomena are not what "I" do. It is more accurate to turn that around and say that my sense of self is a function of what they do. In this way Swedenborg's understanding of our mental life accords with his understanding of how influx operates, both that from the Lord (usually mediately through angels) and that from evil spirits.

This is related to another curious claim that is also contrary to our Cartesian (now "commonsense") expectations but quite consistent with the Buddhist denial of subject-object duality. Swedenborg writes that the divine influx is not experienced as coming from our internals; it is through the forehead into our internals: "The influx of the Lord Himself into man is into his forehead, and from there into the whole face" (251).[8] The strong implication is not (as in so much theistic mysticism) that we must realize the God who resides within us, but rather that the sense of a within apart from the world is the self-delusion that needs to be overcome.

So much of twentieth-century philosophy has been concerned with deconstructing dualisms such as mind/body and mind/matter, which are now generally viewed as problematical and alienating, that it is necessary to remember Swedenborg was writing in the eighteenth century, when it was less obvious that there was any problem or what alternatives there might be. Swedenborg's view of their relation is therefore all the more striking. In the afterworld the body of every spirit is the outer form of that spirit's love, corresponding exactly to the inner form of his soul or mind (e.g., 363). From a person's face, in particular, all the more inward affections are visible and radiate, because faces are the very outward form of these affections (47). From conversation, too, the wiser angels know the whole condition of another person (236). After death, angels carefully examine one's body, beginning with the face, then the fingers, and so on, because the details of one's thought and intention are written on the entire body as well (463). The new spirit is later "devastated" in order for the outward and inward elements to correspond and act as one (498, 503). The result is that the mind and body of a spirit come to correspond so completely that it is no longer meaningful to distinguish between them. This is the basis of that complete conjugal union of couples experienced most fully in the afterworld and sometimes even in this life; for both soul and mind, although they appear to be in the head, are "actually in the whole body" (Swedenborg 1998, 178).

The fact that such union can occur in this world as well reminds us not to draw too sharp a line between the world to come and this one. Bioenergetic therapies such as Rolfing massage seem to confirm that the body is not just a vehicle for mind, for it retains memories of past traumas that can be stimulated and recovered by somatic means.

## The Love of Self

The love of self, which closes our inmost parts to the divine influx (272), is the main problem to be overcome. With the support of his rationality, man has corrupted the output of the spiritual world within himself "through a disorderly life. So he must be born into complete ignorance and be led back from there into the pattern of heaven by divine means" (108).

The need to become ignorant suggests a Buddhist-like critique of conceptualization, which Swedenborg also makes. Insights, being outward truths, do not by themselves save us; what saves us is the way those insights change us (517). Innocence is the essence (*esse*) of everything good, and everything is good to the extent it contains innocence (281). To a Buddhist this sounds like *tathata*, the "just *this!*"-ness that describes the unself-conscious way an enlightened person lives. Having given up the love of self, and let go of the sense of self, we do not attain some other reality but realize the true nature of this one, which is all we need. That is why the essence of Zen can be chopping wood and carrying water.

This is how both traditions solve the problem of life. To be spiritual is nothing more than being open to, and thereby united with, the whole: that is, to accept one's situation and therefrom manifest the whole, in contrast to self-love (Swedenborg) and the delusion of separate self (Buddhism). The essential point is that this is not something that can happen only after we die. We are in heaven right now if our internals are open, according to Swedenborg, and nirvana can be attained here and now, since it is nothing other than the true nature of samsara, according to Mahayana. One version of this is that the passions, just as they are, are wisdom and enlightenment. This contradicts earlier Pali Buddhism, which understands desire as the source of our *dukkha* (suffering, dissatisfaction), but the Mahayana point is that our desires can be transmuted from self-ish cravings into more self-less joys. Swedenborg's attitude toward the pleasures of life makes the same critique of earlier ascetic, life-denying versions of Christianity: "It is by no means forbidden any one to enjoy the pleasures of the body and of sensual things; . . . for these are outermost or corporeal affections from interior affection. The interior affections, which are living, all derive their delight from good and truth; and good and truth derive their delight from charity and faith, and then from the Lord, thus from Life itself; and therefore the affections and pleasures which are from thence are alive" (Swedenborg 1990, 995).

This does not imply that the spiritual life is an epicurean devotion to "higher" pleasures, for there is another aspect of *tathata*-activity that Swedenborg and Buddhism both emphasize: as Swedenborg puts it, the Lord's kingdom is a kingdom of "uses which are ends." Divine worship is not a matter of attending church but living a life of love, charity, and faith (112, 221). "People who like to do good for others, not for their own sakes but for the sake of good, are the ones who love the neighbor; for good is the neighbor" (64). Compare to this the Buddhist proverb that in the beginning one does good deeds for the sake of the neighbor; later (when one has realized that the neighbor also has no self) one does good for the sake of the Dharma; but finally one does good for no reason at all, which in Swedenborg's terms is to attain the highest innocence.

For Buddhism such a life is best exemplified by the bodhisattva, who being un-self-preoccupied is devoted to the endless work of universal salvation. A bodhisattva is so unselfconscious that when he or she gives something to someone, it is without the awareness that he or she is giving, that there is someone else who receives, or even that there is a gift that is given. Such generosity is emphasized as the first and most important (because it is said to include all the others) of the *paramitas*, the "higher perfections" developed by those who follow the bodhisattva path. This corrects the "spiritual materialism" inherent in the more popular Buddhist attitude toward doing good deeds, which is concerned with "making merit" (accumulating good karma). For Swedenborg too, those who are led by the Lord think of nothing less than the merit that their good works might accrue (Swedenborg 1990, 6392). His account of this would fit comfortably into a Mahayana scripture:

> When an angel [or bodhisattva] does good to anyone he also communicates to him his own good, satisfaction, and blessedness; and this with the feeling that he would give to the other everything, and retain nothing. When he is in such communication good flows into him with much greater satisfaction and blessedness than he gives, and this continually with increase. But as soon as a thought enters, that he will communicate his own to the intent that he may maintain that influx of satisfaction and blessedness into himself, the influx is dissipated; and still more if there comes in any thought of recompense from him to whom he communicates his good. (6478)

Unlike those who have retired from the world to live a solitary and devout life, the "angels' life is happy because of its blessedness, and is made up of serving good purposes which are works of charity" (535). Both traditions deny that salvation is effected by performing rituals, or faith alone, or deeds alone, or by having mystical experiences. To be spiritual is to live a certain kind of life, in which love of self is replaced by selfless love.

In order to be able to live this way, however, we must be regenerated, which for Swedenborg involves an opening up of our internals that seems very similar to the enlightenment or *paravrtti* "turning around" of Buddhist liberation. The origin of evil is that "man turned himself backwards, away from the Lord, and round towards himself" (Swedenborg 1998, 444); we need to "turn back around" away from self and toward the Lord. This turning around liberates the Lord's influx to flow into us. This influx is life itself. We have no other life of our own, being receptacles of this divine life. The question is how much of this influx we are open to. Depending on my ruling love, this influx is choked and constricted (by self-love) or flows like a fountain (into love of God and neighbor).

I think this points to the solution of a perennial religious problem, the relationship between personal effort and transcendental grace. This tension recurs in the early Christian argument between Augustine and Pelagius, in the Hindu Vishistadvaita debate about "cat salvation" (a mother cat carries her kittens) versus "monkey salvation" (a baby monkey must cling to its mother's chest), and in the Japanese Buddhist relationship between *tariki* "other effort" (throwing oneself on the mercy of the Buddha) and *jiriki* "self-effort" (which requires one's own efforts to become liberated). All "I" can do is to open up to the spiritual influx by my ego getting out of the way—that is, letting go of myself, whereupon this influx necessarily fills me, just like the sun always shines when the clouds dissipate. Yet this letting go is not subject to my willing. Since self is itself the problem, this is not something that the self can do. In Zen, for example, I indirectly practice "forgetting myself" during *zazen* by concentrating on and becoming one with Mu, for example (as discussed in the previous chapter).[9]

## Identification of the Divine

Although the issue is complicated, Swedenborg's conception of the Divine avoids the extremes of either a personal or an impersonal Absolute in much the same way that Mahayana Buddhism does. The dilemma is that a completely impersonal Absolute, such as found in certain types of Vedanta, must be indifferent to our situation, while a more personal God, understood to have a will and wishes analogous to ours, may choose some people (or some peoples) for a special destiny, perhaps without their doing anything special to deserve it (e.g., through predestination).

Yet there is another alternative, if God is the life-giving force in everything—our very being, as Swedenborg might express it, or our lack of being, as Mahayana might express it, or both our being and our nonbeing, as the thirteenth-century Christian mystic Eckhart does express it. Both descriptions are ways to communicate the same insight that there is no dualism between God and us. So Eckhart can play with the binary terms "Being" and "Nonbeing" by nonchalantly reversing their meaning. Sometimes he refers to the being of creatures and describes God as a nothing, without the slightest bit of existence. At other times Eckhart contrasts the "nullity" of all creatures with the being of God, in which case it is not that God has being, or even that God is being, but that being is God (*esse est deus*). If God is the life or being in everything, then it is just as true to say that nothing has any being of its own. Is this also an adequate explanation of the *shunyata* "emptiness" of beings, according to Mahayana, and of the nature of the Lord for Swedenborg?

The nature of God and the role of Christ for Swedenborg are two difficult issues that are not fully addressed in *Heaven and Hell*, and even when we consider other writings that address those matters more fully—especially

*Divine Love and Wisdom* and *Arcana Cælestia*—I do not find what Swedenborg writes entirely clear or satisfactory. Curiously, however, there is some of the same ambiguity within the Buddhist tradition. Let us consider the two issues separately.

For Swedenborg God is life itself, of which angels and spirits and humans are recipients. This divine essence manifests as love and wisdom, which are inseparable in the same way as the sun's heat and light are—an inspired analogy or rather correspondence that Swedenborg makes much of, since in heaven God appears as (but is not himself) a sun (116–40). When, however, we inquire into the nature of God as he is in himself, apart from all the things infused and the activity of infusing them, what Swedenborg writes is less helpful. He emphasizes repeatedly that God is a man, or human. Three reasons are given for this: humans, like angels and spirits, derive their form from God, "there being no difference as to form, but as to essence" (Swedenborg 2003a, 11); heaven is in the form of a man, both in whole and in part (chaps. VIII–IX); and humans should conceive of God as a man, for it is not possible to think of, love, and be conjoined with something indefinite and therefore incomprehensible (e.g., 3; 1997, 787; 1990, 7211, 8705, 9354).

None of these reasons unambiguously implies theism as that term is usually understood. The first two do not require that God have a self-existence apart from his universe (in general) and from those beings who experience his influx (in particular). They imply something important about the forms we and the universe necessarily embody as recipients of influx, yet nothing about the form-in-itself of the source of that influx. The third reason, the only one that offers an argument rather than assertion, is more difficult to evaluate, because it addresses how one should think rather than what is the case. Swedenborg is concerned about the dangers of conceiving of God in the wrong way, since this can lead us astray. He writes that those who believe in an invisible Divine called the Reality of the Universe, the source of all that exists, end up believing in no Divinity at all, because such a Divine "is no fit subject for thought" (3); those who acknowledge what is incomprehensible "glide in thought into nature, and so believe in no God" (Swedenborg 1990, 9354). Yet no one in heaven "can have any conception of the Divine in itself. . . . For the angels are finite and what is finite can have no conception of the infinite. In heaven, therefore, if they had not an idea of God in the human shape, they would have no idea, or an unbecoming one" (7211).

To sum up: inasmuch as God is infinite, all our conceptions of him must miss the mark, yet inasmuch as we need a conception of him, the best image is that of a man. To a Buddhist, this is reminiscent of the old argument that, since a religion must have a God, Buddhism cannot be a religion. But is it possible to have a religion (such as Buddhism) that criticizes all conceptions of the Divine, including the image of God as human, yet still functions as a religion because its spiritual practices nonetheless promote the Divine influx (to use Swedenborg's terminology)?

Since Swedenborg's quintessential teaching is that the Lord's love and wisdom flow into everything, no being can exist apart from God, and the fact that God is human does not necessarily imply that God exists as humanlike apart from beings. This may be taken a step further. If we extrapolate from Swedenborg's favorite analogy—God as a formless, radiating sun—the Lord may be understood as a *potentiality* that achieves form only in his creation. From that perspective, however, God needs us in order to become fully real, both individually (as we open to his influx) and collectively (as his heaven grows and ramifies).

I think this understanding is consistent with much of Buddhism and may even help to clarify some aspects of Buddhist teaching. Central to Mahayana is the concept of *shunyata*, usually translated as "emptiness." For Nagarjuna, the most important Mahayana philosopher, that things are *shunya* is a shorthand way to express that no thing has any self-being or self-presence of its own. In the succinct *Heart Sutra*, the best known of the Prajñaparamita scriptures, the bodhisattva Avalokitesvara realizes that "form is *shunyata* and *shunyata* is form; form is no other than *shunyata* and *shunyata* none other than form." Unfortunately, the usual English translation "emptiness" does not convey the full connotations of the original, for the Sanskrit root *shu* means "swollen," not only like an inflated balloon but also like a pregnant woman swollen with possibility. According to Nagarjuna, it is only because things are *shunya* that any change, including spiritual development, is possible.

*Shunyata*, then, invites interpretation as a formless spiritual potential that is literally no-thing in itself yet functions as the "empty essence" that gives life to everything and enables it to be what it is. Such an influx is experienced as "empty" for two reasons: it has no particular form of its own, in itself, and insofar as I *am* it I cannot *know* it. This is consistent with Swedenborg's understanding of the Lord as constituting the life in each of us, the heat (love) and light (wisdom) that flow into us to the extent that we are receptive to it. On the Buddhist side, this also helps to avoid the nihilistic interpretation of *shunyata* that the rather-too-negative term has sometimes invited.

Shakyamuni Buddha did not urge his disciples to unite with God or experience God's influx. Instead, he taught them to follow in his own footsteps by pursuing the same types of spiritual practice in order to attain the same nirvana. However, this difference may be less problematical than it seems. For one thing, the nature of nirvana is notoriously obscure, since the Buddha refused to say much about it except that it is the end of suffering and craving. Those who want to know what nirvana is must attain it for themselves. In addition, the comparative study of religion has led us to an insight that is difficult to deny today but would have had less meaning in Swedenborg's time: very similar experiences may be subjected to different and incompatible explanations, according to the tradition one is familiar with. In Shakyamuni's time Indian popular religion was polytheistic, which means that he did not teach in the context of an absolute God transcending or incorporating all other gods; nor does he seem to have been familiar with the Upanishadic conception of an impersonal Brahman, another alternative being developed by other Indian sages at about the same time. So it is hardly surprising that Shakyamuni did not communicate his own spiritual insight—the influx of wisdom and compassion that was liberated by the dissolution of his ego-self?—in either terminology but instead created his own religious categories (nonself, nirvana, etc.), unlike Swedenborg, who naturally understood his own experience in terms of the Christian tradition in which that he had grown up, centered on the idea of an absolute Lord.

Later and in different social contexts, more theistic conceptions did become important in popular Buddhism, such as the Amida Buddha worshiped in more devotional sects of Buddhism. It is worth noticing that these devotional schools—which, as Swedenborg noticed, require that we think of the Divine as human—have been more important for the majority of East Asian Buddhists than have the more meditative paths of Theravada and Chan/Zen Buddhism, not to mention the dialectics of Buddhist philosophers such as Nagarjuna.

In this fashion, Christian theism as Swedenborg explains it—the Lord as our life, due to his influx of love and wisdom—perhaps becomes more compatible with the *shunyata* of Buddha-nature as many Buddhists have understood it.

But what of the unique role of Christ for Swedenborg? It seems to me that he is ambivalent. Taken as a whole, Swedenborg's writings contain a tension between two different positions that never quite become compatible. On the more orthodox side, he defends the uniqueness of Christ as God-Man and the importance of accepting him as our savior. On the other, more ecumenical side, his emphasis on the influx of love and wisdom leads him to reduce the salvific role of Christ so much that he can be reconceptualized without much difficulty as one avatar among many, a view quite compatible with Buddhism.

There is no doubt, however, that Swedenborg thinks of the historical Christ as unique and the Christian church as special. Before his advent, the Lord's influence was mediated through the angelic heavens, yet from the time he became human it has been immediate. Since then the Christian church has formed the heart of the human race on earth and in heaven as well. Christians constitute the breast of the Grand Man, the center toward which all others look. It is not necessary that all or most people accept Christianity, but it is very important that some people do, "for from thence there is light to those who are out of the Church and have not the Word" (Swedenborg 2003a, 233; 1990, 637; 2003b, 256).

Yet who is in the Lord's spiritual church? "[I]t is throughout the whole terrestrial globe. For it is not limited to those who have the Word, and from this have obtained a knowledge of the Lord, and some truths of faith; but it is also with those who have not the Word, and are therefore entirely igno-rant of the Lord, and consequently do not know any truths of faith (for all truths of faith refer to the Lord); that is, with the Gentiles remote from the church ... for in good the Lord is present" (Swedenborg 1990, 3263).

During his visits to hell Swedenborg encountered church dignitaries learned in the Christian Word "but in evils as to life," while in heaven he met both Christians and gentiles "who were in falsities" and "were yet in good as to life" (9192). When we are being regenerated we can fight against falsities "even from truth not genuine if only it be such that it can be conjoined by any means with good; and it is conjoined with good by innocence, for innocence is the means of conjunction" (6765). From passages such as these—and there are many of them—it is difficult to conclude that it is necessary or even important to be a Christian. The point is not simply that we are saved by living a good life, but that we live a good life because we have become receptive to the influx of divine love and wisdom. And insofar as this influx is "innocent," it becomes unclear why it should be necessary to believe in any particular doctrine whatever. If we accept this important ecumenical strand within Swedenborg's writings, a strand that has been even more important in Buddhism, then there is no need for anyone to be a Christian or a Swedenborgian or a Buddhist, except insofar as those teachings and communities help us to turn away from self-love and open up to the influx of self-less love and wisdom.

Why did Christ manifest on earth as man? The internals of humans are under the dominion of either spirits from hell or angels from heaven. When in the course of time the hellish influence became stronger and "there was no longer any faith nor any charity," the Lord's advent was necessary to restore order and redeem man (152). This may be a good reason for the appear-ance of a savior, but it is a poor argument for the uniqueness of Christ as the savior. In fact, it is the same reason given in the *Bhagavad-Gita* for the periodic appearance of avatars,[10] and in Buddhism for the periodic appearance of Buddhas (the next Buddha to come is Maitreya).

## Spiritual Interdependence

In the previous section the *shunyata* "emptiness" of Mahayana Buddhism was interpreted as a formless spiritual potential that gives life to everything, an understanding consistent with Swedenborg's conception of the Lord's influx into each of us. This approach to *shunyata* has been especially important as a way to understand the Dharmakaya (or "Truth-body"), a term for the highest reality in some Mahayana texts, as we shall see shortly when we turn to the *Tibetan Book of the Dead*. However, this has not been the only understanding of *shunyata* in Buddhism, and it is questionable whether it would have been acceptable to Nagarjuna himself, who argued for the *shunyata* of things not by referring to influx but by demonstrating interdependence (things are *shunya* because they have no self-existence, being dependent on many other phenomena).

This emphasis on interdependence became an important Mahayana teaching and in fact the essential teaching of Hua-yen, a Chinese school of Buddhism that describes this relationship using the metaphor of Indra's net:

> Far away in the heavenly abode of the great god Indra, there is a wonderful net that stretches out infinitely in all directions.... [There is] a single glittering jewel in each "eye" of the net, and since the net itself is infinite in all dimensions, the jewels are infinite in number ... in its polished surface there are reflected all the other jewels in the net, infinite in number. Not only that, but each of the jewels reflected in this one jewel is also reflecting all the other jewels, so that there is an infinite reflecting process occurring. (Cook 1977, 2)

Indra's net "thus symbolizes a cosmos in which there is an infinitely repeated interrelationship among all the members of the cosmos" (ibid.). Each jewel is nothing other than a function of the relationships among all the others, and likewise may be said to contain all the others within itself. All is one and one is all: the whole world is contained in each thing, and each thing is nothing other than a manifestation of the whole world.

Is there anything comparable in Swedenborg? The analogy is hard to miss. All the realms of the heavens constitute a whole (1988, chap. VIII)—in fact, a Grand Man—as does hell (553). In that Grand Man who is heaven, for example, infants form the region of the eyes (333). Each of heaven's communities is also a single person (1988, chap. IX), and conversely each angel is a heaven in smallest form (53). The same relationship seems to hold for the hells and the demons in them.[11]

By emphasizing the "ecological" interdependence of each such thing on the functioning of all other things, Indra's net and the Grand Man constitute a type of interdependence that differs from the dependence of non-self-existent things on the influx of spiritual potentiality that gives them being/life. What is significant is that both types of dependence are important both to Mahayana and to Swedenborg. The interpenetration of one in all and all in one in Swedenborg's afterlife presupposes the divine influx that permeates all the realms, including hell, where it is perverted into self-love. In Buddhism these two interpretations of *shunyata* have sometimes been understood as alternatives, but Swedenborg's vision reminds us that they do not need to exclude each other.

This dependence/interdependence must be understood dynamically. Like Buddhism from its inception, Swedenborg emphasizes process (*anicca* "impermanence" in Buddhism) as a way of denying substance (*svabhava* "self-existence"). The persistence of things over time is actually a continual occurrence (106); enduring is a constant emergence (9). This is true even of Swedenborgian regeneration and Buddhist enlightenment. The regenerated are regenerated continually through life and also in the afterlife; heaven as it grows becomes more and more a Grand Man. Most Buddhist schools emphasize the need for continual practice, even for the deeply enlightened, and the urge to deepen one's practice endlessly is a sign of genuine realization. There is a saying in Zen that even Shakyamuni Buddha is only halfway there.

## Consequences of Evil

Perhaps the most profound parallel of all is with Swedenborg's account of evil and its punishment, which is so Buddhist in spirit that it could be used to clarify puzzling Buddhist teachings about karma. Like Shakyamuni Buddha and, for that matter, Christ himself, Swedenborg emphasizes intention, for that is how evil becomes tied to its own punishment:

> Every evil carries its punishment with it, the two making one; therefore whoever is in evil is also in the punishment of evil. And yet no one in the other world suffers punishment on account of the evils that he had done in this world, but only on account of the evils that he then does; although it amounts to the same and is the same thing whether it be said that people suffer punishment on account of their evils in the world or that they suffer punishment on account of the evils they do in the other life, since every one after death returns into his own life and thus into like evils; and the person continues the same as he had been in the life of the body.... But good spirits, although they had done evils in the world, are never punished, because their evils do not return (509).

> The Lord does not do evil to anyone (550).

> Evil has its own punishment, thus hell, and goodness its own reward, thus heaven. (1990, 9033)

This is in effect a sophisticated account of karma that avoids both the problem with a more mechanical understanding of moral cause and effect (common in popular Buddhism) and also the problem with a more juridical understanding of hell as punishment for disobeying divine authority (common in popular Christianity). The central insight is that people are punished not for what they have done but for what they have become, and what we intentionally do is what makes us what we are. That is why in most cases there is no difference between the evil things done in the world and the evil things that one is inclined to do in the afterworld. This conflation makes no sense if karma is understood dualistically as a kind of moral dirt obscuring one's mirrorlike pure self. It makes a great deal of sense if I *am* my intention or "ruling love," for then the important spiritual issue is the development of that ruling love. In that case my actions and my intentions build my character—that is, my spiritual body—just as surely as food is assimilated to become my physical body.

All schools of Buddhism emphasize the importance of our *samskaras*, which are mental tendencies: one's habitual ways of intending and reacting to particular situations. In Buddhism, too, these *samskaras* are the vehicles of karma. They survive death and cause rebirth. In fact, they are what is reborn, since there is no ontological self to be reincarnated. How are such mental tendencies formed?

> We can now see that it is not so hard to lead a heaven-bound life as people think it is because it is simply a matter, when something gets in the way that the person knows is dishonest and unfair, something his spirit moves toward, of thinking that he should not do it because it is against the Divine precepts. If a person gets used to doing this, and by getting used to it gains a certain disposition, then little by little he is bonded to heaven. As this takes place, the higher reaches of his mind are opened; and as they are opened, he sees things that are dishonest and unfair; and as he sees them, they can be broken apart. . . .
>
> But it must be understood that the difficulty of so thinking and of resisting evils increases so far as man from his will does evils, for in the same measure he becomes accustomed to them until he no longer sees them, and at length loves them and from the delight of his love excuses them, and confirms them by every kind of fallacy, and declares them to be allowable and good. (533)

A person suffers not because of "inherited evil" but "because of the realized evil that does belong to him—that is, the amount of inherited evil that he has made his own by his life activities" (342). In this way Swedenborg and

Buddhism both present a psychological version of karma that denies any sharp distinction between the one who intends and the intention itself. "I" *am* my predominant intentions, for habitually acting in certain ways is what constructs my sense of self. That is why people with bad *samskaras*—with a "bad character"—cannot be saved in spite of themselves: because they *are* those *samskaras*, and they cannot dwell in heaven because they would not be comfortable there. Therefore they spontaneously go to where they are comfortable, which happens to be where there are others with similar *samskaras*.

Evil people suffer in the afterworld for the same reason that good people are blessed there: they end up living with others just like themselves.

## A Place in the Spiritual World

Swedenborg's account of the world of spirits has many similarities with the Tibetan understanding of the afterlife and the rebirth process, which provides by far the most detailed account among the various Buddhist traditions. However, there are some problems in working this out. The *Bardo Thodol Chenmo* text first translated by Evans-Wentz and published as *The Tibetan Book of the Dead* is only one of several such Bardo texts in the Tibetan tradition, and because that particular text was composed with reference to a tantric mandala of 110 peaceful and wrathful deities there is much obscure symbolism about those deities.[12]

Yet even if one ignores this difficult iconography there remains a sophisticated description of death, intermediate life, and rebirth that resonates deeply with Swedenborg's account. Both emphasize the importance of one's last thought (444)—in other words, the particular *samskara* activated at the moment of death—and that all one's *samskaras* survive death, along with a psychic body that duplicates one's physical body: "[A]fter death, a person is engaged in every sense, memory, thought, and affection he was engaged in in the world: he leaves nothing behind except his earthly body" (1988, chaps. LXVII, LXVIII). Even as God does not turn his face from anyone and does not cast anyone into hell (545), so the luminosity of the Dharmakaya (experienced as a primordial clear light comparable to the divine sun in Swedenborg's heaven), which is nothing other than one's own *shunyata* mind, does not reject anyone. For both, there is a self-judgment that occurs in the presence of God / the Dharmakaya, in which the true nature of one's *samskaras* / "ruling affections" becomes revealed. In the Bardo tradition, too, the good and wise are attracted to the pure, formless Dharmakaya, and the texts urge them to unite with it. Since it mirrors all one's karma, those less good are repulsed by it and are attracted to the samsaric realm that corresponds to their ruling karma.

Swedenborg emphasizes the limits of the Lord's mercy: no one enters heaven by direct mercy (1988, chap. LIV), for the Lord does not and evidently cannot violate the design that he *is* (523). Since this mercy is constant with each individual and never withdraws, everyone who can be saved is saved, but those whose ruling affection is evil have learned to shut out his influx. In the intermediate Bardo realm, too, even a Buddha cannot stop someone who wants to go somewhere, since (as Swedenborg expresses it) he or she *is* that attraction/affection and could not be stopped without being annihilated (527).

There are, nevertheless, some important differences. For Swedenborg the world of spirits is an intermediate one, because there one is "devastated": that is, outward elements must be changed until they conform with inward elements (426). One's inmost level can no longer be reformed, but the outward elements must be gradually set in order until one's ways of thinking and feeling are consistent with one's deepest intentions. Yet, as the meaning of the Tibetan title ("The Great Liberation through Hearing in the Bardo") suggests, the presupposition of the Bardo "intermediate realm" texts is that it is still possible to exercise some freedom in the Bardo world, that despite the karmic attraction there may still be some choice in the matter—perhaps because there may be more than one "ruling" love?

I can think of two ways to resolve this difference. One is to understand the *Bardo Thodol* less ingenuously as a book meant for the living rather than the dead, as a way of encouraging those still living to reform their lives, their *samskaras*, while they still can. Reading it orally beside the corpse, surrounded by the chastened mourners, certainly serves this function, yet there is another way to look at it. I wonder if there is some inconsistency in the way that *Heaven and Hell* emphasizes that one's ruling love cannot be changed to eternity (477ff.), while also describing incidents such as angels' attempts to influence new spirits (e.g., 450), efforts that would be wasted if they could have no effect whatsoever on their ruling love (and therefore on their eventual place in heaven or hell). It also seems debatable whether we always have only one ruling love. Maybe there are some cases, or many cases, where two or more affections contend with each other throughout one's life and even afterward. If so, perhaps Swedenborg's conception is the disingenuous one?

A difference of emphasis, at least, follows from the distinction between morality and insight. They are closely related, yet to the extent that they may be distinguished Buddhism as a "wisdom tradition" emphasizes wisdom more, while Swedenborg emphasizes morality. One of the ways this difference shows itself is in the distinction that Buddhism makes between "heaven" as one of the six realms of samsara—pleasurable yet complacent, therefore not as good a place as our human realm—and the liberation that is nirvana. From a Buddhist perspective even good karma is troublesome insofar as it operates mechanically. Better is the *prajna* wisdom that frees one from all karma and therefore from all the realms of samsara. A good example of this is the *Bardo Thodol* understanding of what happens after death when a new spirit encounters the pure luminosity of the Dharmakaya. One is encouraged to unite with the white light by realizing that one *is* it. In comparison to this, even the most sublime of the peaceful deities, which represent good karma, is nothing more than a higher form of delusion. I have not found anything comparable in Swedenborg.

This leads us to consider the most important difference between Swedenborg and Buddhism. Swedenborg's Christian conception of the afterdeath drama is orthodox in understanding our present life as a one-chance preparation for heaven or hell, since one's ruling love never changes even to eternity (477, 480). In contrast, all traditional schools of Buddhism understand the alternative to nirvana as rebirth in one of the six samsaric realms (heaven, titan, human, hungry ghost, animal, and hell), which includes the possibility of returning as a human being. We recycle from one realm to another, according to our karma, until we escape samsara by awakening to our true nature.[13]

However, even this difference is complicated by the fact that some *Bardo Thodol* passages warn the spirit about never being able to escape from where one is inclined to go: "[N]ow is the time when by slipping into laziness even for a moment you will suffer for ever." "If you go there you will enter hell and experience unbearable suffering through heat and cold from which you will never get out" (Fremantle and Trungpa 1992, 212–13). Theoretically, though, escape is always possible no matter where you are, if you realize the *shunyata* of your own mind. The corresponding experience in Swedenborg would be regeneration even in hell, by the opening up of one's internals to the Lord's influx and the transformation of one's ruling love. Yet he does not seem to allow for that possibility, despite the fact that the divine love never withdraws from anyone (Swedenborg 2003b, 330).


## Living Correspondences

As a final comparison, let us briefly consider Swedenborg's doctrine of correspondences or representations, a version of afterlife idealism: although the afterworld is in many ways similar to this one, things there are not as fixed or stationary, for their condition varies according to the angels who perceive them, and they disappear when those angels depart (173 ff.). "As all things that correspond to interiors also represent them they are called representatives; and as they differ in each case in accordance with the state of the interiors they are called appearances. Nevertheless, the things that appear before the eyes of angels in heavens and are perceived by their senses appear to their eyes and senses as fully living as things on earth appear to man, and even much more clearly, distinctly, and perceptibly" (175).

This seems similar to some of the claims of Yogachara or Vijñanavada (sometimes translated as "the Representation-Only school"), one of the two main philosophical school of Mahayana, along with Nagarjuna's Madhyamaka, with which it eventually merged. In contrast to the detailed correspondences offered by Swedenborg, Yogachara addresses the issue on a more abstract level, and perhaps more illuminating is the parallel with the *Bardo Thodol*, which understands all postmortem experiences as mentally projected images, making the world beyond "a karmically corresponding image of earthly life": "The descriptions of those visions which, according to the *Bardo Thodol*, appear in the intermediate state (*bar-do*) following death are neither primitive folklore nor theological speculations. They are not concerned with the appearances of supernatural beings . . . but with the visible projections or reflexes of inner processes, experiences, and states of mind, produced in the creative phase of meditation" (Govinda 1969, 122). The challenge of the Bardo realm is to recognize the peaceful and wrathful deities that appear as the karmic projections of one's own mind. "If all the temptations of deceptive visionary images, which are constantly referred to in the texts as hostile forms of the intellect, can be recognized as empty creations of one's own mind and can be immediately penetrated, one will attain liberation" (Lauf 1989, 69).

The difference, as we have already noticed, is that the *Bardo Thodol* urges the deceased not to identify with any such images in order to attain to the liberating luminosity of the formless Dharmakaya, while Swedenborg's angels dwell happily in a mental world that changes constantly according to their affections. Perhaps the common ground between them is that neither spirits are deceived by those correspondences into believing that the things of their world are permanently real, a delusion that occurs when samsaric attachments and delusions motivate one to fixate on them. One who must play cannot play, while those who know that things are correspondences are not trapped by and in those correspondences.

## What is "the Secret of Great Tartary"?

If the above parallels are genuine, they raise a question that should not be ignored: Why are Buddhist and Swedenborg's teachings so similar? There are various possibilities, which readers can work out for themselves, but one ramification in particular deserves to be addressed. Did Swedenborg become acquainted with Buddhism through his travels . . . in the afterworld? One of the most intriguing references in his voluminous works is an allusion to a "Great Tartary" where the teachings of the Ancient Church (which his writings re-present) have been preserved.

I have spoken with spirits and angels who came from there, and
they said that they possess a Word, and have from ancient times;
and that their divine worship is performed according to this Word,
which consists of pure correspondences. . . . They said that they
worship Jehovah, some as an invisible, and some as a visible God.
Moreover they said that they do not permit foreigners to come
among them, except the Chinese, with whom they cultivate peace,
because the emperor of China is from their country. . . . Seek for
it in China, and perhaps you will find it there among the Tartars.
(1912, 11)[14]

What can this refer to? And where? Anders Hallengren discusses this matter
in his article "The Secret of Great Tartary" (Hallengren 1994, 35–54). After
reviewing the historical evidence, he concludes that the most probable reference is the Buddhism of Mongolia and Tibet (since Kublai Khan, founder of
China's Yuan dynasty, was converted by a Tibetan rinpoche in the thirteenth
century, Mongolian Buddhism has been a version of Tibetan Buddhism).

To this I can add only one point, concerning the curious fact that
their worship "consists of pure correspondences." What can this mean? The
Vajrayana Buddhism of Tibet and Mongolia is a Mahayana form of tantra
that employs meditative practices such as mandalas (complex visual images,
usually paintings), mantras (the repetition of sacred sounds), mudras (hand
movements), and so forth. In the case of a mandala, for example, a practitioner
typically meditates on its visual form until he or she is able to reproduce it
completely—indeed, even more sharply—in the mind's eye; the aim of this
practice is to become one with the deities depicted, who represent aspects
of one's own Buddha-nature. Although the complex symbolism of most
mandalas is not very relevant to the theoretical concerns of most Buddhism
philosophy, that symbolism is quite relevant to the more practical concerns
of meditators. Tantra is by nature esoteric because it is a nonconceptual
symbolic system: "[T]he mandala is 'a microcosmic image of the universe';
it is, above all, a map of the cosmos. It is the whole universe in its essential
plan, in its process of emanation and reabsorption" (Lauf 1989, 65). This
suggests that meditations employing these images might involve the "pure
correspondences" that Swedenborg mentions. I do not know how to evaluate this supposition, but in the future I will be less inclined to dismiss such
images as "mere iconography"!

## Conclusion

Here it has been possible to mention only some of the more provocative
parallels between Swedenborgianism and Buddhism. It has nevertheless been

enough to suggest that Swedenborg might become an important bridge in the contemporary dialogue between Christianity and Buddhism. Swedenborg's double emphasis on divine love and wisdom, which forms the core of his theology, is reproduced in the relationship between Christianity and Buddhism, which respectively emphasize the way of love and the way of wisdom—and, as Swedenborg and Buddhism both emphasize, each way entails the other.

Unfortunately, we cannot expect this bridge to carry much traffic, for the same reason that Swedenborg's eschatology has been ignored by the mainstream Christian tradition. His grand conception of the afterworld, and of this world, is too dependent on his own extraordinary spiritual experiences, which few if any of us are able to confirm for ourselves.

Not having visited heaven or hell, I can only hope that, if they exist, they function in the way Swedenborg has described. After one studies his well-structured and extraordinarily detailed eschatology, other conceptions of the afterlife lose whatever credibility they might retain in our skeptical age. If the universe does not work in the way Swedenborg explained, well, maybe it should.

# EIGHT

# The Karma of Women

What does Buddhism have to say about the situation of women?

Needless to say, there is no simple answer to such a question. True to its own emphasis on impermanence and insubstantiality, Buddhism became quite different in different cultures. If Buddhism is not what the Buddha taught but what he started, we are presented with a complicated set of teachings, practices, and historical traditions, which are not always consistent with each other. This chapter focuses specifically on Thailand, one of the most devoutly Buddhist nations in the world.[1] It also has what is probably the largest and best-organized sex trade in the world: according to some estimates up to a million sex workers (out of a total population of about seventy million people), easily dwarfing the declining number of Buddhist monks (less than three hundred thousand *bhikkhu* "monks"). Religions serve a double function in society: they help to mold our most important values, attitudes, and behaviors, even as they absorb and reflect preexisting values, attitudes, and behaviors. So what role does Buddhism presently play in encouraging or rationalizing the Thai sex business? What role might it play in discouraging prostitution, and empowering women generally?

## The Liberation of Women

The earliest Buddhist texts reveal a curious ambivalence about women, which reminds us to place the Buddha's transformative message in its original social context. Although revered as the original words of Shakyamuni Buddha, the Pali Canon was preserved orally for over three hundred years before being written down, providing many opportunities for some passages to be intentionally or unintentionally "corrected" by monks less enlightened than the Buddha. Just as important, however, we need to remember that the historical Buddha was raised in a very patriarchal culture. His teachings as they have come down to us perhaps reveal a struggle against that sexist conditioning.

Buddhism developed largely in response to the Brahmanical culture developing in India in the middle of the first millennium BCE. Brahmanism emphasized caste and the inferiority of women. As later codified in the Laws of Manu, women were fettered to men for life: first as obedient daughters, then as subservient wives, and finally as aging mothers dependent on their sons. A wife's main duty was to produce sons. She was usually confined to the home and had no rights of her own—certainly no opportunity to study the Vedas (reserved for male Brahmins) or engage in most other religious practices.

Religiously, a large part of the problem was that women were believed to be polluted and polluting. This refers not only to their association with blood (the messiness of menstruation and childbirth), but also, and especially, to their role as temptress and seducer, an uncontrollable threat to the chastity of ascetic men trying to follow a spiritual path. Women were chastised for their stronger sex drive, which today seems a classic example of psychological projection: ascetics blaming their own problems with celibacy on women, the objects of their lust.

Early Buddhism did not completely escape this misogyny, for there are many such passages in the Pali Canon, some of them attributed to the Buddha, who warned his monks about the impurity of sexuality generally and the snares of women in particular. One example of this is the three daughters of Mara, the Buddhist archetype of evil (although a rather bland symbol compared to the malevolent Satan of Christianity), who tempted him just before his final enlightenment. Although Mara himself is male, his offspring Raga "lust," Arati "ill will," and Thana "craving," are always depicted as feminine.

In contrast to such patriarchal stereotypes, however, the Buddha's main teaching to householders was almost revolutionary in its historical context. In the *Sigalovada Sutta*, the thirty-first sutra of the *Digha Nikaya*, he instructs a husband to minister to his wife in five ways: by being courteous to her, not despising her, being faithful to her, giving her authority, and providing her with ornaments. From the other side, a wife should show compassion to her husband also in five ways: by performing her duties well, being hospitable to relations and attendants, being faithful, protecting what he brings home, and being skilled and industrious in discharging her duties. Such injunctions may seem unremarkable to us today, but what is extraordinary for the Buddha's time is that the marital relationship is understood to be reciprocal, with both sides having rights and responsibilities—making marriage, in effect, a contract between equals, a momentous step in the male-dominated Iron Age culture of sixth-century BCE India.

But what about the spiritual potential of women? That is the acid test for religious patriarchy, and one that the Buddha passed—but evidently it took him a while. Again, the story as preserved in the Pali Canon suggests some ambivalence. It was not until five or six years after his enlightenment that he agreed to meet with a delegation of women, led by his aunt and foster mother, Mahaprajapati Gotami. They asked for an order of *bhikkhuni* nuns to be established, to parallel the male *sangha* "order" of *bhikkhu*. Several times the Buddha refused, but when his attendant Ananda asked him if women were equal in their capacity for enlightenment, he admitted that they were just as capable of following the contemplative life. He then yielded to their repeated request, but with special conditions: eight additional rules of conduct that made nuns forever subordinate to the monks.[2] Unsurprisingly, internal textual evidence strongly suggests that those rules were added to the passage later. The text then goes on to have the Buddha confide to Ananda that, had women not been admitted as monastics, his teaching would have survived more than a thousand years; due to the admission of women, however, it would only last five hundred years (*Anguttara Nikaya* 8.51/iv 274). Whether or not this prediction was actually made by the Buddha himself, it turned out to be wrong: the Buddhist teachings continue to exist, and in some ways they are flourishing more than ever.

The *bhikkhuni sangha*—the first order of female monastics in human history—initially thrived, although its contributions to Buddhism have been largely neglected by the male monastics who compiled its history. Many of the *bhikkhuni* attained liberation, and the Buddha had occasion to praise at least thirteen of them. Some of their enlightenment verses are included in the Pali Canon, and some of those verses in the *Therigatha* suggest a Buddhist protofeminism. For example, Soma Theri wrote:

> What harm is it
> To be a woman
> When the mind is concentrated
> And the insight is clear?
> If I asked myself
> "Am I a woman
> or a man in this?"
> then I would be speaking
> Mara's language

> (in Murcott 1991, 158–59)

In other words, when it comes to the spiritual path, discriminating according to gender is a delusion.

So far, so good . . . for a while. Once the Buddha was no longer around to keep an eye on things, however, patriarchy began to reassert itself, and the situation of Buddhist women began to deteriorate, for both nuns and laywomen. In Theravada countries the *bhikkhuni* order shrank and disappeared—in

Thailand, apparently only about three hundred years after it had been established.[3] Some Mahayana sutras claimed that women must first be reborn (or magically transformed) into men before they could become fully enlightened Buddhas, and this belief became widespread in Asian Buddhism. Other Mahayana scriptures, however, continued to present more positive images of women that are more consistent with the central Mahayana concept of *shunyata* "emptiness": if men and women are equally *shunya*—both lacking any self-essence—then there is no ground for any gender discrimination. In the Chan/Son/Zen Buddhism of China, Korea, and Japan, respectively, the enlightened mind is neither male nor female, and there are notable examples of female Zen adepts. But such spiritual subtleties did not serve to check the revalidation of male superiority in Buddhist cultures. With the possible exception of Taiwan, where a *bhikkhuni* order is thriving today, women are perceived as inferior to men in Asian Buddhist societies. And there is a Buddhist explanation for that: those unfortunate enough to be born as women are reaping the fruits of their inferior karma.

## The Karma of Women's Suffering

In Buddhist societies where women are not allowed to be fully ordained as monks, women are often told by monks that having been born a woman is a result of bad karma. In order to remedy this problem, the only thing that women can do is to accumulate a lot of merit in this life, so that in their next life they will be born a man, and then they can become a monk if they choose to. This way of thinking makes women feel inferior and that they are to blame for the outcome of their lives. It makes them more willing to accept whatever gender-based violence that they experience, since it is seen as a direct result of their unlucky fate in having been born a woman.

When a woman asks for guidance from a monk when the husband is the cause of her suffering (such as instances where he has another woman, is physically or mentally abusive to her, gambles their money away, drinks alcohol, etc.), the monk's main advice is for her to be patient and compassionate. Often times, the monk will say that karma is the cause of her suffering, so she has no choice but to accept and deal with the situation, and continue to be kind to her husband so that one day the karmic force will subside and everything will be fine. We found that this kind of thinking is not only the belief of the monks themselves but that it is also prominent among the followers of Buddhism

> in Southeast Asia, including women.... It is one of the factors
> that keeps a woman in a marriage even though her life may be
> in danger, and it explains why neighbors and community leaders
> choose not to intervene. (Khuankaew 2002, 23–24)

In this passage Ouyporn Khuankaew shows the relationship between the subordination of women (including the violence they suffer) and the popular Buddhist understanding of karma. Examining this conception and application of karma will be the main focus of the rest of this chapter, especially the implications of this relationship for prostitution and the Thai sex industry.[4]

To begin, it is important to realize that the earliest Buddhist texts do not reflect a disparaging, strongly negative attitude toward women who sell their sexual favors. Unlike in Western Christendom (whose attitude was perhaps unlike the attitude of Jesus himself), sex workers were not condemned as sinful. Prostitution was widespread in the India of his time, and the Buddha did not discriminate against them. Instead, he provided them with the opportunity to join the *bhikkhuni* order (which required them to reform and become celibate, of course) in order to pursue the path to liberation. These early texts even include positive references to some courtesans, such as the wealthy Ambapali, who is well-known in Buddhist literature for her gift of a mango grove to the Buddha and *sangha*. She later renounced her profession, gave away her possessions, and became a *bhikkhuni* whose diligent practice soon led to enlightenment and a new role as a skilled Dharma teacher. Like some other sex workers, she may have progressed so rapidly on the spiritual path because she had experienced the extremes of sensual pleasure and realized the frustration of a life devoted to satisfying such cravings. Or is the problem better understood as the commodification of sexual pleasure, and the degradation of those expected to provide it?

Her midlife career change points to an imbalance that still persists between the Buddhist *sangha* and the position of women in Buddhist cultures: there is a sharp contrast between the high social status of monks and the inferior status of women, who typically suffer from low self-esteem and feelings of worthlessness. Somewhat similar to the Catholic mothers whose sons become priests, Buddhist mothers whose sons become *bhikkhu* are believed to gain lots of merit, as well as an enhanced status in society; but the *sangha* is not an option for their daughters, who therefore may be called upon to serve their families in other ways. This makes the less-judgmental attitude of Buddhism toward prostitution a mixed blessing in practice. Most Thai sex workers, like most of those in other Asian nations, work to send money to their families, which are often large and impoverished. They are trying to fulfill their sense of duty to their parents by sharing the economic burden in the only way they can (although hardly lucrative for the girls themselves, sex work is still much better paid than factory work). The recurring problems of rural agriculture, sometimes aggravated by a father's or a son's gambling debts, not infrequently lead the parents to ask a daughter to "sacrifice" for the sake of the family (Kabilsingh 1991, 78).

One part of a solution to this situation, therefore, might involve (re)introducing the *bhikkhuni sangha*.[5] This would not resolve the economic woes of rural families, but it would raise the status (and therefore the self-esteem) of women whose capacity for enlightenment is thereby acknowledged. Not only would parents also gain merit when their daughter became a nun, but respected *bhikkhuni* would be in a better position to advise other women and offer spiritual guidance.

There have been some recent attempts to reintroduce the *bhikkhuni* order in Sri Lanka, Thailand, and Myanmar, but they continue to be resisted by the established *bhikkhu* hierarchy, and it is too early to know how well they will succeed. Up to now, at least, the response of the Thai Buddhist authorities to the sex industry has also not been helpful. The official *sangha* establishment tends to be quite reserved—which is to say, conservative—toward all social issues, while some individual monks and temples actually profit from emphasizing the inferiority of women in general and the bad karma accumulated by sex workers in particular. Women and prostitutes are encouraged to offer *dana*, "gifts" (usually money and other valuables), to the temple in order to make more merit and guarantee a better rebirth next time. As a result, some temples, especially in northern Thailand, have become wealthy and well adorned as an indirect result of the sex industry (Kabilsingh 2002, 97).[6]

The basic presupposition of this behavior, or social trap, is that one's present life situation, whether good or bad, enjoyable or painful, is a consequence of one's moral behavior in previous lifetimes. Ambapali escaped this bind by joining the *bhikkhuni* order and following the path to enlightenment, which puts an end to the cycle of rebirths. Since the disappearance of that order, contemporary Thai women must try to counteract the negative consequences of their bad karma in other ways. One can gain merit by reciting sutras and other devotions, but the main way is by making *dana* to the monks and temples. With enough merit, one will be reborn into more favorable circumstances—perhaps even as a man.

Unfortunately, the male Thai sangha benefits enormously from this understanding, or rather misunderstanding, of Buddhist teachings about karma and rebirth. So do all those who organize and profit from the sex industry, who are relieved of any guilt feelings they might otherwise have, and also spared any resistance on the part of their sex workers, who have no one else to blame but themselves (in a past life) for their present situation. The responsibility for their own abuse is really in their own hands, not in the powerful men and patriarchal social structures that seem to exploit them. It is a classic case of "blame the victim," protecting the perpetrators and wrapping the structures of exploitation in invisibility and inevitability (Brock and Thistlewaite 1996, 237). Moreover, if some women want to rebel against this system, they are only creating more bad karma for themselves (Gross 1993, 143).

Obviously, this understanding of karma and rebirth has important implications for much more than the Thai sex industry. The connections with other types of physical and structural violence against women could also be discussed, as well as many other nongendered consequences regarding the rationalization of racism, economic oppression, birth handicaps, and so forth. Karma is used to justify both the authority of political elites, who therefore deserve their wealth and power, and the subordination of those who have neither. It provides the perfect theodicy: there is an infallible cause-and-effect relationship between one's moral actions and one's fate, so there is no need to work toward social justice, which is already built into the moral fabric of the universe.

For these reasons, karma is perhaps the most critical issue for contemporary Buddhist societies. That brings us to our main concern: Has it been misunderstood? Is it a fatalistic doctrine, or is it an empowering one?

By the power of my merit, may I be reborn a male. . . .

—fifteenth century CE inscription of a Queen Mother

The previous sections imply that karma (along with its correlative, rebirth) has become a problem for modern Buddhists that can no longer be evaded. To accept the popular understanding about it as literal truth—that karmic determinism is a "moral law" of the universe, with an inevitable and precise calculus of cause and effect comparable to Newton's laws of physics—leads to a severe case of cognitive dissonance for contemporary Buddhists, since the physical causality that modern science has discovered about the world seems to allow for no mechanism for karma or rebirth to operate. How should modern Buddhists respond to this situation?

In the *Kalama Sutta*, sometimes called "the Buddhist charter of free inquiry," the Buddha emphasized the importance of intelligent, probing doubt: we should not believe in something until we have established its truth for ourselves. To accept karmic rebirth in a literal way, simply because it has traditionally been accepted as part of the Buddha's teaching, may thus be unfaithful to the best of the tradition. Given a healthy skepticism about the Iron Age belief systems of the Buddha's time, one should hesitate before making such an enormous leap of faith. Instead of tying one's social role, and spiritual path, to belief in such a doctrine, is it wiser for contemporary Buddhists to be agnostic about it?

Consider how the *Kalama Sutta* concludes. After emphasizing the importance of evaluating for oneself the spiritual claims of others, the Buddha finishes his talk by describing someone who has a truly purified mind:

> " 'Suppose there is a hereafter and there is a fruit, result, of deeds done well or ill. Then it is possible that at the dissolution of the body after death, I shall arise in the heavenly world, which is possessed of the state of bliss.' This is the first solace found by him.
>
> " 'Suppose there is no hereafter and there is no fruit, no result, of deeds done well or ill. Yet in this world, here and now, free from hatred, free from malice, safe and sound, and happy, I keep myself.' This is the second solace found by him.
>
> " 'Suppose evil (results) befall an evil-doer. I, however, think of doing evil to no one. Then, how can ill (results) affect me who do no evil deed?' This is the third solace found by him.
>
> " 'Suppose evil (results) do not befall an evil-doer. Then I see myself purified in any case.' This is the fourth solace found by him." (*Kalama Sutta*, in *Anguttara Nikaya* 3.65)[7]

These intriguing verses can be understood in different ways. The Buddha is speaking to non-Buddhists, so he does not presuppose a Buddhist worldview in describing the fruits of a purified mind. Yet there is another way to take this passage, which is more relevant for twenty-first-century Buddhists. Do our actions bear fruit in a hereafter? For the sake of argument, at least, the Buddha adopts an agnostic view in this important sutta. Maybe they do, maybe they do not. Perhaps what is needed today is not a new version of Pascal's wager but a refusal to wager for or against an afterlife. In either case, a purified mind finds solace by cherishing good deeds and avoiding bad ones.

In this sutra the Buddha's lack of dogmatism shines forth. We can understand his tactful words as a skillful means for speaking with the Kalamas, who were weary of doctrinaire assertions. Or we can focus instead on the agnosticism about rebirth, which implies a different understanding of karma and its consequences. If those of us who are Buddhists are honest with ourselves, we must admit that today we really do not know what to think about karma and rebirth. We wonder if testimony about near-death experiences supports a literal view. At the same time, a literal understanding hardly seems compatible with what modern science has discovered about the physical world. So are karma and rebirth fact or myth? If I consider myself a Buddhist, do I have to take them literally? Here the Buddha speaks directly to our skeptical age: in the most important sense, it does not matter which is true, because if we know what is good for us (and those around us) we will endeavor to live the same way in either case.

Challenging the usual literal understanding is not to dismiss or disparage Buddhist teachings about karma and rebirth. Rather, it highlights the need for modern Buddhism to *interrogate* them. Given what is now known about human psychology, including the social construction of the self, how might they be understood today?

Although one of the most basic principles of Buddhism is interdependence, I wonder how many Buddhists realize what that implies about the original teachings of the Buddha. Interdependence means that nothing has any "self-existence," because everything is part of everything else. Nothing is self-originated, because everything arises according to causes and conditions. But Buddhism, it is believed, originates in and remains grounded in the unmediated experience of Shakyamuni, who became "the Buddha" upon his attainment of nirvana under the Bodhi tree. Although different Buddhist scriptures describe that experience in different ways, for all Buddhist traditions his awakening is the *fons et origo* of Buddhism, which unlike Hinduism does not rely upon ancient revealed texts such as the Vedas.

Buddhists usually take the above for granted, yet there is a problem with it: the Buddha's enlightenment story, as usually told, is a myth of self-origination. If the interdependence of everything is true, the truth of Buddhism could not have sprung up independently from all the other spiritual beliefs of the Buddha's time and place (Iron Age India), without any relationship to them. Instead, the teachings of Shakyamuni must be understood as a *response* to those other teachings, but a response that, inevitably, also *presupposed* many of the spiritual beliefs current in that cultural milieu—that took for granted, perhaps, popular notions of karma and rebirth.

Consider the following insightful comment that Erich Fromm made about another (although quite different!) revolutionary, Sigmund Freud:

> The attempt to understand Freud's theoretical system, or that of any creative systematic thinker, cannot be successful unless we recognize that, and why, every system as it is developed and presented by its author is necessarily erroneous. . . . [T]he creative thinker must think in the terms of the logic, the thought patterns, the expressible concepts of his culture. That means he has not yet the proper words to express the creative, the new, the liberating idea. He is forced to solve an insoluble problem: to express the new thought in concepts and words that do not yet exist in his language. . . .
>
> The consequence is that the new thought as he formulated it is a blend of what is truly new and the conventional thought

which it transcends. The thinker, however, is not conscious of this contradiction. (Fromm 1982, 1, 3)

Fromm's point is that even the most revolutionary thinkers cannot stand on their own shoulders. They too remain dependent upon their context, whether intellectual or spiritual—which, to say it again, is precisely what Buddhist emphasis on impermanence and causal interdependence implies. Despite many important differences between Freud and Shakyamuni, the parallel is nevertheless very revealing. The Buddha, too, expressed his new, liberating insight in the only way he could, in the religious categories that his culture could understand and that he himself was a product of. Inevitably, then, his way of expressing the Dharma was a blend of the truly new (for example, teachings about *anatta* "nonself" and *pratitya-samutpada* "dependent origination") and the conventional religious thought of his time (karma and rebirth?) "which it transcends." .

Earlier Indian teachings such as the Vedas tended to understand karma more mechanically and ritualistically. To perform a sacrifice in the proper fashion would invariably lead to the desired consequences. If those consequences were not forthcoming, then either there had been an error in procedure or the causal effects were delayed, perhaps until one's next lifetime (a reason for believing in rebirth). The Buddha's spiritual revolution transformed this ritualistic approach to controlling one's life into an ethical principle by focusing on *cetana* "motivations." That most popular of early Buddhist texts, the *Dhammapada*, begins by emphasizing the preeminent importance of our mental attitude:

> Experiences are preceded by mind, led by mind, and produced by mind. If one speaks or acts with an impure mind, suffering follows even as the cart-wheel follows the hoof of the ox.
>     Experiences are preceded by mind, led by mind, and produced by mind. If one speaks or acts with a pure mind, happiness follows like a shadow that never departs. (Mascaro 1973, 35)

To understand the Buddha's innovation, it is helpful to distinguish a moral act into its three aspects: the *results* that I seek; the *moral rule or regulation* I am following (for example, a Buddhist precept or Christian commandment, but this also includes ritualistic procedures); and my mental attitude or *motivation* when I do something. Although these aspects cannot be separated from each other, we can emphasize one more than the others—in fact, that is what we usually do. In modern moral theory, for example, utilitarian theories focus on consequences, deontological theories focus on moral principles such as the Decalogue, and "virtue theories" focus on one's character and motivations.

In the Buddha's time, the Brahmanical understanding of karma emphasized the importance of following the detailed procedures (rules) regulating each ritual; naturally, however, the people who paid for the rituals were more interested in the outcome (results). Arguably, the situation in some Theravada Buddhist countries, including Thailand, is not much different today. Male monastics are preoccupied with following the complicated rules regulating their lives (which according to the popular view is what makes them "good" monks), while laypeople are preoccupied with accumulating merit by giving gifts to them (which makes them second-class Buddhists, focused on the future karmic consequences of their commodified relationship with monks). Both of these attitudes miss the point of the Buddha's spiritual innovation.

Earlier, I cited evidence of error and/or alteration in some passages of the Pali Canon, the earliest Buddhist texts we have. There also seem to be inconsistencies in what the Buddha said about karma. Some statements—and perhaps it is no coincidence that these tend to work in favor of the material benefit of the *bhikkhu*—support a more deterministic view (e.g., the *Culakammavibhanga Sutta*, where karma is used to explain various differences between people, including physical appearance and economic inequality). However, there are several other texts where the Buddha clearly denies moral determinism—for example, the *Tittha Sutta* in which the Buddha argues that such a view denies the possibility of following a spiritual path:

> "There are priests and contemplatives who hold this teaching, hold this view: 'Whatever a person experiences—pleasant, painful, or neither pleasant nor painful—that is all caused by what was done in the past.' . . . Then I said to them, 'Then in that case, a person is a killer of living beings because of what was done in the past. A person is a thief . . . unchaste . . . a liar . . . a divisive speaker . . . a harsh speaker . . . an idle chatterer . . . greedy . . . malicious . . . a holder of wrong views because of what was done in the past.' When one falls back on what was done in the past as being essential, monks, there is no desire, no effort [at the thought], 'This should be done. This shouldn't be done.' When one can't pin down as a truth or reality what should and shouldn't be done, one dwells bewildered and unprotected. One cannot righteously refer to oneself as a contemplative." (*Tittha Sutta*, in *Anguttara Nikaya* 3.61)[8]

In another short sutta, an ascetic named Sivaka asked the Buddha about a view held by some ascetics and Brahmins that " 'whatever a person experiences, be it pleasure, pain or neither-pain-nor-pleasure, all that is caused by previous action.' Now, what does the revered Gotama [Buddha] say about this?"

"Produced by (disorders of the) bile, there arise, Sivaka, certain
kinds of feelings. That this happens, can be known by oneself;
also in the world it is accepted as true. Produced by (disorders of
the) phlegm . . . of wind . . . of (the three) combined . . . by change
of climate . . . by adverse behavior . . . by injuries . . . by the results
of Karma—(through all that), Sivaka, there arise certain kinds
of feelings. That this happens can be known by oneself; also in
the world it is accepted as true. Now when these ascetics and
Brahmins have such a doctrine and view that 'whatever a person
experiences, be it pleasure, pain or neither-pain-nor-pleasure, all
that is caused by previous action,' then they go beyond what they
know by themselves and what is accepted as true by the world.
Therefore, I say that this is wrong on the part of these ascetics and
Brahmins." (*Moliyasivaka Sutta*, in the *Samyutta Nikaya* 36.21)[9]

Although other texts could be cited, this is not the place for a close textual
analysis of all the relevant passages.[10] The point to be gleaned from the above
references is that the earliest Buddhist teachings about karma are not only
sometimes humorous ("produced by wind . . .") but also somewhat ambiguous
and therefore insufficient by themselves as a guide for understanding karma
today. That brings us back to the Buddha's insight into the moral preeminence of the motivations of our actions. How should we today understand
the originality of his approach?

The original Sanskrit term *karma* literally means "action" (*phala* is the
"fruit" of action), and, as this suggests, the basic point is that our actions
have consequences. More precisely, our morally-relevant actions have morally
relevant consequences that extend beyond their immediate physical effects. In
the popular Buddhist understanding, the law of karma and rebirth is a way
to manipulate how the world treats us, which also implies, more immediately,
that we must accept our own causal responsibility for whatever is happening
to us now.

This misses the revolutionary significance of the Buddha's reinterpretation. The most important point about karma is not whether it is a moral law
involving some inevitable and precise calculus of cause and effect. Karma is
better understood as the key to spiritual development: *how our life situation
can be transformed by transforming the motivations of our actions right now.*
When we add the Buddhist teaching about *anatta* "not-self"—the claim,
consistent with modern psychology, that one's sense of self is a mental construct—we can see that karma is not something the self *has*, but what the
sense of self *is*, and that sense of self changes according to one's conscious
choices. "I" (re)construct myself by what "I" intentionally do, because "my"
sense of self is a precipitate of my habitual ways of thinking, feeling, and

acting. Just as my body is composed of the food I eat, so my character is composed of my consistent, repeated mental attitudes. People are "punished" or "rewarded" not for what they have done but for what they have become, and what we intentionally do is what makes us what we are. An anonymous verse expresses this well:

> Sow a thought and reap a deed
> Sow a deed and reap a habit
> Sow a habit and reap a character
> Sow a character and reap a destiny

What kinds of thoughts and deeds do we need to sow? Buddhism does not have much to say about evil per se, but our *dukkha* "unhappiness" is attributed to the three "unwholesome roots" (*akusala-mula*) of action: greed, ill will, and delusion.[11] These need to be transformed into their positive counterparts: greed into nonattached generosity, ill will into friendliness, and the delusion of separate self into the wisdom that realizes our interdependence with others.

Such an understanding of karma does not necessarily involve another life after we physically die. As Spinoza expressed it, happiness is not the reward for virtue; happiness is virtue itself. Likewise, we are punished not for our sins but by them. To become a different kind of person is to experience the world in a different way. When your mind changes, the world changes. And when we respond differently to the world, the world responds differently to us. Since we are actually nondual with the world—our sense of separation from it being a delusion—our ways of acting in it tend to involve reinforcing feedback systems that incorporate other people. People not only notice what we do, they notice why we do it. I may fool people sometimes, but over time my character becomes revealed in the intentions behind my deeds. The more I am motivated by greed, ill will, and delusion, the more I must manipulate the world to get what I want, and consequently the more alienated I feel and the more alienated others feel when they see they have been manipulated. This mutual distrust encourages both sides to manipulate more. On the other side, the more my actions are motivated by generosity, loving-kindness, and the wisdom of interdependence, the more I can relax and open up to the world. The more I feel part of the world and nondual with others, the less I am inclined to use others, and consequently the more inclined they will be to trust and open up to me. In such ways, transforming my own motivations does not only transform my own life, but it also affects those around me, since I am not separate from them.

This more naturalistic understanding of karma does not mean we must necessarily exclude other, perhaps more mysterious possibilities regarding the consequences of our motivations for the world we live in; there may well be other aspects of karmic cause and effect that are not so readily understood. What is clear in either case, however, is that karma-as-how-to-transform-my-life-situation-by-transforming-my-motivations-right-now is not a fatalistic doctrine. Quite the contrary: it is difficult to imagine a more empowering spiritual teaching. We are not enjoined to accept the oppressive circumstances of our lives. Instead, we are encouraged to improve our spiritual lives and social situation by addressing those circumstances with generosity, friendliness, and wisdom.

With regard to women, patriarchal institutions are not inevitable, for this "new" understanding of karma implies that our social analysis should highlight and expose the selfish (and deluded) motivations of those who benefit from the suffering of women. Rita Gross puts it well: "[W]hat causes the negativity of women's existence under patriarchy is not women's karma, but the self-centered, fixated, habitual patterns of those in power, of those who maintain the status quo. . . . This explanation, which locates the cause of women's misery under male-dominated systems in *present* ego-patterns and self-interest, rather than in past karma, also has the advantage of being a thoroughly *Buddhist* analysis, in addition to making sense in feminist terms" (Gross 1993, 145).

The sex industry in Thailand and elsewhere, like other forms of physical, cultural, and institutional violence against women, should not be accepted by Buddhists but rather challenged as un-Buddhist—indeed, as anti-Buddhist, because incompatible with its liberatory message. Properly understood, the karma doctrine does not imply passive acceptance of any type of violence against women, but rather inspires us to challenge the rationalizations that have attempted to naturalize such violence. It teaches us not only how to transform our lives by transforming our own unwholesome motivations, but also that male and female Buddhists should confront the unwholesome motivations of those who maintain patriarchal systems of domination.

# NINE

# The West Against the Rest?

## A *Buddhist Response to* The Clash of Civilizations

The next world war, if there is one, will be a war between civilizations.

—Samuel Huntington

Did September 11 vindicate Samuel Huntington's claim in "The Clash of Civilizations," that the new battle lines today are the fault lines between the world's civilizations? Or has his argument become a self-fulfilling prophecy—because, for example, the U.S. response to September 11 has deepened those fault lines?

The collapse of most communist states in 1989 and the end of the Cold War raised worldwide hopes that were short-lived. Francis Fukuyama claimed that we had reached "the end of history," but history did not seem to notice. Although neither the United States nor the Soviet Union needed to engage in proxy wars anymore, violent conflicts continued, even in the backyard of a paralyzed Europe that could not figure out how to respond to Yugoslavia's disintegration. Despite the preeminence of the United States, now unchallengeable as the only hyperpower, the world did not become any less messy. Other nations and peoples were not falling into line, not accepting their proper places in the Pax Americana. What was going on? What new description of the world could make sense of it all?

The first Gulf War of 1991 gave a hint. Saddam Hussein was not a very good Muslim, and Iraq was hardly an Islamic state, but the aggressive U.S. response to his aggression against Kuwait aroused widespread support for his cause among other Muslim peoples (although less so among their more cautious governments). Few of them agreed that the sanctions afterward imposed on Iraq, which caused widespread misery, including the deaths of over half a million Iraqi children, were "worth the cost," as Secretary of State Madeleine Albright famously put it. A civil war in eastern Europe had Christians fighting

Muslims. In southern Asia there were more tensions between Hindu India and Muslim Pakistan, including periodic battles in Kashmir. China, too, continued to be difficult, modernizing in its own way: a growing source of cheap labor and occasionally a big market for Western products, but unwavering in its own political direction and suppression of all dissent.

The penny finally dropped for Samuel P. Huntington. When he wrote "The Clash of Civilizations," Huntington was Eaton Professor of Government and director of the Olin Institute for Strategic Studies at Harvard University. His now-famous (or infamous) essay was originally written for an Olin Institute project on "the changing security environment and American national interests." It was published in *Foreign Affairs* in 1993, and then expanded into a book. As this genesis suggests, what it offers us is not some impartial overview of global civilization, but rather the postwar world as perceived by the U.S. foreign-policy elite—the "best and brightest" that previously gave us the Vietnam War, justified by a "domino theory" that also rationalized U.S. support for Pinochet, the shah of Iran, Marcos, Suharto, Mobutu, and many other dictators around the world. Huntington himself was a consultant for the State Department in 1967; at that time he wrote a long position paper that supported U.S. goals in Vietnam but criticized the military strategy for attaining them.

I mention this not to make an ad hominem attack on Huntington but to clarify the purpose for his essay: determining the new security needs of the United States in the post–Cold War world. This becomes apparent in its second half, which is more obviously concerned about defending "the values and interests of the West" against those of other civilizations. Although this subtext is not always explicit, it determines what Huntington sees and what he is unable to see.

What he sees is a new global paradigm that brings the new global mess into focus. The era of struggle between nation-states and rival ideologies is over. Democratic societies, in particular, do not go to war against each other. The new conflicts are between civilizations, which have different languages, histories, institutions, and—most importantly—different religions. Huntington lists seven or eight civilizations: Western, Confucian, Japanese, Islamic, Hindu, Slavic-Orthodox, Latin-American, "and possibly African" (1996, 3). We are told that the differences between them are more fundamental than the old differences between political regimes or ideologies. Huntington claims that increasing interaction among people of different civilizations is enhancing the historical "civilization-consciousness" of peoples in ways that "invigorate differences and animosities stretching or thought to stretch back deep into history" (4).

This challenges the common and more irenic perception that increasing contact tends to decrease tensions. Today, more than ever, people from different parts of the world not only buy one another's commodities but enjoy one another's music, films, TV shows, fashions, and cuisines. When they have the opportunity, many are eager to travel to faraway countries, to meet other people, and occasionally even to intermarry. Is this increasing contact and awareness increasing intercivilizational intolerance and strife, or decreasing it? Or does that question miss the point because the effects of all this interaction are too complicated to generalize about in such a black-and-white way?

Civilizations, Huntington tells us, are the broadest level of cultural identity that people have, "short of that which distinguishes humans from other species" (2). Yet why such cultural differences should be emphasized more than our similarities as fellow humans is not immediately obvious, except perhaps for the unfortunate if common tendency to identify ourselves by distinguishing our own interests from those of some "other group." This is no minor point, if the subtext of Huntington's argument—U.S. national security—itself exemplifies such an "in-group" defending its own interests at the cost of others. U.S. relations with Latin America is an obvious example. History suggests that the Monroe Doctrine of 1823 was promulgated less to protect Central American and South American countries from European interference than to monopolize U.S. interference.

How are present global tensions viewed by those who are not part of the Western elite? What other perspectives are possible? Although born and raised a U.S. citizen, I lived and traveled in East Asia and Southeast Asia for almost thirty years (1977–2005), and although these regions are home to three or four of Huntington's civilizations, what I was able to observe was quite different from Huntington's clash of civilizations. While there are certainly clashes of values and interests, it seemed to me (and still seems to me) that predominant tensions are more readily understood as due to the efforts of a West "at the peak of its power" (5) to transform the rest of the globe in ways that suit the self-perceived interests of its own elites (especially the managers of transnational corporations). From an Asian perspective, Western-led economic, political, technological, and cultural globalization is the main event of our times, and resistance to it is where the main fault lines have been forming.

Of course, globalization is not one development but a web of related processes, usually (although not always) augmenting one another. From this alternative perspective, the fissures that matter most today are not civilizational differences but rather the conflicting social forces promoting or challenging different aspects of globalization, resulting in various stresses, most obviously due to economic changes or pressures to change.

This is not a small point. Huntington's clash of civilizations assumes a pluralism of irreconcilable values and interests in the world, which paradoxically implies value-relativism ("Since there is really no such thing as 'the best civilization' . . .") even as it supposedly justifies our Western ethnocentrism (". . . we should defend and promote our own values and interests"). If, however, the real issue is Western-sponsored globalization, then that globalization can and should be evaluated according to the ways it is changing societies, including Western ones.

Asking whether globalization is good or bad misses the point. To say it again, globalization is too complicated to characterize so simply. For example, many of those who want more human rights and more consumer goods are also suspicious of the self-preoccupied individualism that seems to encourage social problems in some Western countries. Then the most important question becomes: Who is entitled to decide which changes a society will embrace, and which to reject? The World Trade Organization? The International Monetary Fund? A West defending its own interests? Or the people most affected by those changes?

By no coincidence, the same fissures are deepening within the West, too. Huntington's West is more or less monolithic, yet if we do not focus so much on the differences between civilizations we can see the same tensions at home, especially inside the United States. Internationally, globalization has been increasing the gap between rich and poor; the same thing is happening within the United States, which now has more poor people than any other Western nation. Internationally, globalization is increasing corporate influence on governments, as well as corporate dominance of economies and natural resources; obviously the same thing has been happening in the United States. Internationally, an antiglobalization movement has sprung up to challenge these developments; a similar resistance has developed within the United States, probably the strongest domestic movement since the Vietnam War. Because the pressures of globalization tend to affect different civilizations in some similar ways, many of the same tensions and ruptures are recurring within different civilizations.

One way to focus this point is by considering the role of religion in these struggles. Religion is crucial for Huntington. It is the most important way that civilizations differentiate themselves from each other. In his *Foreign Affairs* response to his critics, he claims that "in the modern world, religion is a central, perhaps the central force, that motivates and mobilizes people" (1996, 63). His original article quotes George Weigel—to the effect that the "unsecularization of the world is one of the dominant social facts of life in the late twentieth century"—and emphasizes that this revival of religion serves as a basis for identity and commitment transcending nations and unifying civilizations (4).

Religions unite civilizations by providing people with a common identity, which they are often willing to die for and kill for. Religions are also the source and repository for our most cherished values—except perhaps in the modern West, where traditional religious values have been losing a war of attrition with this-worldly values such as Enlightenment rationalism, secular nationalism, "moneytheism," and consumerism. For Huntington the social scientist and foreign-policy mandarin, what is most important about religions is that the identity they provide is irreconcilable with other religious identities. A Jew is a Jew, a Muslim is a Muslim, and ne'er the twain shall meet. That is why religious differences are at the heart of the civilizational clash.

Again, things look somewhat different from a perspective more sensitive to religious concerns than to "realist" foreign policy (i.e., nationalist) values. The struggle over globalization is, at its heart, not just a clash of identities but a clash of values: the different values that people of different cultures want to live by. In order to understand the contemporary conflicts that religions are involved in, it is necessary to realize in what way modern Western culture does not really offer an alternative to religious values. Rather, it offers this-worldly values that are nonetheless religious, in the most important sense of the term. Religion is notoriously difficult to define, yet if we understand it functionally—as teaching us what is really important about the world, and therefore how to live in it—modern identities such as secular nationalism and modern values such as consumerism are best understood not as alternatives to religion but as *secular religions*. They offer this-worldly solutions to the problem of ultimate meaning in life: for example, patriotic identification with one's country (a poor impersonal substitute for genuine community) or the promise of a more immediate salvation in consumerism (it is always the next thing we buy that will make us happy).

The Cold War victory of the West means that capitalism now reigns unchallenged, so it has been able to remove its velvet gloves. Because capitalism evolved within a Christian culture, the two have been able to make peace with each other, more or less, in the contemporary West. Christ's kingdom is not of this world, we should render unto Caesar what is Caesar's, and as long as we go to church on Sunday we can devote the rest of the week to this-worldly pursuits. From premodern and nonmodernized religious perspectives, however, the values of globalizing capitalism look more problematical.

Buddhism, for example, emphasizes that in order for us to become happy our greed, ill will, and delusion must be transformed, respectively, into generosity, compassion, and wisdom. Such a transformation is difficult to reconcile with an economic globalization that seems to encourage greed (producers never have enough profit, advertising ensures that consumers are never satisfied), ill will (an inevitable consequence of "looking out for number one"), and delusion (the world—our mother as well as our home—desacralized by commodifying everything).

Buddhism provides other problems for Huntington's thesis, since it straddles the Indian, Chinese, and Japanese civilizations he identifies. Buddhism is now beginning to make significant inroads into the West as well, another phenomenon that does not quite fit into his paradigm of faults between civilizations. If religious identity provides the core of civilizations, why was

Buddhism so successful not only in India (its homeland) and other South Asian and Southeast Asian cultures, but also in China, Tibet, Korea, Japan, and so on? Why did many Chinese syncretically embrace Confucianism, Taoism, *and* Buddhism? Why do many Japanese celebrate birth at a Shinto shrine, wed in a Christian ceremony, and perform Buddhist funeral rites?

As the Buddhist example shows, it is too simple to say that tensions arise because of a clash of fissured, irreconcilable value systems, in which we need to focus on promoting our own. In the contemporary world all religions are under tremendous pressure to adapt to new circumstances, including new worldviews and new values, for globalization means that renegotiation with modern developments is constant. Fundamentalism—clinging to old verities and customs—is a common response, but the fact that some fundamentalists are willing to die and kill for their cause does not quite disguise the reality that the fundamentalist reaction to modernity is defensive, cramped, and in the long run untenable in a fast-shrinking world where all civilizations are increasingly interconnected.

This does not mean that religious beliefs and values are incompatible with globalization. It means that the tension between globalization and anti-globalization is, in part, an ongoing struggle between traditional religious concerns—most importantly, love and responsibility to something greater than our own individual egos—and the corrosive effects of a secular modernity that too often promotes individualistic self-centeredness.

For either side to "win" this struggle would be disastrous. Traditional religions need the challenge of modernity to wake them from their dogmas and institutional sclerosis, to encourage them to ask again what is essential in their teachings and what is cultural baggage that can be shed. On the other side, the unrestrained dominance of corporate capitalism and its commodifying values would be catastrophic not only for human communities but for the entire biosphere.

The real test case for their negotiation is Islam. Huntington discusses many clashes between civilizations, and most of them involve Islam. "Islam has bloody borders" (1996, 5), he writes. Without Islam, it would be difficult for him to make his case; thanks to Islam, it is easy, since the Islamic world seems to have trouble getting along with any other world.

Or so it seems from a Western perspective. That perspective, however, is hardly an objective or a neutral one. For most of their histories, the Christian West and the Islamic world have been each other's chief rivals. At first Islam had the edge, culturally as well as militarily. Medieval Christian theology and philosophy were revived by the rediscovery of classical Greek texts preserved by Islamic scholars; European science developed on an Arabic foundation. That is part of Islam's burden today. In contrast to early Christianity, which had to endure centuries of Roman persecution, Islam was immediately triumphant, establishing a mythic legacy that makes eclipse (including colonial and now economic subordination) by the modern West all the more difficult to bear.

There are other ways in which Islam stands out from other missionary religions such as Christianity and Buddhism. Unlike Jesus and Shakyamuni, Muhammad was not only a spiritual teacher but also a political and military leader, in ways that were usually quite progressive for his time, although some of them have become problematical as the world has changed. Because neither Jesus nor Shakyamuni provided that kind of leadership, it has been easier to adapt their teachings to radically different cultural conditions, including secular modernity. Today a "good" Christian can pray in church on Sunday and more or less serve Mammon the rest of the week. A "good Muslim" prays five times a day and follows more than a few customs from seventh-century Arabia, including studying and often memorizing the Qur'an in Arabic.

Partly as a result of these differences, Islam has remained more traditionalist than either Christianity or Buddhism. No religion is monolithic, and all major religions have deep fissures of their own, including an unavoidable one between literal interpretations of scriptures and more flexible metaphorical readings. There have been rationalist movements in Islam, such as the Mutazilites in the ninth century and, more recently, many other attempts at modernist reform, yet they have generally been less successful than similar movements in Christianity and Buddhism. As a result, the contemporary image of Islam among most non-Muslims is of an extremely conservative, ritualistic, and literalistic faith. Among the major religions, Islam is having the most difficulty adjusting to the modern distinction between an enervated sacred sphere and a more dynamic secular sphere. There are also political problems due to the legacy of Western colonialism (including the imposition of a nation-state structure that evolved in Europe and has often grafted poorly onto non-Western cultures) and economic problems due to the neocolonialism of Western-led globalization.

Yet there is another way to look at Muslim difficulties today. Of the world's missionary religions, Islam is arguably the one most deeply concerned with social justice—and social justice is an increasingly important issue in the struggles over what kind of globalization we shall have. That is the other side of Muhammad's legacy as a political leader as well as a spiritual one. Although this theme is missing in Huntington, we cannot understand Islamic values and present concerns without it. That is why it is not enough simply to emphasize the fissure between Islam and the West, a clash between their values and ours. A demand for social justice has become essential in a world where, according to the 1999 *Human Development Report* by the United Nations Development Program, almost a billion people in seventy countries consume less today than they did twenty-five years ago; where the world's five hundred billionaires are worth more than the combined incomes of the poorest half of humanity (a gap that globalization is aggravating); where, as a result, a quarter million children die of malnutrition or infection every week, while hundreds of millions more survive in hunger and deteriorating health.

Allah is merciful but also a God of justice and will judge us harshly if we do not accept personal and collective responsibility for the less fortunate. The third pillar of Islam is *zakat*, "alms." *Zakat* is not so much charity as an essential expression of the compassion that all Muslims are called upon to show to those who need it. Muslims believe that everything really belongs to God, and material things should be used as God wishes them to be used. This means not hoarding but sharing with others in need. For example, the often-quoted Sura 102:1 of the Qur'an declares, "The mutual rivalry for piling up (the things of this world) diverts you (from more serious things)" and Sura 92:18 praises those who use their wealth for increase in self-purification. That is why the capitalist idea of using capital to gain ever more capital—you can never have too much!—is foreign, even reprehensible, to many devout Muslims.

By adapting so well to the modern world of secular nationalism, capitalism, and consumerism, most Christians in the West have learned to finesse such concerns. The Bible tells us that the poor will always be among us, and in any case we must accept what the "social science" of economics tells us are laws of supply and demand, the importance of free trade, and so on. Admittedly, the main effect of transnational capitalism so far has been to make the rich richer, yet we must have faith (this is a religion, after all) that a rising tide of worldwide wealth will eventually lift all boats.

Islam is less willing to accept such equivocations, because it recognizes no God other than Allah. The need to "have faith" that corporate globalization will eventually work to benefit almost everyone points to what is increasingly apparent: as Western culture has lost faith in any afterlife salvation, the West's economic system has also become its religion, because it now has to fulfil a religious function for us. Economics today is less a social science than the theology of that moneytheistic religion, and its god, the Market, has been able to become a vicious circle of ever-increasing production and consumption by promising us a this-worldly salvation. Western-led globalization means that the Market is becoming the first truly world religion, rapidly converting all corners of the globe to a worldview and set of values whose religious role we overlook only because we insist on seeing them as secular.

Although few people yet understand pro-globalization versus antiglobalization struggles in such spiritual terms, many instinctively feel what is at stake, in a way that Huntington does not. The clash of civilizations is a convenient paradigm for foreign-policy mandarins who take globalization for granted, and who prefer to insulate the culture-specific values of different religions from one another. Let them have their values, and we will have ours! For those who can see how the West is imposing new "religious" values on other civilizations in the economic guise of "free trade," Huntington's paradigm is a smoke screen that obscures more than it reveals about the ways the world is now groaning and travailing together.

The issue of social justice also brings me to my final point: a gaping fissure that runs right through the middle of Huntington's own essay. Although he concludes by calling upon the West to develop a better understanding of the religious and philosophical foundations of other civilizations, Huntington has more specific short-term recommendations for Western (read "U.S.") foreign policy, including: to maintain Western military superiority, to exploit differences among Islamic and Confucian states (he is worried about a nascent Confucian-Islamic axis), to support non-Western groups that are "sympathetic to Western values and interests," and "to strengthen international institutions that reflect and legitimate Western interests and values" (1996, 24–25). Huntington the hardheaded realist has no illusions about a world community of civilizations, but his oft-repeated phrase "Western values and interests" deserves some attention for the way it merges two different concepts.

In the only place where he identifies Western values, Huntington trots out the usual shibboleths: "individualism, liberalism, constitutionalism, human rights, equality, liberty, the rule of law, democracy, free markets, the separation of church and state"—which "often have little resonance" in other cultures. And what is the relationship between these Western *values* and Western *interests*? Huntington never addresses this uncomfortable question, perhaps because it is difficult to square these mostly commendable ideals with the ways that the United States has actually treated other nations when its own short-term interests have been at stake.

We have supported constitutionalism, human rights, liberty, the rule of law, and democracy in other countries when those values have produced leaders amenable to our own national interests. Those same values evidently resonate less loudly for us when they produce leaders who have different ideas, such as Chávez in Venezuela. In 1954, for example, the United States sponsored a coup against the democratically elected government of Guatemala, which over the following years led to the deaths of over one hundred thousand peasants. In 1965 the United States overthrew the government of the Dominican Republic and helped to kill some three thousand people in the process. In 1973, the United States sponsored a coup against the democratically elected government of Chile that murdered or "disappeared" several thousand people. In the 1980s the United States sponsored a terrorist war by the contras against the government of Nicaragua, which led to the deaths of over thirty thousand innocent people and to a World Court declaration that the U.S. government was a war criminal for mining Nicaragua's harbors. Another U.S.-supported war in the 1980s, against El Salvador, resulted in the deaths of eighty thousand more innocent people. Lots of "collateral damage."

All those recent examples are from Latin America alone. In 1965 the United States also sponsored or assisted a military coup in Indonesia that led to the deaths of over half a million people, and the military dictatorship of Suharto, who invited Western corporations back into the country. When President Bush declares that Iran is part of a new "axis of evil," we should remember why many Iranians return the compliment, viewing the U.S. government as "the Great Satan." When Western oil interests in that country were challenged by a democratically elected prime minister in the early 1950s, the CIA helped to sponsor a brutal coup that installed the widely detested shah of Iran, whose notorious Savak secret service then proceeded to torture and kill over seventy thousand Iranians between 1952 and 1979.

There are many more examples, unfortunately, yet the point is made. Clearly the problem here is something more than not quite living up to our own ideals. It is not that we just keep making mistakes, such as innocently backing the wrong sort of people. Once can be a mistake, twice may be stupidity, but this pattern of repeated violations of our own self-declared values amounts to something more sinister. "By their fruits shall you know them," as someone once put it. It is difficult to avoid the conclusion that our so-called values are not really our values, at least not when it comes to international relations. The basic problem is not a clash between our values and theirs, but between our (declared) values and our (short-term) interests.

Huntington admits that a world of clashing civilizations is inevitably a world of double standards (1996, 13), but with such a clash between U.S. ideals and U.S. interests, one need not look any further to understand why our international goals so often meet resistance. Given how little most Americans know about the rest of the world, it is not surprising that other civilizations—on the receiving end of U.S. foreign policy—are more aware of this clash than we are. As long as our preeminent foreign policy value continues to be narrow and often brutal self-interest, we will not need a sophisticated new paradigm to explain why the new Pax Americana is not working.

Surely Huntington, a distinguished Ivy League professor of international relations, knows about these violations of the Western ideals he identifies. Why does he ignore such a gaping fissure between U.S. values and U.S. interests? Perhaps he regards such incidents as regrettable but unavoidable consequences of the Cold War, whereas the clash of civilizations is a new post–Cold War paradigm. Yet such rationalizations will not do. If we were concerned to combat communism in Latin America, we picked some of the worst ways to do it—ways that alienated many of the best people in those countries and made them more sympathetic to alternatives such as communism. No, the basic problem is that U.S. foreign policy in Latin America has been more concerned with the best interests of the United Fruit Company, and other such corporations, than with the best interests of Latin Americans.

And what about today? Even if we ignore recent military and more covert actions, in the year 2001 alone the U.S. refused to join 123 other nations in banning the use and production of antipersonnel bombs and mines (February); President Bush declared the Kyoto global warming protocol "dead" and refused to participate in revising it, because that might harm the U.S. economy (March); the United States refused to participate in OECD-sponsored talks in Paris on ways to crack down on offshore tax and money-laundering havens (May); the United States was the only nation to oppose the U.N. Agreement to Curb the International Flow of Illicit Small Arms (July); and the United States withdrew from the landmark 1972 Antiballistic Missile Treaty, to the dismay of virtually every other country (December). In addition, the United States has not ratified the Comprehensive (Nuclear) Test Ban Treaty, signed by 164 nations but opposed by Bush, and the United States has rejected the Land Mine Treaty, concluded in Ottawa in December 1997 and signed by 122 countries, because the Pentagon finds land mines useful.

Do these examples support a clash of civilizations, or show that the United States is unwilling to work with other civilizations? As the only superpower, the United States cherishes its sovereignty, because it wants to be free to do whatever it wants to do, regardless of what the rest of the world may think. In that case, however, is the clash of civilizations a valid paradigm for understanding the world, or a self-fulfilling rationalization for self-serving behavior in the world?

As a citizen of the United States, I value most of the ideals that Huntington identifies as Western: liberalism, constitutionalism, human rights, equality, liberty, the rule of law, democracy, and so forth. As someone who practices Buddhism—an intercivilizational traitor?—I also believe that a life lived in accordance with such ideals will nevertheless not be a happy one unless I also make efforts to transform my greed into generosity, my ill will into compassion, and my delusions into wisdom. Buddhism teaches me that this not only works to make others happier but is even more important for my own happiness, because that is the only way to overcome the illusory, self-defeating duality between myself and other people.

Is the same also true collectively, for the relations between peoples and cultures? If the answer is yes, there are immense consequences for U.S. relations with the rest of the world and for the West's relationship with other civilizations. Instead of dismissing such Buddhist ideals as foreign, by relativizing them as the attributes of an alien civilization, another option is to learn from them, and perhaps even assimilate some of them into our own culture, as Sri Lanka, Southeast Asia, China, Tibet, Korea, and Japan have done.

The rest of the world still has much to learn about the Western ideals that Huntington cites: human rights, equality, liberty, the rule of law, and democracy. For that matter, so does the West. The West may also have much to gain from a more profound understanding of the basic religious and philosophical values underlying other civilizations—as Huntington perhaps implies in the last paragraph of his essay.

Any American who lives outside the United States for long cannot help but be reminded, repeatedly, how important the United States is for the rest of the world. It is not just that others enjoy our pop culture or crave our consumer goods. Most other nations look to the United States for international leadership, and all too often they are dismayed when a nation that is already by far the wealthiest and most powerful responds by promoting its own short-term economic interests at the cost of the larger good—and at the cost of its own long-term interests in an increasingly interdependent world. September 11 showed us that this attitude is dangerous as well as selfish and arrogant, and our government's response to that tragedy has only made things worse.

# TEN

# Terrorism as Religion

## *The Identity Crisis of Secularism*

Hell is truth seen too late.

—Anonymous

Why would a small group of people want to crash hijacked airplanes into skyscrapers, killing thousands (including themselves) and terrorizing millions? Perhaps only religion can provide sufficient motivation and collective support for such heinous deeds.[1] Does this mean that religious terrorism can be dismissed as just another example of irrational fanaticism? Or is there a kind of logic to fundamentalist terrorism, which makes it a regrettable but nonetheless understandable reaction to modernity?

Mark Juergensmeyer and Karen Armstrong have shown that religious fundamentalism is not a return to premodern ways of being religious. Jewish, Christian, and Islamic fundamentalisms are all recent developments reacting to what is perceived—to a large extent correctly, I shall argue—as the failure of secular modernity. Such fundamentalism, including the violence it occasionally spawns, is the "underside" of modernity, its Jungian *shadow*. Although such responses are themselves flawed, of course, there is nevertheless something insightful in their perception of the need for an alternative to secularity as we now experience it. While deploring its recourse to violence, we also need to appreciate the crucial problem that religiously inspired terrorism points to: the "God-shaped hole" in the modern world that motivates it.

Although religious critiques of modernity usually focus on our faith in self-sufficient human reason, that is not the central point to be explored in this final chapter. The key issue is *identity*, especially the security that identity provides—and the anxiety that lack of secure identity arouses. Traditional premodern religion provided an *ontological security*, by grounding us in an all-encompassing metaphysical vision that explains the cosmos and our role ⌐ relating to being, existence within it. Modernity and postmodernity question such transcendental narratives, and therefore leave us with *ontological anxiety* about the apparent meaninglessness of the universe and the ungroundedness of our lives within it. The result is that we are afflicted with "a deepening condition of metaphysical homelessness" that is psychologically difficult to bear (Berger 1979, 77).

By promoting secular values and goals, the modern world cannot avoid undermining the cosmic identity and therefore the ontological grounding that religion traditionally provides. Modernity offers us some other identities—as citizens, as consumers—but this-worldly alternatives cannot provide the ultimate security that we cannot help craving. Modern identities are more obviously humanly constructed roles that can be exchanged, which therefore offer no privileged place or special responsibility in a meaningful cosmos.

This highlights our fate as moderns. Lack of ontological security manifests as aggravated anxiety, which we usually experience as this or that *fear of...* —most recently, of course, fear of terrorism. The problem is not merely that modern identities involve a different sense of self-worth that is more individualistic and competitive. Even the most successful among us remain essentially ungrounded. To be grounded one needs to fit into a larger scheme of value and meaning—something that a sacred worldview provides but contemporary secularity does not. This ungroundedness means, among other things, that we do not have a solution to death, or to what I have elsewhere described as our "sense of lack." We experience this lack as the gnawing suspicion that "there is something wrong with me," yet we never quite get a handle on what that something is. Sartre said that the death of God in the modern world has left a "God-shaped hole" at our core. Many of our problems today derive from the fact that we compulsively try to fill this hole or bottomless pit, which gives a manic quality to our secular projects. If this is also true collectively—if societies and nations can also be obsessed with a group sense of ungroundedness—we begin to see why modernity (and now postmodernity) has become so problematic.

A Buddhist way to describe this situation is with the basic Mahayana categories of form and emptiness (the latter term understood, in this case, as formlessness). Identity is form: because formlessness (the original meaning of "chaos") terrifies us, we cling to fixed identities for stability, a secure ground. The traditional premodern guarantor of fixed identity has been religion, which teaches us who we really are and what we need to do to feel grounded, but such myths were anathema to the eighteenth-century Enlightenment, which promoted in their place the freedoms we cherish today.

The destabilizing effects of modernity mean that modern fundamentalists must cling to their doctrines (orthodoxy) and rituals (orthopraxy) more tightly than their premodern forebears needed to do. Unavoidably, such contemporary identifications are not only more literalistic but more self-conscious, which means they are less effective at allaying anxiety—and that means that greater, often more violent measures are needed in defense of one's religious commitments in a secular world that constantly challenges those commitments. Even a hundred years ago, Christianity for Westerners was (with few exceptions[2]) fate; today Christian commitment is a choice, even for those raised in all-Christian communities, since they need only turn on the television or open a magazine to be exposed to seductive secular alternatives. Religious choice today is often motivated by the perception that there is something wrong with those secular alternatives. I will argue that this understanding is largely correct, which of course does not necessarily imply that a fundamentalist response is better.

Linking the issue of religious terrorism with ontological identity may seem too abstract and metaphysical. The problems that this relationship reveals, however, are all too real and immediate. Their linkage gives us insight not only into the violent tendencies of religious fundamentalism, but into the basic problem with modernity itself, revealing why the cause of fundamentalism is modernity, and why modern attempts to deal with the problems created by modernity have been so unsuccessful. In Mahayana terms, our identity, like all other forms, is always empty (*shunya*), but realizing that is not problematic, because emptiness/formlessness is liberated to take on the form or forms appropriate to the situation. If form is empty, emptiness is also form. Ironically, this implies that the "spiritual home" that awareness seeks can be found only in homelessness itself, because confronting our lack—facing and accepting the groundlessness we dread—transforms it.

## Terrorism Is a Force that Gives Us Identity

> A society provides an accepted—even heroic—social role for its citizens who participate in great struggles and have been given the moral license to kill. They are soldiers. Understandably, many members of radical religious movements see themselves that way.
>
> —Juergensmeyer, *Terror in the Mind of God*

Engaging in terrorist mass murder / suicide is so horrific that it normally requires special support, not only to provide the material means but to reinforce the internal conviction necessary to carry out something so extreme. A legitimating ideology is needed, maintained by a community that encourages such desperate measures, by emphasizing, among other things, the violence-supporting texts to be found somewhere within almost all religious traditions. Although such passages are normally a minor part of the tradition, they can be decontextualized from other doctrines, and groups can construct their belief systems upon violent historical events or myths. We should not be surprised that individuals can internalize terrorist-promoting beliefs. Despite our self-image as rational beings, the usual reason—or cause—for our beliefs is that other people whom we respect (and those whom we want to respect us) believe the same thing. Accepting their beliefs makes us part of the group, and membership provides us with a reassuring identity.

This by itself is not sufficient to understand the lure of terrorism, yet a community of believers supplies the conscious ideology that allows other, less reputable factors the space to operate. Violence, once morally justified, opens the door not only to illusions of power but to fantasies of personal recognition that involve "proving oneself" in a virile, testosterone-fueled way. Popular culture also celebrates violence as the solution to many problems. It can be cathartic, and it can also be a way to be noticed, to prove to others that *I am real* and need to be taken account of. As the novelist Don DeLillo has put it, terrorism is "the language of being noticed" (in Juergensmeyer 2000, 139) If one's self-image involves internalizing the perceptions that others have of us, the anonymity of mass society is part of modernity's lack-of-identity problem. How can one distinguish oneself, if, as DeLillo has also said, "only the lethal believer, the person who kills and dies for faith," is taken seriously in modern society (in Juergensmeyer 2000, 125)? Better to be known as someone who was willing to die for his beliefs, than not to be known at all—than to *be* no one at all.

This helps us to understand why terrorist attacks such as those on the World Trade Center and the Pentagon, which seem strategically absurd and self-defeating, can nevertheless seem desirable to some people. They are not instrumental means to realize political goals but are *symbolic*. As David Rapaport has observed, terrorism and religion fit together not only because of a violent streak in the history of most religions, but also because there is a ritualistic aspect to terrorist acts that mimics religious rites. Victims are chosen not primarily because they are threatening but because they are representative symbols that tie into "a special picture of the world" (in Juergensmeyer 2000, 125). Juergensmeyer himself emphasizes that religion is crucial for such dramatic statements, because it "provides images of cosmic war that allow activists to believe that they are waging spiritual scenarios" (2000, xi). This brings us back to the question of how religion offers ontological identity.

In *War Is a Force that Gives Us Meaning* Chris Hedges, writing from his own experience as a war correspondent, reflects on why war is so addictive, despite all the suffering and danger it involves:

> The enduring attraction of war is this: Even with its destruction and carnage it can give us what we long for in life. It can give us purpose, meaning, a reason for living. Only when we are in the

midst of conflict does the shallowness and vapidness of much of
our lives become apparent. Trivia dominates our conversations
and increasingly our airwaves. ... [War] allows us to be noble.
(Hedges 2002, 3)

Peace had again exposed the void that the rush of war, of battle,
had filled. Once again they [victims of the Bosnian war] were, as
perhaps we all are, alone, no longer bound by that common sense
of struggle, no longer given the opportunity to be noble, heroic,
no longer sure what life was about or what it meant. (7)

The communal march against an enemy generates a warm, unfamil-
iar bond with our neighbors, our community, our nation, wiping
out unsettling undercurrents of alienation and dislocation. War, in
times of malaise and desperation, is a potent distraction. (11)

Notice the contrast: war provides a meaning lacking in peacetime. Despite
its horrors, war remains attractive because it fills the void—the shallowness,
loneliness, alienation, and malaise—of everyday life. Because it conceals better
the lack of our everyday identities? That is the important question Hedges's
book suggests. Is this lack of purpose a general description of all peacetime
life, which suggests a grim prognosis indeed, or is it particularly descriptive
of the sense of lack in modern secular life, which seems to doom our lives
to triviality insofar as it provides us with no cosmic role greater than consumerism or (occasionally) patriotism? Is it the secular alternative that makes
religious war so attractive?

The return to a peaceful environment was often difficult for Hedges
and other correspondents, who had become addicted to the excitement of
war. But what if there is a grand spiritual war that is going on all the time,
even in times of peace, although mostly unbeknownst to those who do not
have the spiritual insight to perceive what is at stake? In that case, the vapidness of everyday life may be avoided indefinitely, since the noble struggle
continues indefinitely.

Such soldiers have found new battles: the grand spiritual and
political struggles in which their movements envision themselves to
be engaged. These cosmic wars impart a sense of importance and
destiny to men who find the modern world to be stifling, chaotic,
and dangerously out of control. The imagined wars identify the
enemy, the imputed source of their personal and political failures;
they exonerate these would-be soldiers from any responsibility
for failures by casting them as victims; they give them a sense

of their own potential for power; and they arm them with the
moral justification, the social support, and the military equipment
to engage in battle both figuratively and literally. (Juergensmeyer
2000, 190)

Transcendental struggle can provide a heroic identity that transcends even
death, for death is not checkmate when you are an agent of God. What
grander destiny is possible, than to be part of the cosmic forces of Good
fighting against Evil? It is a heady alternative to languishing in a refugee camp
without much hope for the future—or, for that matter, to channel surfing and
shopping at the mall.

In such a war it is okay to kill "innocent bystanders," for there are really
no bystanders, just people unaware of whose side they are on, who do not
understand the role they are already playing in this cosmic struggle. One's
own violence is a defensive response to evil aggression, in an ongoing war
that may have started a long time ago. To feel that one is on the side of the
Good it is necessary to demonize the enemy—easy to do, since the primary
enemy here usually *is* Satan, in one or another of his nefarious roles. This
means that no quarter should be given, for evil must be destroyed. One's own
death as a martyr (literally, "witness") becomes a sacrifice (literally, "making holy") that ennobles one's victims as well as oneself. All this is justified
because the context and the meaning of this struggle transcend this world
and its inhabitants. The salvation—the spiritual identity and home—of such
cosmic warriors is not to be found on this earth except insofar as its mundane
events are related to higher, invisible spiritual developments.

The need for ideological support reminds us of the importance of religious collectives in scripting such cosmic dramas. Of course, some groups
have a more important role than others to play in this spiritual war, so they
cannot be held to the same standards of behavior that those others must
follow. The Hebrews became a chosen people due to their covenant with
God; Christians who worship the true Son of God are obliged to convert the
heathen; the extraordinary military success of the first Muslims suggested that
God looked upon them with special favor; and ever since the first Puritan
settlers, Americans have tended to view their new nation as a New Jerusalem,
charged with unique responsibility to bring salvation (whether religious or
secular) to the rest of the world. According to a 2002 Pew poll, 48 percent
of Americans believe that the United States has had special protection from
God for most of its history.

To have a special role is also to have a privileged destiny. According to the Israeli rabbi Eleazar Waldman of the Gush movement, "[T]he
Redemption of the world *depends* upon the Redemption of Israel. From this
derives our moral, spiritual, and cultural influence over the entire world. The

blessing will come to all of humanity from the people of Israel living in the whole of its land" (in Armstrong 2000, 286). Since world redemption is the most important thing of all, if it involves expelling more Palestinians from Greater Israel—well, in the long run that will be for their own (spiritual) good, too.

A juxtaposition of special destinies can lead to some peculiar alliances, as in the support of many conservative U.S. Christians for Israeli expansion into Palestinian homelands. According to their reading of the Book of Revelation, the Last Days will not occur until the Jewish people return to the Holy Land.[3] According to the same 2002 Pew poll, 44 percent of Americans believe that God gave the land that is now Israel to the Jewish people, and 31 percent think that "the state of Israel is a fulfillment of the biblical prophecy about the second coming of Jesus." Although the turbulent days to follow, including the Second Coming, will condemn to eternal damnation those Jews who do not convert to Christianity—well, that may be unfortunate, but the important thing is to do whatever is necessary to encourage his return.

It ends up a hypocritical contract, or Faustian compact, between two chosen peoples each eager to use the other for its own higher destiny (and identity). In such a cosmic struggle, of course, the welfare of "bystanders" such as the Palestinians is trumped by the superior role of Jews and/or Christians. In Armstrong's words, a "literal reading of highly selected passages of the Bible had encouraged them [Christian fundamentalists] to absorb the Godless genocidal tendencies of modernity" (2000, 218). The same is true for those Zionists who will do anything deemed necessary to promote the redemption of Israel. One's identity as a spiritual warrior justifies the oppression of the less spiritually important Other.

It is quite remarkable how often the literature on terrorism cites identity as the basic issue. For example, the Sikh terrorist leader Bhindranwale "echoed the common fear that Sikhs would lose their identity in a flood of resurgent Hinduism, or worse, in a sea of secularism." Many Japanese have understood the attraction of Aum Shinrikyo, which released sarin gas in a Tokyo subway, as "the result of a desperate searching for social identity and spiritual fulfill-ment" (Juergensmeyer 2000, 94, 103). Juergensmeyer concludes that the modern world as experienced by religious terrorists and their supporters is

> a dangerous, chaotic, and violent sea for which religion was an anchor in a harbor of calm. At some deep and almost transcen-dent level of consciousness, they sensed their lives slipping out of control, and they felt both responsible for the disarray and a victim of it. To be abandoned by religion in such a world would mean a loss of their own individual identity. In fashioning a "traditional religion" of their own, they exposed their concerns not so much

with their religious, ethnic or national communities as with their own personal, imperiled selves. (223)

Juergensmeyer describes a syndrome that "begins with the perception that the public world has gone awry, and the suspicion that behind this social confusion lies a great spiritual and moral conflict, a cosmic battle between the forces of order and chaos, good and evil," in which a delegitimized government is seen as allied with the forces of chaos and evil (224).

Of course, there are other ways in which the world might have gone awry. But then one would not have recourse to the familiar, even comfortable concept of war, and the heroic identity it provides for those engaged in it.

> The idea of warfare implies more than an attitude; ultimately it is a world view and an assertion of power. To live in a state of war is to live in a world in which individuals know who they are, why they have suffered, by whose hand they have been humiliated, and at what expense they have persevered. The concept of war provides cosmology, history, and eschatology and offers the reins of political control. Perhaps most important, it holds out the hope of victory and the means to achieve it. In the images of cosmic war this victorious triumph is a grand moment of social and personal transformation, transcending all worldly limitations. One does not easily abandon such expectations. To be without such images of war is almost to be without hope itself. . . . Like the rituals provided by religious traditions, warfare is a participatory drama that exemplifies—and thus explains—the most profound aspects of life. (Juergensmeyer 2000, 155)

Hedges's book shows us that the worldview, meaning, and power provided by warfare are addictive for many. Elevate this struggle into a cosmic war between Good and Evil and the attraction of warrior-identity is multiplied many times over.

## Apocalypse Tomorrow

A striking characteristic of almost all the grand cosmic wars is the apocalyptic resolution that is just about to occur. Despite great variety in fundamentalist belief about the nature of this spiritual struggle, everyone seems to know that the last days are at hand. Often this includes the return of a Messiah, whose advent will set off (or crown) the final chain of events. In addition to the Book of Revelation, Juergensmeyer refers to the "catastrophic messianism" dear to

Rabbi Meir Kahane, founder of Israel's right-wing Kach Party: the Messiah will come—"fairly soon"—when Jews win a great conflict and praise God through their successes. The "messianic Zionism" taught by Avraham Kook, Israel's first chief rabbi, was much encouraged by the euphoria after Israel's success in the 1967 Six Days' War, which was taken to imply that "history was quickly leading to the moment of divine redemption and the recreation of the biblical state of Israel" (Juergensmeyer 2000, 54–55). "Kook really believed that he was living in the last age and would shortly witness the final fulfillment of human history." The tragic vision of Shiite Islam views the martyrdom of Muhammad's descendants as symbolizing a spiritual war in which evil always seems to get the upper hand, but the last days will bring the final reappearance of the Hidden Imam (Armstrong 2000, 187, 45). Shoko Asahara, the Japanese founder of Aum Shinrikyo, predicted an Armageddon in which evil forces will use the most vicious weapons—including radioactivity and poison gas—to destroy almost everyone. Only the members of Aum Shinrikyo and a few others with "great karma" will survive. The Tokyo subway attack in March 1995, which released sarin gas that killed twelve people and injured thousands, was expected to hasten the climactic cataclysm (Juergensmeyer 2000, 113).

How shall we understand this widespread expectation of an imminent apocalyptic resolution? Its historical recurrence suggests a persistent psychological need perhaps aggravated by modernity's preoccupation with temporal progress. The traditional self-understanding of premodern societies unites cosmology and temporality: rituals must be performed at certain times because they are needed at those times. An orderly continuation of the world cycle is preserved, and the identity of participants thus grounded, not by transcending the past but by reliving it. Premodern history is not a weight to be overcome but a harmonious pattern to be reenacted. Our role in the cosmos is to keep enacting it, so the cosmic cycle will continue. Apocalyptic movements arise when reenactment fails to resolve accumulated tension/lack; often it is social or economic crisis that inspires the quest for a spiritual alternative.

In contrast, secular modernity focuses on the future. The past is to be superseded; our own identities, like the world in general, can and should be improved upon. Yet technological developments and economic growth do not address our need for a spiritual grounding. Our sense of sin (or lack) is all the more difficult to cope with today, since we are not supposed to have it and therefore lack the religious resources to deal with it. Our greater freedom is shadowed by greater anxiety.

Impending apocalypse is a solution to this tension. We can no longer secure ourselves by reenacting the ancient rituals; the traditional cycle of time has been broken by our linear obsession with progress. If the solution to the awfulness of the present cannot be found in the past, it must be sought in the future—and not a distant future, for that would project the object of our hopes, the end of our lack, too far away to reassure and motivate us now. The event that will wipe away the past and purify the world, destroying the corrupt and redeeming the faithful, must be just around the corner. Life would be unbearable without that imminent prospect. We are about to attain our spiritual home! The greater our anxiety, the greater our need for such a resolution, and the sooner the better.

## A Distorted Insight?

Should this cosmic war between Good and Evil be understood as merely a fantasy of the spiritually unsophisticated? Or might it be a somewhat confused but nevertheless insightful realization that we are indeed in the midst of a worldwide spiritual/psychological struggle?

Karen Armstrong describes the "battle for God" as an attempt to fill the empty core of a society based on scientific rationalism. "Confronted with the genocidal horrors of our century, reason has nothing to say. Hence, there is a void at the heart of modern culture, which Western people experienced at an early stage of their scientific revolution" (2000, 365), or *began* to experience. The void is still there; we have just gotten used to avoiding or repressing the great anxiety associated with modernity—and not noticing the consequences. Armstrong reminds us of Nietzsche's madman in *Zarathustra* and *The Gay Science*, who declares that the death of God has torn humanity from its roots and cast us adrift "as if through an infinite nothingness," ensuring that "profound terror, a sense of meaningless and annihilation, would be part of the modern experience" (2000, 97). Today politicians and economists urge us to keep the (secular) faith; they keep telling us that we are approaching the promised land, but "at the end of the twentieth century, the liberal myth that humanity is progressing to an ever more enlightened and tolerant state looks as fantastic as any of the other millennial myths" her book examines (366). The nameless dread still haunts us. Fundamentalists and secularists seem to be "trapped in an escalating spiral of hostility and recrimination" (371). And the stakes, after September 11, have become much higher.

Juergensmeyer notices three aspects common to the violent religious movements he has studied. All of them reject the compromises that more mainstream religious organizations have made with liberal and secular values. They refuse to observe the sacred/secular distinction that is so sacred to modernity, which banishes religion from the public sphere by consigning it to private life. Finally, they replace modernity's attenuated religious forms with more vigorous and demanding expressions. He "was struck with the intensity of their quests for a deeper level of spirituality than that offered by the superficial values of the modern world" (2000, 221–22).

These three attributes can be summed up as *a rejection of modern secularity*. The secularity of contemporary life is a hard-won historical legacy that seems necessary for the freedoms we enjoy today, including freedom of religious commitment and expression. Nevertheless, the fundamentalist perception that there is something basically problematical about the modern distinction between sacred and secular is fundamentally valid. Although the separation between those spheres is one of the finest achievements of Western civilization, it is also *the* basic problem of Western civilization, the tragic flaw that may yet destroy it. The contemporary struggle between them can indeed be understood as a spiritual war, whose significance is difficult to exaggerate.

## Denying the God-Shaped Hole

We have never been so prosperous. Yet we have never been so secular and pagan. . . . We are making secularism our national religion.

—Jerry Falwell, "A National Rebirth Needed"

The basic problem for Falwell and other fundamentalists is not so much other religions as *the ideology that pretends not to be an ideology*. Juergensmeyer concludes by focusing on the widespread loss of faith in the values of secular nationalism (2000, 226). Mahmud Abouhalima, convicted for his role in the 1993 World Trade Center bombing, was emphatic that the problem with America is not Christianity but its ideology of secularism; secularism has no life, and secular people are "just moving like dead bodies" (Jurgensmeyer 2000, 69).

Sayyid Qutb, the Islamic scholar who became the intellectual inspiration for most Islamic terrorist groups including al Qaeda, built his philosophy on a critique and rejection of secularism. His major work, *In the Shade of the Qur'an*, emphasizes that the modern world has reached *jahiliyya*, a pathological "moment of unbearable crisis," not only because of its faith in human reason but more generally because of the Christian split between the sacred and secular dimensions of life, which later evolved into the modern Western separation of church and state. For Qutb, secularist morality is "ersatz religion," and a life in *jahiliyya* is "hollow, full of contradictions, defects and flaws" (in Euben 1991, 21–22). This "hideous schizophrenia" becomes worse when Christians try to impose it on Islam, because secularist morality is alien to shari'a, the Islamic moral code that regulates everyday life in great detail. Qutb rejected the Muslim leaders of his time (including "the Pharaoh" Nasser, who jailed and then executed him in 1966), as modernized and pagan products of the "new ignorance" sweeping the world. Their secularism is an attempt to destroy Islam, hence it must be resisted by any means possible (Berman 1991, 26–28; Euben 1991, 20).

We do not need to accept Qutb's call for violent resistance to benefit from his perspective: the modern Western bifurcation between sacred and secular remains foreign to the core teachings of Islam. Muhammad was a social and political leader as well as a spiritual adviser, and his legacy includes detailed instructions on how to incorporate one's religious commitment into the practices of everyday life. The fact that some of those guidelines no longer seem appropriate in the twenty-first century is part of Islam's difficulty today, but the challenge of modifying them does not imply that Muslims should accept the basic premise of Western modernity. "Western thinkers rightly note that Islam has never grasped the need for a secular realm. They fail to note that what passes for secular belief in the West is a mutation of religious faith" (Gray 2003, 11). This mutation is inconsistent with Islam.

Before raising questions about what is, in effect, the foundation of our modern world, let me first emphasize that I share the usual appreciation of the freedoms usually associated with the distinction between sacred and secular. In particular, the liberty to believe what one wants, or not believe, is a hard-won and essential right. Nevertheless, the "naturalness" of the secular worldview must be challenged, in order to gain a better understanding of what has been lost as well as gained.

The fundamental problem is that our sense of lack remains oblivious to any distinction we might make between a sacred worldview and a secular one. Our lack continues to fester regardless, although a secular understanding of the world (e.g., a world without Abrahamic sin or Buddhist delusion) tends to repress it, since a rationalistic and humanistic orientation acknowledges no such basic deficiency at our core. The result is that we end up trying to fill up that lack in ways that are doomed to fail, by grasping at something or other *in* the secularized world. We need to appreciate the fundamentalist insight that no solution to lack can be found in this way.

## The Spirituality of Secularity

The main problem with our usual understanding of secularity is that it is taken for granted, so we are not aware that it *is* a worldview. It is an ideology that pretends to be the everyday world we live in. Most of us assume that it is simply the way the world really is, once superstitious beliefs about it have been removed. Yet that is the secular view of secularity, its own self-understanding, no more to be accepted at face value than Falwell's or Qutb's neo-orthodox alternatives to secularity. The secularity we presuppose must be "denaturalized" in order to realize how unique and peculiar such a worldview is—and how inherently unstable.

Western secularity, including its capitalist economy, originated as the result of an unlikely concatenation of circumstances. To survive within the Roman Empire, early Christianity had to render unto Caesar what was Caesar's and keep a low profile that did not challenge the state; spiritual concerns were necessarily distinguished from political issues. Later struggles between the emperor and the papacy tended to reinforce that distinction. By making private and regular confession compulsory, the late medieval church also promoted the development of a subjective interiority that encouraged more personal religiosity. New technologies such as the printing press made widespread literacy, and hence more individualistic religion, possible.

All that made the Reformation possible. By privatizing an unmediated relationship between more individualized Christians and a more transcendent God, Luther's emphasis on salvation by faith alone eliminated the intricate web of mediation—priests, sacraments, canon law, pilgrimages, public penances, and so on—that in effect had constituted the sacred dimension of this world. Desacralization of the world occurred not because God disappeared, but because God became understood to dwell far above this corrupted world, and also deep inside the human heart—but no longer in the everyday world of our social lives. The religiously saturated medieval continuity between the natural and the supernatural was sundered by *internalizing* faith and *projecting* the spiritual realm far above our struggles in this one. The newly liberated space between them generated something new: the secular (from the Latin *saeculum*, "generation, age," thus the temporal world of birth and death). The inner freedom of conscience was distinguished from our outer bondage to secular authorities. "These realms, which contained respectively religion and the world, were hermetically sealed from each other as though constituting separate universes" (Nelson 1981, 74–75). The sharp distinction between them was a radical break with the past, and it led to a new kind of person. The medieval understanding of our life as a cycle of sin and repentance was replaced by a more internalized conscience that did not accept the need for external mediation.

As God slowly disappeared up into the clouds, the secular became increasingly dynamic, accelerating into the creative destruction to which we today must keep readjusting. What often tends to be forgotten in the process is that *this distinction between sacred and secular was originally a religious distinction*, meant to empower a new type of (Protestant) spirituality—that is, a more privatized way to address our sense of lack and fill up the

God-shaped hole. By allowing the sacred pole to fade away, however, we have lost the original religious raison d'etre for that distinction. That evaporation of the sacred has left us with the secular by itself, bereft of the spiritual resources originally designed to cope with it, because secular life is increasingly liberated from any religious perspective or moral supervision.

Does this historical understanding give us the context we need to understand the much-maligned shari'a? Like the Judaic emphasis on ritual law (dietary prohibitions, etc.), its primary purpose is not punitive. Both are designed as ways to sacralize everyday life, by instilling patterns of behavior that work to infuse this world with a sense of the divine. We may want to question how successful some of those ways remain today, but the Judaic and Islamic approach is to structure our life in the world with rituals that remind us of the sacred and offer us ceremonial access to it. By privatizing religious commitment and practice as something that occurs primarily "inside" us, modern Christianity encourages the public/private split and aggravates the alienation of subject from object. When religion is understood as an individual process of inner faith-commitment, we are more likely to accede to a diminished appreciation of the objective world "outside" us, denuding the secular realm of any sacred dimension. With fewer spiritual identity-markers remaining outside our own psyches, we are supposed to find or construct an identity "inside," a challenge not easy to meet: "On the one hand, modern identity is open-ended, transitory, liable to ongoing change. On the other hand, a subjective realm of identity is the individual's main foothold in reality. Something that is constantly changing is supposed to be the *ens realissimum*" (Berger 1979, 74).

The basic problem with the sacred/secular bifurcation has become more evident as the sacred has evaporated. The sacral dimension provided not only ritual and morality but also a grounding identity that explained the meaning of our life in the world. Whether or not we now believe this meaning to be fictitious makes no difference to the transcendent security and ultimate foundation that it was felt to provide. A solution was provided for death and our God-shaped sense of lack, which located them within a larger spiritual context and therefore made it possible to endure them. Human suffering and striving were not accidental or irrelevant but served a vital role within the grand structure of our spiritual destiny.

What may be misleading about this discussion of an enervated sacral dimension is that it still seems to suggest superimposing something (for example, some particular religious understanding of the meaning of our lives) onto the secular world (that is, the world "as it really is"). My point is the opposite: our usual understanding of the secular is a deficient worldview (in Buddhist terms, a delusion) distorted by the fact that one half of the original duality has gone missing, although now it has been absent so long that we have largely forgotten about it.

This may be easier to see if we think of God and the sacral dimension as symbols for the "spiritual" aspect of life in a more psychological sense—that is, the dimension that encompasses our concerns about the meaning and value of human life in the cosmos. The sacred becomes that sphere where the mysteries of our existence—birth and death, tragedy, anxiety, hope, transformation—are posed and contemplated. From this perspective, the secular is not the world as it really is when magic and superstition have been removed, but the supposed objectivity that remains when "subjectivity"—including these basic issues about human role and identity—has been brushed away as irrelevant to our understanding of what the universe really is. In the process our spiritual concerns are not refuted; rather, there is simply no way to address them in a secular world built by pruning value from fact, except as subjective preferences that have no intrinsic relationship with the "real" material world we just happen to find ourselves within.

A metaphorical understanding of the spiritual makes it more obvious that the sacred cannot be avoided, although it can be repressed if we accept a diminished understanding of ourselves to accommodate our diminished understanding of the world. It is easy to dismiss the outdated beliefs and antiquated rituals of traditional religions, while missing the fact that these are expressions, however unsatisfactory today, of *a basic human orientation to sacralize the world one lives in, which includes integrating practices that address one's sense of lack.* By throwing out the spiritual baby with the bathwater, we overlook the fact that the "objective" secular always has very particular implications for our subjectivity. *The secular world is secular only in relation to a particular kind of subject,* which understands its lack in a particular way—or, more precisely, does not understand its lack in a way that helps to successfully resolve it. The deep-rooted anxiety that accompanies life in a rationalized world, which deprives us of the spiritual identity that traditionally served to ground us, is not some accident of modern history. Metaphysical terror is implicit in the basic figure-ground relationship that secularized humans have with their secularized world.

The secular world is deficient in the sense that we do not experience that world as it really is, but as distorted perceptually and emotionally by our repressed, unacknowledged need to find something in it that will fill up the gaping wound at our core. Obsessed with the emptiness of a God-shaped hole that our rationality cannot understand and so does not recognize, we now try to *make ourselves real* by making the best of the possibilities that the secular world offers. Individually, we are obsessed with symbolic reality-projects such as money, fame, and power. Collectively, our lack empowers transnational corporations that are never big or profitable enough, nation-states that are never secure enough, and accelerating technological innovation that is never innovative enough to satisfy us for very long. Insofar as these preoccupations are driven by a compulsion to fill up a lack they cannot fulfill, they tend to become addictive and demonic.

In short, we do not understand what is unique about the secular world without also acknowledging the unique identity-crisis haunting the people who live in that world. By liberating us from the more confining identities of the premodern world, modernity also liberated our lack, and secularity implies that we can seek a solution to that lack only by identifying with something *in* the world. In contrast, Buddhism emphasizes that there is nothing to successfully identify with, because the impermanence of everything provides no fixed perch anywhere.

That brings us to what Buddhism has to say about samsara, literally "going round and round." Samsara is the way this world is experienced due to our greed, ill will, and delusion, which makes it a realm of suffering. One could argue that technological development has given us the opportunity to reduce suffering, but for Buddhism the greatest suffering is due to the sense of lack that shadows a deluded sense of self. In one way, a secular world is more samsaric and addictive for us than a premodern one, because it is more haunted by the modern loss of traditional securities. The Buddhist solution is to undo the habitual thought-patterns and behavior-patterns that cause us to experience the world in the diminished way that we normally now do. The point is not to self-consciously try to resacralize the world, but to realize something about everyday life that has always been there although we have been unable to see it.

I am arguing that religious fundamentalists are right, in a way. The tragedy of secular identity projects is that they cannot succeed. The modern world can keep many of us alive longer, and sometimes makes death less physically painful, but it has no answer to the groundlessness that plagues us, for nothing *in* the world can fill up that bottomless God-shaped hole at our core. That is implied by the Buddhist critique of attachment. Without understanding what motivates us, all we can do is cling—not only to physical things but to symbols and ideologies, which tend to be more troublesome—insofar as we are driven to fixate our identities one way or another. The basic problem, at least for those likely to read these words, is not securing the material conditions of our existence but grounding our constructed identities in an impermanent world of accelerating change where everything, including ourselves, is constantly being reconstructed.

To sum up, the distinction between sacred and secular originally developed as *a new way to be religious.* And the fact that our lack cannot be evaded means that our secular world remains a way (although an inadequate way) to be religious. That we do not usually understand what motivates us does not make our motivations any less religious. It means only that our concern to ground ourselves is expressed in compulsive ways that never quite work. This has meant, most of all, an obsession with power, including of course that convertible form of congealed power known as money. If we focus on reason as the defining characteristic of modernity, the emphasis must be on instrumental reason, as Max Weber and other critical theorists have argued. Human rationality itself is no substitute for a sacral dimension, whereas individual and collective craving for power is perhaps inevitable in a world where human meaning must define itself in secular terms. Insofar as this craving is a secular substitute for a now-unobtainable spiritual goal, it too can never give us the sense of ontological security we seek from it, although, if we do not know what else to try, we may conclude that our problem is *not enough* power.

The Reformation distinction between sacred and secular ended up bifur-cating between the otherworldly *ends* of life and the *means* that this world provided. For the Protestant reformers our life in this world still derived its meaning from reference to a world to come. Secular life is a preparation for our eternal destiny. As God slowly evaporated, however, that spiritual purpose evaporated along with him, leaving . . . only the means, now liberated from any relationship to its original ends. Disappearance of an otherworldly sacred did not lead to a resacralization of this world. Old habits die hard, especially when they have been internalized (the disciplined, more goal-oriented charac-ter of post-Reformation individuals) and institutionalized (in capitalism and the nation-state). From this perspective, our obsession with various types of power is not so much a new goal as increased preoccupation with the old means now divested of any other ends. Or we may give up the struggle and abandon ourselves to the hedonism of consumerism.

In other words: since our ever-itching lack means that the issue of ends (the meaning of life, etc.) cannot be evaded, the disappearance of the original ends (eternity with God in heaven) has, by default, left the original means as our ends. Max Weber pointed out that capitalism is the archetypal victory of means over ends: instead of providing us with what is needed for a good life, now ever-more profit, growth, and capital accumulation have become understood as the good life itself. Money lubricates the whole as the most quantified form of power, convertible into anything we like. Yet power, by definition, can only be a means—although we may not notice that until we have enough of it, which means never.

Darwinism provided the transition to such a secular ethic. Evolution by natural selection undermined the strongest remaining reason for believing in God, the argument from design. There was no longer any good reason to postulate a deity that created us; all species including *Homo sapiens* are produced by an impersonal biological process. Although random mutation does not really support a doctrine of progress, Darwin's theory was used to rationalize a new secular paradigm: life as struggle, in which only the fittest survive. This seemed to justify the most ruthless forms of competition, both economic (the plutocrats of the late nineteenth century, the globalizing corporations of the late twentieth century) and political (the imperialistic rivalries of Western nation-states, resulting in two horrendous world wars, followed by the Cold War between the two remaining superpowers).

Let me now carry the argument one step further. Not only are fundamentalists right to be suspicious of such a secularism, I believe they are also correct to believe that there is a spiritual war going on. To use the favorite Christian term, there is indeed an Antichrist that needs to be challenged, in fact one that parallels the original coded reference to the Roman Empire in Revelation: the corporate-military-state, which has become the main institutional beneficiary of the unbridled secular authority that Luther effectively liberated from sacred supervision.

The Reformation created a need and a place for secular divinities, to replace the Big One about to disappear into the clouds. The compulsion to find a more worldly solution to our lack enabled European rulers to become absolute monarchs. With enhanced authority deriving from the aura of their new religious charisma, their now-majestic being became a secular substitute wherein their subjects were encouraged to ground their own lack of being. The political revolutions that eventually overthrew these monarchs did not dissolve the concentration of power that had accumulated around them. State power merely became more impersonal, invested now in the bureaucracy of the administrative apparatus. In short, the unrivaled power of the contemporary nation-state, as the political authority of our secular world, is another legacy of Luther's spiritual innovation.

Unfortunately, a self-destructive tension is built into the nation-state system. Each state is a *secular god*, because the Reformation eventually freed states from any authority external to themselves. Unlike the Holy Roman Emperor who was (at least in principle) spiritually subordinate to the church, a state's "national interest" acknowledges nothing higher than itself that it is subordinate or responsible to. As Hitler is reputed to have said, "We wish to have no other God, only Germany." There are, however, many other such gods, each having a monopoly on authority (including violence) within its own physical territory delimited by others'. This makes for an unstable polytheism, given that the power of each is, in principle, sovereign. "If men recognize no law superior to their desires, then they must fight when their desires collide" (Tawney 1920, 42). That has turned out to be even more true for the secular nation-state, which by definition acknowledges no law superior to itself.

The implications of this tension were evident from the beginning, as war became woven into the fabric of the nascent states. The need to finance large standing armies and their campaigns led to the development of modern banks. New military technologies and forms of human organization were also required—for example, the drill techniques that integrated recruits into a more efficient fighting machine. In short, "war made the state and the state made war" (Tilly 1975, 42). It is no coincidence, then, that periods of peace have been the exception over the last five hundred years. Since its inception, the nation-state system has been more or less synonymous with war. According to Lewis Mumford, "[A]ll the great national states, and the empires formed around a national core, are at bottom war states; their politics are war politics; and the all-absorbing preoccupation of their governing classes lies in collective preparation for armed assault" (Mumford 1970, 349).

Of course, the international political system can function this way only because we have created these secular gods, by collectively identifying with them. Nationalism has flourished because it offered itself as an alternative identity providing a this-worldly security in shared beliefs and communal values.

> War is the health of the State. It automatically sets in motion throughout society those irresistible forces for uniformity, for passionate cooperation with the Government in coercing into obedience the minority groups and individuals which lack the larger herd sense . . . the nation in war-time attains a uniformity of feeling, a hierarchy of values culminating at the undisputed apex of the State ideal, which could not possibly be produced through any other agency than war. . . . The State is intimately connected with war, for it is the organization of the collective community when it acts in a political manner, and to act in a political manner towards a rival group has meant, throughout all history—war. . . . (Bourne 1918, 31)

International events such as the second Gulf War remind us forcefully that the basic unit of political and military power remains the nation-state, which if powerful enough may act without any constraints on its behavior. There are no other gods—certainly not religious ones!—to trump its sovereign power.

Today, however, we do better to refer to the *corporate-military-state*, since little effective distinction remains between the economy and the government. As Dan Hamburg concluded from his experience as a U.S. congressman (D-CA): "The real government of our country is economic, dominated by large corporations that charter the state to do their bidding. Fostering a secure environment in which corporations and their investors can flourish is the paramount objective of both [political] parties" (Hamburg 1997, 25). This is increasingly true of all "economized" nations: their governments have become so preoccupied with the vicissitudes of the economy that they operate largely to service its needs. Economic growth is almost unanimously endorsed by political leaders as the criterion by which to judge the well-being of a nation, and one that justifies whatever burdens might be imposed upon society (Poggi 1978, 133). So in the days after September 11 President Bush told the shocked and grieving American people to go shopping. Don't stop consuming! We cannot let the economy be damaged by what has happened! Consumption has become a sacred rite because consumerism serves the national-economic goal of capital accumulation and GNP growth. This is inculcated into us, with pervasive advertising, as another secular solution to the (essentially religious) question about the meaning of one's life.

To sum up, the secular corporate-military-state deserves the label "Antichrist" because its dominion depends upon exploiting not only the biosphere but also the spiritual motivations of the people who constitute it and who end up being used by it. Consumer-nationalism takes advantage of our spiritual groundlessness, feeding upon our lack by seeming to provide a secular solution to the God-shaped hole. By diverting what is basically a spiritual drive (to resolve our lack), such solutions gain their attraction; without it they would lose their power over us. Our spiritual insecurities are manipulated by the corporate-military-state for its own self-aggrandizing purposes.

If our God-shaped hole is oblivious to whatever distinction we may make between sacred and secular—if we cannot avoid trying to fill up our lack, one way or another—then secular values and identities cannot avoid competing with more ostensibly religious ones. Is there another alternative to the void at the heart of modern secular identities, on the one side, and the traditional religious identities that fundamentalisms promote, on the other?

## Postmodern Identity: Half an Awakening?

> We burn with desire to find solid ground and an ultimate sure foundation whereon to build a tower reaching to the infinite. But our groundwork cracks, and the earth opens to abysses.
>
> —Pascal, *Pensées*

The distinction between modernity and postmodernity—where the one ends and the other begins—is controversial, but according to one perspective (Jameson 1992) the postmodern is an *acceleration* of the modern. By deconstructing the self to reveal our groundlessness, postmodernity aggravates the God-shaped hole in a way that makes us more aware of it, even while continuing to deny (as modernity does) that our groundlessness is really a problem. With this denial postmodernity remains true to its own secular roots, rubbing our noses in the lack it cannot see.

Karen Armstrong points out that no culture before the modern West could have afforded the constant innovation we take for granted today. Premodern societies are naturally conservative in that social order and stability are viewed as more important than freedom of expression or action, which can be destabilizing. Traditional societies fulfill their potential by modeling themselves on past ideals (the Golden Age); novelty threatens that security (Armstrong 2000, 33–34). Today Protestant fundamentalists try to fill the God-shaped hole with absolute certainty in inerrant doctrinal correctness. Ultra-Orthodox Jews seek ritual certainty by minutely observing divine law and other traditions. Fundamentalist Muslims seek literalist certainty in God's words (the Qur'an) and by making shari'a the law of the land. Each form of spirituality "reveals an almost ungovernable fear which can only be assuaged by the meticulous preservation of old boundaries, the erection of new barriers, a rigid segregation, and a passionate adherence to the values of tradition" (Armstrong 2000, 204).

Psychoanalytically, this is recognizable as a repetition-compulsion, which attempts to ward off anxiety—lack—that cannot or will not be more directly confronted. There are, of course, other types of repetition-compulsion. More secular and popular examples are the addictions reflected in the high rates of obesity, gambling, and substance abuse in the United States. All these repetition-compulsions provide the context to keep in mind as we evaluate the new liberatory prospects of the polyvalent world that postmodernists herald. They raise the essential question: How well are we able to cope with this liberation?

Kenneth Gergen's *The Saturated Self: Dilemmas of Identity in Contemporary Life* remains one of the best accounts of how new technologies of social saturation (air travel, cell phones, Internet and e-mail, etc.) expose us to a much wider range of persons and to novel types of relationships. Like it or not, this leads to "a populating of the self, the acquisition of multiple and disparate potentials for being" (Gergen 1991, 69). "Under postmodern conditions, persons exist in a state of continuous construction and reconstruction: it is a world where anything goes that can be negotiated. Each reality of self gives way to reflexive questioning, irony, and ultimately the playful probing of yet another reality. The center fails to hold" (7).

He argues that the sense of psychological *depth* formerly attributed to individuals was an effect of print technologies and the widespread literacy they made possible. Electronic media, especially television and the Internet, shatter that self-unity by dissociating our experience. According to Jean Baudrillard, "[W]e no longer exist as playwrights or actors, but as terminals of multiple networks" (in Gergen 1991, 69) We become pastiches of one another, splitting into a multiplicity of self-investments that Gergen calls "multiphrenia" (1991, 73). He is not oblivious to the downside of this. "One bears the burden of an increasing number of oughts, self-doubts and irrationalities" (80), yet he emphasizes the new possibilities for self-expression: "[A]s the technologies are further utilized, so do they add to the repertoire of potentials. It would be a mistake to view this multiphrenic condition as a form of illness, for it is often suffused with a sense of expansiveness and adventure. Someday there may indeed be nothing to distinguish multiphrenia from simply 'normal living' " (74). Gergen suggests that there are three phases of postmodern self-construction. In the first, one "increasingly and distressingly" finds oneself playing roles to obtain one's goals. The second and third phases, however, are described in wholly positive terms. The stage of pastiche personality liberates one from essence, as one learns to "derive joy" from new forms of self-expression, and the final stage of relational self leads to immersed interdependence in which relationships construct the self (147).

From a Buddhist perspective, this is an insightful account, especially Gergen's presentation of the last phase, which resonates with Buddhist claims about our emptiness (*shunyata*) and interdependence. Nonetheless, this optimistic description tends to downplay the sometimes-paralytic anxiety involved, which can subvert the process or distort the outcome. Gergen quotes the sociologist Louis Zurcher, whose concept of the "mutable self" affirms its openness, tolerance, and flexibility, but who also notices that this tends to give rise to a narcissism suffusing everyday life with the search for a self-gratification that makes others into implements to satisfy one's own impulses (154). That is exactly the problem we would expect if the sense of lack at one's core has not been squarely addressed in the process of postmodern self-reconstruction. Inability to resolve our lack makes us narcissistic and obsessive.[4]

For Buddhism, intuiting our lack of self is more than just temporarily distressing, since it requires realizing and adjusting to our groundlessness. Does the multiphrenic lifestyle that Gergen celebrates address the sense of lack at the core of our being, or does it involve new ways of evading what Buddhism understands to be the fundamental spiritual challenge?

The usual answer, which Gergen elaborates, is that the self is normally constructed/reconstructed in a largely unconscious fashion, by internalizing aspects of other selves. This understanding offers no answer to the sense of self's sense of lack, because it remains unaware of any intrinsic lack. A more Buddhist response is that our lack reflects something unknown at our empty core, an unfathomed center that offers new potentialities unbeknownst to secular multiphrenia, but potentialities that require further transformation in order to be actualized.

Buddhism agrees that our sense of self is a delusive construction. The doctrine of *pratitya-samutpada*, "dependent origination," explains how that construction occurs. It deconstructs our experience into a set of twelve impermanent processes, each conditioned by and conditioning all the others. The interaction of all these impersonal processes creates and sustains the sense of self, but the most crucial factor is *upadana*, "clinging." Early Buddhist texts identify four types of *upadana*, which, curiously, correspond quite closely to the types of modern clinging that were identified a few paragraphs earlier as our main responses to secular groundlessness. "There are these four kinds of clinging: clinging to *kama* [sensual pleasures], clinging to *ditthi* [views], clinging to *sila* [rules and observances], and clinging to *atta* [a doctrine of self] (*Majjhima Nikaya* 1.9, in Bhikkhu Bodhi 1995, 137–38). Clinging to *kama* is consumerism and other types of hedonism. Clinging to *ditthi* includes the obsession with orthodoxy (preoccupation with correct belief in inerrant doctrine). Clinging to *sila* is the obsession with orthopraxy (preoccupation with precise ritual). Narcissistic obsession with *atta* is delusive, because there is no self to cling or to cling to. In postmodern terms, even a protean, multiphrenic self is *shunya*, "empty." Until we are able to realize that, we continue to be haunted by the groundlessness at our core.

The translators of the above passage about clinging append a note to it: "Clinging in any of its varieties represents a strengthening of craving, its condition" (Bhikkhu Bodhi 1995, 1186–87n.125). In other words, none of these four types of clinging can solve the problem of the lack of our God-shaped hole; instead, they strengthen it. Fredric Jameson (1992) refers to our present situation as "late capitalism," and I wonder if we can also describe it as "late secularism," in which individual and collective clinging becomes intensified because our groundlessness is becoming more apparent and therefore more threatening. As the secular sense of self becomes more problematic, the gravitational pull of the black hole at our core becomes more insistent. We are driven to more extreme ways of filling it up (but nothing can fill it up): stronger drugs and other diversions, more dogmatic views and rigid observances, more narcissistic multiphrenia.

## Transforming Religion

It is time to recap what has been said. Terrorism provided our initial entry into these issues, yet the problem of post/modern lack of identity led to a broader critique of secularity that focuses on how much we are afflicted by the desacralization of the world, including the desacralization of ourselves. A figure-in-field approach means we cannot understand our secular world except in relation to the lack of our secular identities within it, which tend to become burdened by compulsions we do not understand.

For individuals, the Buddhist response, which emphasizes the problem of clinging and the importance of a spiritual practice to help us realize our groundlessness/formlessness, has been mentioned several times. But what about the social dimension?

That the secular is incomplete by itself means, among other things, bringing religious partners into the public conversation and decision-making process now dominated by the corporate state, by allowing more of a role for spiritual and ethical concerns. Gandhi believed that the modern state needs to be "civilized" by integrating spirituality and morality into it, something that could be realized through "democratic-political engagements with the basic teachings of the different religions." His version of Indian secularism would still preserve the relative autonomy of the political and the religious (ethical, spiritual) spheres, "so they can engage each other in a reconstructive way" (Pantham 1991, 183). Juergensmeyer's study of religious terrorism leads him to conclude that rapid global transformation provides an occasion for religions and their ideas to reassert themselves as a public force. The devaluation of purely secular authority highlights the need for alternative conceptions of public order (Juergensmeyer 2000, 15).

Such a recommendation seems ironic, given the role of fundamentalist Christianity in recent U.S. politics—not a very good example of the engagement that Gandhi and Juergensmeyer call for. However, if and when we learn to approach religious traditions from a perspective that highlights the problem of our identity and its groundlessness, we will realize that what remains most important about religion today is its role in encouraging personal and social transformation, and that its dogmas and practices can be used for heuristic devices to achieve that. The forms of religious clinging described earlier, such as preoccupation with orthodoxy and orthopraxy, should be recognized as types of repetition-compulsion that are often, in the end, counterproductive to the transformations that are needed.

We should have no illusions that this understanding of religion will soon or easily become the most prominent aspect, but it may have become inescapable, due to the accelerated communication and transportation systems that are globalizing us whether we want it or not. As the world becomes smaller, we find ourselves rubbing elbows with other people and other cultures sometimes living literally next door. This offers a particularly serious challenge to traditional religions, which have always interacted with one another but have usually had more time and space to develop according to their own internal dynamics. Living among a plurality of religious traditions puts us in a new, often uncomfortable, but potentially liberatory position, one that encourages us—and in the end may require us—to confront the implications of different orthodoxies and orthopraxes.

*In the Wake of 9/11: The Psychology of Terror,* published by the American Psychological Association, concludes with a dilemma. All of us are more or less securely embedded within some humanly created system of meaning and value, but which is the most beneficial, or least harmful? The most secure and comfortable worldview is rigid in its certainties, while more relativistic and tolerant worldviews, being less certain, may not be enough to base the meaning and value of our lives upon. Is there a middle ground? "Is there a vision of reality substantial enough to serve our deep psychological needs for death-transcending meaning and value—but flexible enough to endure peaceably the existence of alternative worldviews? If we are unable to find this safer place, then perhaps the human race is doomed to ignominious self-extermination" (Pyszczynski, Solomon, and Greenberg 2003, 198).

Pyszczynski and his coauthors conclude with questions, because none of us know if such a safer place will be found. Given the paramount role that religions still serve in the collective consciousness of humankind, however, it is safe to say that the religious traditions will need to be deeply involved for any such middle ground to be developed. The solution, I suggest, is religion understood not as orthodoxy or as orthopraxy but as transformative spiritual path.

# Notes

## Chapter One: Awareness Bound and Unbound

I am grateful to Tony Black, Charles Muller, Joseph O'Leary, Gene Reeves, Michio Shinozaki, Ken Tanaka, Jonathan Watts, and especially two anonymous *Philosophy East and West* reviewers for their helpful comments on earlier drafts of this chapter.

1. The terms "awareness" and "attention" will be used interchangeably, although neither is completely satisfactory because both have dualistic connotations: awareness is cognate with "wary (of)," and attention suggests the effort implied by "tension." But in this context their more homely, everyday meanings make them preferable to the more abstract, theoretical connotations of "mind" and "consciousness."

2. Yampolsky 1967, 133 n. 41. The Dunhuang version that Yampolsky translates does not mention this particular line from the *Diamond Sutra*, only that Hui-neng awakened when he heard the sutra expounded to him.

3. Blofeld's translation nevertheless gives Huang-po's teachings a transcendentalist bias. It begins: "The Master said to me: All the Buddhas and all sentient beings are nothing but the One Mind, besides which nothing exists. This Mind, which is without beginning, is unborn and indestructible..." (Blofeld 1958, 29). For a critique of Blofeld's translation, see Wright 1998, chap. 9.

4. For many other examples, see Gomez 1976.

5. Of course, the distinction between duality and nonduality is another duality. One way to make this point is to say that Buddhism does not reject duality in favor of nonduality but is careful not to take bifurcations as dichotomies.

6. I have adapted Mervyn Sprung's translation in Candrakirti 1979, 262. *Lucid Exposition of the Middle Way* is Chandrakirti's classical commentary on the *Mulamadhyamakakarikas*. Making his own transcendentalizing gestures, Sprung translates *shiva* as "beatitude" and capitalizes "truth."

7. Candrakirti 1979, 259–60. Sprung gives "the everyday world" for *samsara* and "ontic range" for *koti*. Cf. 16:9–10: "Those who delight in maintaining 'without the grasping I will realize nirvana; nirvana is in me' are the ones with the greatest grasping. When nirvana is not [subject to] establishment and samsara not [subject to] disengagement, how will there be any concept of nirvana and samsara?"

8. See Loy 1988, pp. 224–38.

9. There is a more extended discussion of karma in chap. 8, "The Karma of Women."

10. This approach tries to evade the ontological controversies that preoccupy much of Buddhist philosophy, while benefiting from their basic insights: the Madhyamaka emphasis on not "settling down" with any concepts, and the Yogachara realization that a dualistic grasper/grasped epistemology is inadequate for describing the experience of liberated awareness.

11. Might realizing Bankei's Unborn encourage the conclusion that one has awakened to such a Transcendental Mind? Is that how belief in Brahman, and so forth, arose?

12. The same argument is repeated on Waddell 1984, 35, to prove that "in the Unborn, all things are perfectly resolved," for "you were listening by means of the Unborn."

13. This sheds light on a famous passage: "When the gods . . . seek a bhikkhu who is thus liberated in mind, they do not find [anything of which they could say]: 'The consciousness of one thus gone is supported by this.' Why is that? One thus gone, I say, is untraceable here and now." *Majjhima Nikaya* 1.140, in Bhikkhu Bodhi 1995, 233. The bracketed material is bracketed in the original.

14. According to many Mahayana texts and teachers, the primary concern that arises in awakened awareness is compassion for others. One spontaneously wants to help those who are suffering, and in particular wants to help beings realize the true nature of their awareness. Compassion is also important in Pali Buddhism, of course, but apparently without the same assumption of spontaneity; there seems to be more emphasis on the need to cultivate it. Is this more consistent with the nondwelling emptiness of truly liberated awareness, which has no characteristics of its own—not even compassion? How can we understand this difference of emphasis? Perhaps the familiar *Heart Sutra* equation is helpful here. "Form is no other than emptiness" emphasizes the lacking-nothing quality of truly awakened awareness, which needs nothing and needs to do nothing because it is, in itself, nothing. "Emptiness is form," stressed as much by Mahayana, has some other implications. For attention to awaken to its own nature is to wake up from preoccupation with one's own *dukkha* only to become that much more aware of the world's *dukkha*. Since we are social beings, liberated emptiness becomes more sensitive to the forms of others, most of whom are not aware of the true nature of their own awareness. Nonduality means that the liberation of attention does not detach us from the world but enables us to be more responsive to it.

15. Harris 2005. No doubt the lobbying of pharmacological companies has also been a factor in this increase.

16. In one of his last papers, "Guarding the Eye in the Age of Show," (2000), Illich traces "the route on which the image mutated to the point of becoming a trap for the gaze. . . . An ethics of vision would suggest that the user of TV, VCR, McIntosh [*sic*] and graphs protect his imagination from overwhelming distraction, possibly leading to addiction." He contrasts the earlier tradition of ocular *askesis*: "During the Middle Ages and well into modern times, it dealt primarily with protecting the heart from distracting or destructive images. The question that is profoundly new today is a different one: How can I eschew not pictures, but the flood of shows?" (Illich 2000).

17. The *Financial Mail* quotation is from Rowe 2001. *Carpe callosum* means, in Latin, "seize the brain." For Michael Goldhaber, "obtaining attention is obtaining a kind of enduring wealth, a form of wealth that puts you in a preferred position to get anything this new economy offers" (Goldhaber 2005). See also Davenport and Beck 2001, and the online discussion of it at http://www.alamut.com/subj/economics/attention/attent_economy.html.

18. The rest of this section summarizes Rowe's argument.

19. The child reference is from Freedland 2005. The other examples cited in this paragraph, except for the special *New Yorker* issue, are mentioned by Rowe 2001.

20. This does not amount to an argument for Marxism. From a Buddhist perspective, capitalism and Marxism share the same delusion insofar as they imply that there is an economic (or technological) solution to human *dukkha*.


## Chapter Two: Language Against Its Own Mystifications

1. My references to the original Sanskrit text are from J. W. de Jong's 1977 edition of Nagarjuna's *Mulamadhyamakakarika*.

2. For example, Kalupahana translates the first half of 25:24 as "the appeasement of all objects, the appeasement of obsession" (Kalupahana 1991, 369); in *The Fundamental Wisdom of the Middle Way* Jay Garfield translates the same as: "the pacification of all objectification / And the pacification of all illusion" (Garfield 1995, 76). But elsewhere (e.g., in his discussion on pp. 353–59) Garfield too emphasizes the cessation of predication and conceptual construction. My version of 25:24 follows Sprung (in Candrakirti 1979, 262). The basic difficulty is that, although important both in Pali Buddhism and in Madhyamaka, the meaning of *prapanca* is unclear and controversial. Etymology yields *pra + panc*, "spreading out" in the sense of manifoldness and ramification; it refers to some indeterminate "interface" between perception and thought. In his book on the concept, Nanan. nda defines its primary meaning as "the tendency towards proliferation in the realm of concepts," but this loses the connection with perception. See Nananada 1971, 3–4.

3. See also 18:7; 22:11, 12, 15; and 24:18.

4. In this context the final verse of Wittgenstein's *Tractatus Logico-Philosophicus* is often quoted, yet the previous one is just as relevant as an elucidation of the Madhyamaka position: "6.54. My propositions serve as elucidations in the following way: anyone who understands me eventually recognizes them as nonsensical, when he has used them—as steps—to climb up beyond them. (He must, so to speak, throw away the ladder after he has climbed up it.) He must transcend these propositions, and then he will see the world aright" (1961, 151).

5. For more examples see Kim 1985, 54–82. The typology is on pp. 61–78. My analysis of Dogen's deconstructive techniques largely follows this paper, with the exception of the discussion of time (in technique number 3), which offers my own understanding of Dogen's view of time.

6. In the *Muchu-setsumu* fascicle; see Kim 1985, 71–72.

## Chapter Three: Dead Words, Living Words, Healing Words

1. See, for example, Coward and Foshay 1992. This includes two essays by Derrida: "Of an Apocalyptic Tone Recently Adopted in Philosophy" and "How to Avoid Speaking: Denials," as well as Christian, Buddhist, and Hindu reactions to those essays, with responses by Derrida.

2. Caputo 1989, 24–39.

3. The self-existence (Sanskrit, *sva-bhava*) that Madhyamaka refutes corresponds to the "self-presence" that Derrida criticizes in textual terms, by showing that every process of signification, including self-consciousness, is an economy of differences. Self-presence "has never been given but only dreamed of and always already split, incapable of appearing to itself except in its own disappearance." Discussions of this argument tend to focus on the *-presence* of self-presence, but the *self-* needs to be emphasized as much. It is "the hunger for/of self" that seeks fulfillment in "the absolute phantasm" of "absolute self-having." See Derrida 1998, 112; Derrida in Coward and Foshay 1992, 90, 91.

4. Scruple is from the Latin *scrupulus*, itself derived from *scrupus*, "a rough (hard) pebble," used figuratively by Cicero for a cause of uneasiness or anxiety. The Latin *opportunus* means fit, suitable, convenient, seasonable; advantageous, serviceable.

5. In this section it is necessary to repeat some of the examples cited in chapter 2, "Language Against Its Own Mystifications."

6. This apparent paradox may be understood as an East Asian version of Nagarjuna's argument in the *Mulamadhyamakakarikas*, which uses causality to refute the self-existence of anything, and then denies causal relationships: "That which, taken as causal or dependent, is the process of being born and passing on, is, taken non-causally and beyond all dependence, declared to be nirvana." (25:19, in Candrakirti 1979, 255).

7. Caputo refers to Tobin 1986, 171–79.

8. *On Grammatology* privileges writing as a better metaphor for understanding language than the supposed self-presence of speech. Yet speech remains a better metaphor for the *ippo-gujin* of language. Yes, speech does give us an illusion of wholeness and unity, but the point of *ippo-gujin* is that that is not merely an illusion.

9. I am indebted to Professor Caputo for this felicitous way of expressing the difference (in a personal communication).

## Chapter Four: Zhuangzi and Nagarjuna on the Truth of No Truth

1. For a more detailed discussion of rationalism and antirationalism, see Graham 1985 and Graham 1992.

2. "It is well worth remarking that most philosophical work, down to the humblest journal article, has been presented with the air of 'Here is the truth; the inquiry into this topic may now cease, because all alternative views are incorrect.'... if a philosopher understands that a final, definitive account is impossible, and chooses to mirror this in his or her manner of presentation, this could change everything. The

philosophy must then be tentative and exploratory. It cannot be serious in the way in which most philosophy is serious" (Kupperman 1989, 316).

3. In accordance with the linguistic turn in contemporary philosophy, some commentators understand this and similar passages to be about language: for example, the nominalistic realization that "names have only a conventional relation to objects," or that no language-game is absolute, for each is only internally self-justifying. (See, e.g., Hansen, in Mair 1983, 45–47.) Such interpretations overlook or de-emphasize the integral relationship between the words we employ and the world we experience. When our concepts change, the world they organize also changes. John Searle makes this point well: "When we experience the world we experience it through linguistic categories that help to shape the experiences themselves. The world doesn't come to us already sliced up into objects and experiences. What counts as an object is already a function of our system of representation, and how we experience the world is influenced by that system of representation" (in Magee 1978, 184). When our conceptual categories change, so does the world *for us*.

4. In the *Zhuangzi* inner chapters, Huzi "levels out the impulses of the breath" and the True Men of old "breathe from their heels" (Graham 1981, 97, 84).

5. As P. J. Ivanhoe points out (1993, 651), Zhuangzi's examples are all benign, for we do not encounter any assassins or pickpockets. If grasping the Dao is a matter of knowing-how, however, then (contra Graham) it is not clear why their skills should not also qualify them. We cannot cross-examine wheelwright Pian about his personal life, but the twentieth century provides some counterexamples. Consider the case of Picasso, arguably its greatest painter, yet, if we can believe half the stories told by friends and acquaintances, often a moral monster due to his egoism, a *self-* centeredness usually insensitive to those around him. We cannot deny his genius—that the Dao often flowed into his painting—but that was not enough to make him a sage. Although romanticism has familiarized us with such inconsistencies, it remains difficult to reconcile Picasso as a master-artist who knew-how with a view of the Dao as simply knowing-how. In order to understand what makes someone a sage, we seem to need something more: what the "knowing-how" of *living* is.

6. P. J. Ivanhoe describes Zhuangzi as a "connoisseur of words" (Ivanhoe 1993, 640).

## Chapter Five: CyberBabel

1. See, for example, Sanders et al. 2000.

2. Quoted in Associated Press 2006.

3. See Berger 1979.

4. See Schwartz 2005.

5. "The use of drugs to treat attention-deficit hyperactivity disorder in younger adults more than doubled from 2000 to 2004" (Harris 2005).

6. Quoted in Burkeman and Johnson 2005.

7. In Borges 1999, 112–28; the quotes that follow are from pp. 114–16. See also Borges's 1944 story "Funes the Memorious."

8. These examples are cited in Wilber 1977, 92–93.

9. Quoted in Associated Press 2006.

10. See Brubaker 1991, 10 and 36ff.

11. This point is expressed much better by Michael Ende in his wonderful novel *Momo* (Penguin, 1984).

## Chapter Six: Dying to the Self that Never Was

1. For more on the koan process, see Isshu and Sasaki 1984; Kapleau 1966; Hori 2003; Heine and Wright 2000. A short "working paper" by Robert Aitken Roshi lists "nine principal points of interchange" between the koan method and *The Cloud of Unknowing*: nonintellectual method; brevity of meditation theme; abruptness of experience; intimacy of experience; joy of experience; resoluteness after experience; avoiding sentimental devotion; don't falter; and longing. See Aitken 1981.

2. McCann 1952, 50. All subsequent *Cloud* references are to this edition.

3. See Yasutani's "Introductory Lectures" in Kapleau 1966, 58–60.

4. In "Genjo-koan," the first fascicle of his *Shobogenzo*.

5. This practice is usually followed during a *sesshin*, a secluded and intensive meditation retreat of three to seven days, when all distractions can be reduced to a minimum.

6. Eckhart: "The moment you get ideas, God fades out and the Godhead too. It is when the idea is gone that God gets in.... If you are to know God divinely, your own knowledge must become as pure ignorance, in which you forget yourself and every other creature" (Blakney 2004, 127).

7. According to Eckhart (and later Swedenborg), God's grace (influx) must flow into us once the obstacle of self-love is removed.

8. Buddhism can explain this as due to practice in previous lifetimes.

9. I am grateful to Professor David Chappell for this information and for other comments on an earlier draft of this paper.

10. From a typescript of the lecture "Zen and Christianity," presented at a Buddhist-Christian dialogue conference in Berkeley, California, August 1987.

11. See, for example, Waldenfels 1980.

## Chapter Seven: The Dharma of Emanuel Swedenborg

I am grateful to Leonard Fox, Donald L. Rose, and especially Jane Williams-Hogan for their comments on an earlier draft of this chapter.

1. Dasa 1887, 14. I am grateful to Leonard Fox for providing me with a photocopy of this book. The Dasa epigraph ("[H]idden under Judaic-Christian names...") is from p. 7.

2. Did Suzuki read the *Buddhist Ray* while he was working for the Open Court Publishing Company? It is likely that Paul Carus was aware of it.

3. Translated by Tatsuya Nagashima in Nagashima 1993, 202–17. Later in the first chapter, Suzuki makes a seemingly ingenuous remark that is worth quoting because it touches on one of the most attractive qualities of Swedenborg's "dreary, dogmatic, and soporific octavos": "Swedenborg's writings have a sphere of consistent sincerity and honesty. He is not a man of fraudulence and deception. He just writes honestly what he sees and hears. There is no pretension in him. Whether or not one believes in him, we must admit that there is a reason why one feels his sincerity coming from what he writes" (Nagashima 1993, 214). Suzuki's book has recently been translated into English by Andrew Bernstein and published by the Swedenborg Foundation in 1996 as *Swedenborg: Buddha of the North*; this includes the 1927 article by Suzuki I mention later, as well as an earlier version of this present chapter as an afterword. My Suzuki epigraph ("Revolutionary in theology . . .") is from the preface. I am grateful to Mr. Nagashima and to Ms. Mihoko Bekku for providing me with information about Suzuki's Swedenborgian background.

4. Mihoko Bekku, personal communication. Ms. Yukie Dan, formerly secretary of the Eastern Buddhist Society (which publishes the *Eastern Buddhist*, a journal founded by Suzuki), has provided me with a list of Swedenborg references in Suzuki's *Collected Writings* (in Japanese): a total of ten, in addition to the studies and translations already mentioned. "Generally, Swedenborg is not thought to be of much importance to Suzuki, who does not mention him overtly. But this information sheet listing fairly explicit mentions of ES would suggest that Swedenborg was never apart from Suzuki. So we now believe he is significant, but significant in which way has yet to be elucidated" (Yuki Dan, personal communication).

5. Contact between India and Europe occurred long before Alexander's conquests (326–323 BCE), and Marco Polo gives an account of the legend of the Buddha. In the thirteenth century papal envoys visited the Mongol khan, and their accounts aroused much interest in Europe. Later missionaries also sent back numerous reports, but since few of these were published it is difficult to determine how much correct information on Buddhism reached Europe before the nineteenth century. The important exception, curiously, was Tibet. At the end of the sixteenth century Jesuit missionaries believed that Christians lived there, and a series of Catholic missionaries visited, beginning in 1624. One of them, Ippolito Desideri, stayed in Lhasa for five years (1716–21) and acquired an excellent knowledge of Tibetan language and religion. He wrote a *relazione* on his studies during his return, but this was not published until 1904. Only in the nineteenth century did systematic studies of Buddhism begin and reliable translations begin to appear. See De Jong 1987, 5–15.

6. Unless otherwise noted, numbers in the text refer to the numbered sections (or, in roman numerals, chapter headings) in Ager's translation of Swedenborg 1988. All other Swedenborg references also refer to numbered sections rather than pages.

7. As quoted in Kapleau 1966, 205. Although the original reference is from the "Sokushin-zebutsu" fascicle of Dogen's *Shobogenzo*, the same point is made by Dogen in other fascicles as well.

8. See also Swedenborg 1988, 145. While the spiritual importance of the forehead and the top of the head (the parietal aperture left by the fontanelle) has been largely ignored in the Christian tradition, it has been emphasized in the Buddhist tantric and Indian yogic traditions, which have a system of seven chakras that puts

greatest importance on the "third eye" in the middle of the forehead and the chakra at the top of the head (according to the Tibetan tradition, the latter chakra is the proper way for the mental body to exit the physical body after death).

9. Swedenborg has little to say about meditation practices, although Swedenborg 1997, no. 767 mentions the Lord appearing before angels when they practice spiritual meditation. Swedenborg's own preferred practice was meditating on the meaning of the Bible and allowing his mind to be guided by the Lord into an awareness of its spiritual significance.

10. Krishna: "Whenever righteousness falters and chaos threatens to prevail, I take on a human body and manifest myself on earth. In order to protect the good, to destroy the doers of evil, to ensure the triumph of righteousness, in every age I am born" (Mitchell 2002, 74).

11. Much of Swedenborg's vision of the afterworld, and this aspect in particular, is compatible with John Hick's conclusion in *Death and Eternal Life*, an almost exhaustive historical study of Christian eschatology that, characteristically of modern theology, ignores Swedenborg. "The distinction between the self as ego and the self as person suggests that as the human individual becomes perfected he becomes more and more a person and less and less an ego. Since personality is essentially outward-looking, as a relationship to other persons, whilst the ego forms a boundary limiting true personal life, the perfected individual will have become a personality without egoity, a living consciousness which is transparent to the other consciousnesses in relation to which it lives in a full community of love. Thus we have the picture of a plurality of personal centres without separate peripheries. They will have ceased to be mutually exclusive and will have become mutually inclusive and open to one another in a richly complex shared consciousness. The barrier between their common unconscious life and their individual consciousnesses will have disappeared, so that they experience an intimacy of personal community which we can at present barely imagine" (Hick 1976, 459–460). Not a bad description of Swedenborg's heaven. Compare Swedenborg 1990, 2057: "Mutual love in heaven consists in this, that they love the neighbor more than themselves. Hence the whole heaven presents as it were a single man; for they are all thus consociated by mutual love from the Lord. Hence it is that the happiness of all are communicated to each, and those of each to all. The heavenly form is therefore such that every one is as it were a kind of center; thus a center of communication and therefore of happiness from all; and this according to all the diversities of that love, which are innumerable."

12. On the *Bardo Thodol*, see Mullin 1986, 21–22.

13. Section 256 gives an alternative explanation for the belief that people "can return to a former life": occasionally a confused "recollection" can occur due to experiencing the memories of spirits that always accompany us.

14. See also Swedenborg 1998, 77; *The Coronis*, part of Swedenborg 1997, 39; and Swedenborg 2002, 6077.

## Chapter Eight: The Karma of Women

1. From a Buddhist perspective there are good reasons for focusing on Thai Buddhism. Thailand is the only Buddhist nation never conquered or colonized by

the West, which means that Thai Buddhism has been less affected by other religious traditions, and Buddhism continues to play a major role in Thai society.

2. The eight additional rules are: (1) any *bhikkhuni*, no matter how senior, must respectfully salute any *bhikkhu*, no matter how junior; (2) an aspiring *bhikkhuni* must undergo a two-year training period and then be ordained by both the *bhikkhu sangha* and the *bhikkhuni sangha*; (3) *bhikkhuni* must not criticize *bhikkhu*; (4) *bhikkhuni* must not receive alms before *bhikkhu*; (5) *bhikkhuni* who violate rules are subject to disciplinary action and then must ask to be reinstated by both the *bhikkhu sangha* and the *bhikkhuni sangha*; (6) every fortnight *bhikkhuni* should ask *bhikkhu* for instruction; (7) *bhikkhuni* must spend the rainy season retreat near a group of *bhikkhu*; (8) *bhikkhuni* should request the ceremony marking the end of the rainy season retreat from both the *bhikkhu sangha* and the *bhikkhuni sangha*. The *Bhikkhuni vibhanga* commentary on the *Bhikkhuni-patimokkha* includes other sets of lesser rules for women monastics.

3. This claim is controversial: the evidence is limited, and some scholars argue that the *bhikkhuni sangha* was never fully established in Thailand.

4. The role of Buddhism should not be overemphasized. The main causes of the Thai sex industry are economic and political: the poverty of most Thai families, the increasing role of consumerism (including desire for a higher income), and the new business opportunities opened up in the 1960s and 1970s by the "rest and recreation" of a large number of American GIs fighting in Vietnam.

5. See Puntarigvivat 2001, 211–38.

6. There have also been accusations of widespread pedophilia (mainly sexual abuse of boys) within the Thai *sangha*, especially among those in positions of authority, but these are difficult to confirm: those with the power to investigate this evidently do not want to do so. If true, the similarity with recent problems in the Catholic Church, especially in the United States, reinforces questions about the viability of required celibacy in religious institutions—and, perhaps more fundamentally, about the tendency to identify the spiritual life with celibacy, which has been called "the strangest of the sexual perversions."

7. *Anguttara Nikaya* 3.65. This translation by Soma Thera is at http://buddhism. kalachakranet.org/resources/kalama_sutra.html.

8. *Tittha Sutta*, in the *Anguttara Nikaya* 3.61. This translation by Thanissaro Bhikkhu is at http://www.buddhistinformation.com/ida_b_wells_memorial_sutra_ library/tittha_sutta.htm.

9. *Moliyasivaka Sutta*, in the *Samyutta Nikaya* 36.21. This translation by Nyanaponika Thera is at http://www.buddhistinformation.com/ida_b_wells_memorial_ sutra_library/tittha_sutta.htm.

10. See Nagapriya 2004.

11. "There are, O monks, three causes for the origination of action. What three? Greed (*lobha*), hatred (*dosa*) and delusion (*moha*)" (*Anguttara Nikaya* 3, in Nyanaponika and Bodhi 1999, 49–50).

## Chapter Ten: Terrorism as Religion

1. Nazism, Stalinism, and the Khmer Rouge movement remind us that religion can include the modern nation-state, the dominant secular God today.

2. The main exception within Europe was Jews; outside Europe it was Muslims. Because both demonstrated an alternative to Christianity, they threatened the "natural" ontological security of Christians.

3. Revelation is the most political book of the New Testament, but not quite in the way that many conservative Christians understand it today. Many, and perhaps most, scholars today agree that the "Antichrist" is a coded reference to the Roman Empire; in contemporary terms, therefore, the closest parallel would seem to be the new U.S. empire.

4. Christopher Lasch's work on narcissism in American culture (1979) comes to similar, although more negative, conclusions about the changing character of the contemporary self.

# Bibliography

Aitken, Robert. 1981. "The Method of Meditation: Zen Buddhist and Roman Catholic." *Buddhist-Christian Studies* 1.
———. 1991. *The Gateless Barrier: The Wu-Men-Kuan (Mumonkan).* San Francisco: North Point Press.
Armstrong, Karen. 2000. *The Battle for God: Fundamentalism in Judaism, Christianity, and Islam.* London: HarperCollins.
Associated Press. 2006. "Lonely Nation" (article). July 31, 2005.
Aveni, Anthony F. 1991. *Empires of Time.* New York: HarperCollins.
Berger, Peter. 1979. *The Heretical Imperative.* New York: Doubleday.
Berger, Peter, Brigitte Berger, and Hans Kellner. 1973. *The Homeless Mind.* Harmondsworth, UK: Penguin.
Berman, Paul. 2003. "The Philosopher of Islamic Terror." *New York Times Magazine.* March 23.
Betty, L. Stafford. 1983. "Nagarjuna's Masterpiece—Logical, Mystical, Both, or Neither?" *Philosophy East and West* 33, no. 2.
Blakney, Raymond B., trans. and ed. 2004. *Meister Eckhart: A Modern Translation.* Kila, MT: Kessinger.
Blofeld, John, trans. and ed. 1958. *The Zen Teaching of Huang Po on the Transmission of Mind.* New York: Grove Press.
———, trans. and ed. 1969. *The Zen Teaching of Hui Hai.* London: Rider.
Bodhi, Bhikkhu, trans. and ed. 1995. *The Middle Length Discourses of the Buddha.* Boston: Wisdom.
———, trans. and ed. 2000. *The Connected Discourses of the Buddha: A New Translation of the Samyutta Nikaya.* 2 vols. Boston: Wisdom.
Borges, Jorge Luis. 1999. "The Library of Babel." In *Collected Fictions,* trans. Andrew Hurley. New York: Penguin.
Bourne, Randolph. 1918. "The State." Unpublished manuscript. New York: Columbia University Libraries.
Boyer, E. L. 1996. "The Scholarship of Engagement." In *The Third Mission: Service and the Academy* 1, no. 1. http://www.uga.edu/jheoe/abs1_1.htm.
Brock, Rita Nakashima, and Susan Brooks Thistlewaite. 1996. *Casting Stones: Prostitution and Liberation in Asia and the United States.* Minneapolis: Fortress Press.
Brown, Norman O. 1961. *Life Against Death: The Psychoanalytic Meaning of History.* New York: Vintage.

Brubaker, Rogers. 1991. *The Limits of Rationality: An Essay on the Social and Moral Thought of Max Weber.* London: Routledge.

Burkeman, Oliver, and Bobbie Johnson. 2005. "Search and You Shall Find." *Guardian,* February 2.

Candrakirti. 1979. *Lucid Exposition of the Middle Way.* Trans. and ed. Mervyn Sprung. Boulder, CO: Prajna Press.

Caputo, John D. 1989. "Mysticism and Transgression: Derrida and Meister Eckhart." In Silverman, 1989.

Carey, Alex. 1996. *Taking the Risk out of Democracy: Corporate Propaganda versus Freedom and Liberty.* Champaign: University of Illinois Press.

Chang, Chung-yuan. 1971. *Original Teachings of Ch'an Buddhism.* New York: Vintage.

Chang, Garma C. C., trans. and ed. 1970. *The Practice of Zen.* Perennial Library ed. New York: Harper & Row.

Conze, Edward, trans. and ed. 1973. *The Perfection of Wisdom in Eight Thousand Lines and Its Verse Summary.* Bolinas, CA: Four Seasons Foundation.

Cook, Francis H. 1977. *Hua-Yen Buddhism: The Jewel Net of Indra.* University Park: Pennsylvania State University Press.

Coward, Harold, and Toby Foshay, eds. 1992. *Derrida and Negative Theology.* Albany: State University of New York.

Crary, David. 2006. "Isolated Americans Trying to Connect." Associated Press (AP), August 6.

Dallmayr, Fred., ed. 1991. *Border Crossings: Toward a Comparative Political Theory.* Boston: Lexington.

Darwin, Charles. 1995. *The Origin of Species.* New York: Gramercy.

Dasa, Philangi. 1887. *Swedenborg the Buddhist; or, The Higher Swedenborgianism, Its Secrets and Thibetan Origin.* Los Angeles: Buddhistic Swedenborgian Brotherhood.

Davenport, Thomas H., and John C. Beck. 2001. *The Attention Economy: Understanding the New Currency of Business.* Cambridge, MA: Harvard Business School Press.

Dawson, Lorne. 2001. "Doing Religion in Cyberspace: The Promise and the Perils." *Council of Societies for the Study of Religion Bulletin* 30, no. 1.

de Jong, J. W. 1987. *A Brief History of Buddhist Studies in Europe and America.* Delhi: Sri Satguru Publications.

Derrida, Jacques. 1981. *Positions.* Trans. Alan Bass. Chicago: University of Chicago Press.

———. 1998. *Of Grammatology.* Baltimore: Johns Hopkins University Press.

Dogen. 1985. *Moon in a Dewdrop: Writings of Zen Master Dogen.* Trans. and ed. Kazuaki Tanahashi. San Francisco: North Point Press.

Ende, Michael. 1986. *Momo.* Trans. J. Maxwell Brownjohn. Harmondsworth, UK: Penguin.

Eriksen, Thomas. 2001. *Tyranny of the Moment: Fast and Slow Time in the Information Age.* London: Pluto Press.

Euben, R. L. 1991. "Mapping Modernities, 'Islamic' and 'Western.'" In Dallmayr 1991.

Freedland, Jonathan. 2005. "The Onslaught." *Guardian*. October 25. http://media. guardian.co.uk/site/story/0,14173,1600020,00.html/.

Fremantle, Francesca, and Chogyam Trungpa, trans. and eds. 1993. *The Tibetan Book of the Dead*. Boulder, CO: Shambhala.

Fromm, Erich. 1982. *The Greatness and Limitations of Freud's Thought*. London: Sphere Books.

Garfield, Jay. 1995. *The Fundamental Wisdom of the Middle Way: Nagarjuna's "Mulama-dhyamakakarika."* New York: Oxford University Press.

Gergen, Kenneth. 1991. *The Saturated Self: Dilemmas of Identity in Contemporary Life*. New York: Basic Books.

Getches, Catie. 2004. "Wired Nights: In the 24-Hour Universe, There's No Winding Down." *Washington Post*, October 17.

Goldhaber, Michael. 2005. *The Attention Economy and the Net*. http://www.firstmonday. org/issues/issue2_4/goldhaber/.

Gomez, Luis O. 1976. "Proto-Madhyamika in the Pali Canon." *Philosophy East and West* 26 no. 2 (April): 137–65.

Govinda, Lama Anagarika. 1969. *Foundations of Tibetan Mysticism*. New York: Samuel Weiser.

Graham, A. C., trans. and ed. 1981. *Chuang-tzu: The Inner Chapters*. London: George Allen & Unwin.

———. 1985. *Reason and Spontaneity*. London: Curzon Press.

———, trans. and ed. 1990. *The Book of Lieh-tzu*. New York: Columbia University Press.

———. 1992. *Unreason within Reason: Essays on the Outskirts of Rationality*. LaSalle, IL: Open Court Press.

Gray, John. 2003. *Al Qaeda and What It Means to Be Modern*. London: Faber and Faber.

Gross, Rita M. 1993. *Buddhism after Patriarchy: A Feminist History, Analysis, and Reconstruction of Buddhism*. Albany: State University of New York Press.

Hallengren, Anders. 1994. "The Secret of Great Tartary." *Arcana* 1, no. 1 (Fall): 35–54.

Hamburg, Dan. 1997. "Inside the Money Chase." *Nation*. May 5.

Harris, Gardiner. 2005. "Use of Attention-Deficit Drugs Is Found to Soar among Adults," *New York Times*, September 15. http://www.nytimes.com/2005/09/15/health/15/disorder.html/.

Hedges, Chris. 2002. *War Is a Force that Gives Us Meaning*. New York: Public Affairs.

Heine, Steven, and Dale S. Wright, eds. 2000. *The Koan: Texts and Contexts in Zen Buddhism*. New York: Oxford University Press.

Herman, Edward S., and Noam Chomsky. 2006. *Manufacturing Consent: The Political Economy of the Mass Media*. New York: Vintage.

Hershock, Peter. 1999. *Inventing the Wheel: A Buddhist Response to the Information Age*. Albany: State University of New York Press.

Hick, John. 1976. *Death and Eternal Life*. London: Collins.

Hori, Victor Sogen. 2003. *Zen Sand: The Book of Capping Phrases*. Honolulu: University of Hawaii.

Huntington, Samuel. 1996. "The Clash of Civilizations." Reprinted in *The Clash of Civilizations? The Debate.* New York: Foreign Affairs Press.

Illich, Ivan. 1973. *Tools for Conviviality.* New York: Harper & Row. http://todd.cleverchimp.com/tools_for_conviviality/.

———. 1999. *Deschooling Society: Social Questions.* London: Marion Boyars.

———. 2000. "Guarding the Eye in the Age of Show." http://homepage.mac.com/tinapple/illich/.

Isshu, Miura, and Ruth Fuller Sasaki. 1984. *The Zen Koan: Its History and Use in Rinzai Zen.* New York: Harvest Books.

Ivanhoe, Philip J. 1993. "Skepticism, Skill and the Ineffable Tao." *Journal of the American Academy of Religion* 61, no. 4: 639–54.

Jameson, Fredric. 1992. *Postmodernism, or, The Cultural Logic of Late Capitalism.* Durham, NC: Duke University Press.

Juergensmeyer, Mark. 2000. *Terror in the Mind of God: The Global Rise of Religious Violence.* Berkeley and Los Angeles: University of California Press.

Kabilsingh, Chatsumaarn. 1991. *Thai Women in Buddhism.* Berkeley, CA: Parallax Press.

———. 2002. "Prostitution and Buddhism." *WFB Review: Journal of the World Federation of Buddhists* 39, nos. 3/4: 94–98.

Kalupahana, David J. 1991. *"Mulamadhyamakakarika" of Nagarjuna: The Philosophy of the Middle Way.* Delhi: Motilal Banarsidass.

Kapleau, Philip ed. 1966. *The Three Pillars of Zen.* Tokyo: Weatherhill.

Khuankaew, Ouyporn. 2002. "Buddhism and Domestic Violence." *WFB Review: Journal of the World Federation of Buddhists* 39, nos. 3/4.

Kim, Hee-Jin. 1975. *Dogen Kigen—Mystical Realist.* Tucson: University of Arizona Press.

———. 1981. "Method and Realization: Dogen's Use of the Koan Language." Paper presented at the conference on "The Significance of Dogen." Tassajara Zen Mountain Center, October 8–11, 1981.

———. 1985. " 'The Reason of Words and Letters': Dogen and Koan Language." In *Dogen Studies,* ed. William R. LaFleur. Honolulu: University of Hawaii Press.

Kupperman, Joel L. 1989. "Not in So Many Words: Chuang-tzu's Strategies of Communication." *Philosophy East and West* 39 no. 3: 311–17.

Lasch, Christopher. 1979. *The Culture of Narcissism.* New York: Norton.

Lauf, Detlef Ingo. 1989. *Secret Doctrines of the Tibetan Books of the Dead.* Boston: Shambhala.

Levine, Robert. 1997. *A Geography of Time.* New York: Basic Books.

Leys, Simon. 1996. "One More Art." *New York Review of Books* 43, no. 7. 18 (April): 28–31.

Lifton, Robert J. 1993. *The Protean Self.* New York: Basic Books.

Lin, Derek, trans. 2006. *Tao Te Ching.* Woodstock, NY: SkyLight Paths.

Loy, David. 1988. *Nonduality: A Study in Comparative Philosophy.* New Haven, CT: Yale University Press.

———. 1996. *Lack and Transcendence: The Problem of Death and Life in Psychotherapy, Existentialism, and Buddhism.* Atlantic Highlands, NJ: Humanities Press.

———. 1997. "The Religion of the Market." *Journal of the American Academy of Religion* 65, no. 2: 275–90.

———. 2002. *A Buddhist History of the West: Studies in Lack.* Albany: State University of New York Press.

Magee, Bryan, ed. 1978. *Men of Ideas.* New York: Viking Press.

Mair, Victor, ed. 1983. *Experimental Essays on Chuang-tzu.* Honolulu: University of Hawaii Press.

Mascaro, Juan, trans. 1973. *The Dhammapada.* Harmondsworth, UK: Penguin.

Matsunaga, Reiho, trans. 1972. *A Primer of Soto Zen: A Translation of Dogen's Zuimongi.* London: Routledge and Kegan Paul.

McCann, Abbot Justin, ed. 1952. *The Cloud of Unknowing,* 6th rev. ed. London: Burns Oates.

Mitchell, Stephen, trans. 2002. *The Bhagavad-Gita: A New Translation.* New York: Three Rivers Press.

Mullin, Glenn H. 1986. *Death and Dying: The Tibetan Tradition.* London: Arkana.

Mumford, Lewis. 1970. *The Culture of Cities.* New York: Harcourt Brace Jovanovich.

Murcott, Susan. 1991. *The First Buddhist Women: Translations and Commentaries on the Therigatha.* Berkeley, CA: Parallax.

Nagapriya. 2004. *Exploring Karma and Rebirth.* Birmingham, UK: Windhorse.

Nagarjuna. 1977. *Mulamadhyamakakarika.* Ed. J. E. de Jong. Madras: Adyar Library and Research Centre.

Nagashima, Tatsuya. 1993. "Daisetsu T. Suzuki, Internationally Known Buddhist: CryptoSwedenborgian?" *New Church Life,* May.

Nanananda. 1971. *Concept and Reality in Early Buddhist Thought.* Kandy, Sri Lanka: Buddhist Publication Society.

Nelson, Benjamin. 1981. *On the Roads to Modernity.* Totowa, NJ: Rowman and Littlefield.

Nietzsche, Friedrich. 1968. *The Will to Power.* Trans. Walter Kaufmann and R. J. Hollingdale. New York: Vintage.

———. 1969. *Twilight of the Idols.* Trans. and ed. R. J. Hollingdale. Harmondsworth, UK: Penguin.

———. 1986. *Human, All Too Human.* Trans. R. J. Hollingdale. Cambridge: Cambridge University Press.

Nyanaponika Thera and Bhikkhu Bodhi, trans. and eds. 1999. *Numerical Discourses of the Buddha: An Anthology of Suttas from the "Anguttara Nikaya."* New York: Altamira.

Pantham, Thomas. 1991. "Indian Secularism and Its Critics: Some Reflections." In Dallmayr 1991.

Peter, Lawrence J., ed. 1977. *Quotations for Our Time.* New York: Morrow.

Pew Poll. 2002. Pew Research Center for People and the Press. http://www.faithand-values.com/tx/csm-1376/1/.

Poggi, Gianfranco. 1978. *The Development of the Modern State: A Sociological Introduction.* London: Hutchinson.

Polanyi, Karl. 1957. *The Great Transformation.* Boston: Beacon Press.

Price, A. F., and Wong Mou-lam, trans. 1974. *The Diamond Sutra and the Sutra of Hui-Neng.* Boulder, CO: Shambhala.

Puntarigvivat, Tavivat. 2001. "A Thai Buddhist Perspective." In Raines and Maguire 2001.

Pyszczynski, Thomas A., Sheldon Solomon, and Jeff Greenberg. 2003. *In the Wake of 9/11: The Psychology of Terror.* Washington, DC: American Psychological Association.

Raines, John C., and Daniel C. Maguire, eds. 2001. *What Men Owe to Women: Men's Voices from World Religions.* Albany: State University of New York Press.

Reiho, Masunaga. 1958. *The Soto Approach to Zen.* Tokyo: Layman Buddhist Society Press.

Rowe, Jonathan. 2001. "Carpe Callosum." *Adbusters* 9, no. 6: unpaginated.

Sanders, C. E., et al. 2000. "The Relationship of Internet Use to Depression and Social Isolation among Adolescents." *Adolescence,* Summer. http://www.findarticles.com/p/articles/mi_m2248/is_138_35/ai_66171001.

Schwartz, Barry. 2005. *The Paradox of Choice: Why More Is Less.* New York: Harper.

Silverman, Hugh J., ed. 1989. *Derrida and Deconstruction.* New York: Routledge.

Streng, Frederick J. 1967. *Emptiness: A Study in Religious Meaning.* Nashville, TN: Abingdon.

Stryck, Lucien, and Takeshi Ikemoto, trans. 1973. *Zen Poems of China and Japan: The Crane's Bill.* Garden City, NY: Anchor.

Suzuki, D. T. 1950. *Essays in Zen, 2nd Series.* London: Rider.

———. 1956. *Zen Buddhism.* Ed. William Barrett. New York: Anchor.

———. 1996. *Swedenborg: Buddha of the North.* Trans. Andrew Bernstein. West Chester, PA: Swedenborg Foundation.

Swedenborg, Emanuel. 1912. *Apocalypse Revealed.* Trans. John Whitehead. New York: Swedenborg Foundation.

———. 1988. *Heaven and Hell.* Trans. John C. Ager. West Chester, PA: Swedenborg Foundation.

———. 1990. *Arcana Coelestia.* Trans. William Ross Woffenden. West Chester, PA: Swedenborg Foundation.

———. 1997. *True Christian Religion.* Trans. John C. Ager. West Chester, PA: Swedenborg Foundation.

———. 1998. *Conjugial* [sic] *Love.* Trans. Samuel S. Warren. West Chester, PA: Swedenborg Foundation.

———. 2002. *Spiritual Diary.* Trans. George Bush. 5 vols. West Chester, PA: Swedenborg Foundation.

———. 2003a. *Divine Love and Wisdom.* Trans. George F. Dole. West Chester, PA: Swedenborg Foundation.

———. 2003b. *Divine Providence.* Trans. George F. Dole. West Chester, PA: Swedenborg Foundation.

Tawney, Richard H. 1920. *The Acquisitive Society.* New York: Harcourt Brace and Co.

———. 1938. *Religion and the Rise of Capitalism.* Harmondsworth, UK: Penguin.

Tilly, Charles. 1975. *The Foundation of the National States in Western Europe.* Princeton, NJ: Princeton University Press.

Tobin, Frank. 1986. *Meister Eckhart: Thought and Language.* Philadelphia: University of Pennsylvania Press.

Tucci, Giuseppe. 1969. *The Theory and Practice of the Mandala*. London: Rider.

Tweed, Thomas, and Helen Tworkov. 1991. "The Original Ray." *Tricycle: The Buddhist Review* 1, no. 1: 6–7.

United Nations Development Program. 1999. *Human Development Report*. Oxford: Oxford University Press.

United Nations University Workshop. 2001. "The Contribution of Education to the Dialogue of Civilizations: Observations and Recommendations." May 3–5. www.unu.edu/dialogue/workshops/education-e.doc/.

Virilio, Paul. 1997. *Open Sky*. Trans. Julie Rose. London: Verso.

Waddell, Norman, trans. and ed. 1984. *The Unborn: The Life and Teaching of Zen Master Bankei*. San Francisco: North Point Press.

Waldenfels, Hans. 1980. *Absolute Nothingness: Foundations for a Buddhist-Christian Dialogue*. New York: Paulist Press.

Watson, Burton, trans. 1996. *Chuang Tzu: Basic Writings*. New York: Columbia University Press.

Weber, Max. 2001. *The Protestant Ethic and the Spirit of Capitalism*. Trans. Talcott Parsons. London: Routledge.

Wilber, Ken. 1977. *The Spectrum of Consciousness*. Wheaton, IL: Theosophical Publishing House.

Williams, Raymond B. 2004. Quotation accessed online December 1, 2004 at http://www.intrust.org/magazine/pastarticle.cfm?id=47&CFID=3330914&CFTOKEN=93993326/.

Wittgenstein, Ludwig. 1961. *Tractatus Logico-Philosophicus*. Trans. D. F. Pears and B. F. McGuinness. London: Routledge and Kegan Paul.

Wright, Dale. S. 1992. "Rethinking Transcendence: The Role of Language in Zen Experience." *Philosophy East and West* 42, no. 1: 113–38.

———. 1998. *Philosophical Meditations on Zen Buddhism*. Cambridge: Cambridge University Press.

Yampolsky, Philip B., trans. and ed. 1967. *The Platform Sutra of the Sixth Patriarch*. New York: Columbia University Press.

# Index